Managing in
Different Cultures

Managing in Different Cultures

Edited by

Pat Joynt and Malcolm Warner

UNIVERSITETSFORLAGET AS

Norwegian University Press (Universitetsforlaget AS), 0608 Oslo 6
Distributed world-wide excluding Scandinavia by
Oxford University Press, Walton Street, Oxford OX2 6DP

London   New York   Toronto
Delhi   Bombay   Calcutta   Madras   Karachi
Kuala Lumpur   Singapore   Hong Kong   Tokyo
Nairobi   Dar es Salaam   Cape Town
Melbourne   Auckland

and associated companies in
Beirut   Berlin   Ibadan   Mexico City   Nicosia

British Library Cataloguing in Publication Data
Managing in different cultures.
   1. Management. Cultural aspects
   I. Joynt, Pat   II. Warner, Malcolm, *1937–*
658.

ISBN 82-00-07287-8

Printed in England by
Page Bros (Norwich) Ltd.

Contents

PREFACE

Preface

One of the major changes that has occurred in International Management courses is the introduction of the subject of cross-cultural management. To illustrate this point, one can refer to a recent experience at the Norwegian School of Management where one of the central features on the agenda for the International Management course was guest speakers from practical business life.

One of the speakers pointed to an experience he had in an African country where his patience paid off. He had been invited to a public official's home for the first time after having lived in the country for approximately two months. No business was discussed during the first six hours—however, well into the night the host complimented him on being the first Western business person who had not talked business right away. The end result was a substantial contract for a Norwegian firm.

The second incident involved a Norwegian company that was started in Scotland some years ago. The managing director used a management style which involved a great deal of informal activity with his staff. He even used the same entrance door as the staff, and this informality was not lost on the employees when a union was being formed. They were not interested in joining the national union, which had a history of conflict with their bargaining counterparts. Rather a Norwegian type of union based on cooperation and 'soft' bargaining was formed.

The above incidents are stories that can be told in many lands with only some of the key factors in the situation at hand changed. Perhaps Croziers' (1964:210) message from twenty years ago is more appropriate today!

Incentively . . . people have always assumed that bureaucratic structures and patterns of action differ in different countries . . . Men of action know it and never fail to take it into account. But contemporary social scientists . . . have not been concerned with such comparisons.

This book takes issue with the above, only on one point. The social scientists involved in this publication *are* concerned with the differences in bureaucratic structures as well as with the patterns of behaviour and action across cultures. We feel others are beginning to share with us this interest, and this is the 'raison d'être' for this publication.

This book constitutes an attempt to explain the often misunderstood notion of cross-cultural management and its development in the context of our modern world. We also feel that there is a need to illustrate the division between the old and the new methods of analysis when studying cross-cultural management. As such, this is *not* a book full of statistics with large questionnaires and appendices. Rather, it is a group of readings from a many-faceted world of ideas and actions that include a variety of actors who often operate in very complex settings.

A work of this nature also runs into problems of time. We felt that the topic would emerge as one of the main topics during the 1980s— but when? Recently two special issues of the *Journal of International Studies of Management and Organization* were devoted to the topic. Many other journals in the management area are also beginning to write on the subject. In addition, many workshops and seminars are being filled by both academics and practitioners who want (and need) to know more about Cross-Cultural Management.

The book is a result of a seminar sponsored by EIASM (The European Institute for Advanced Studies in Management). The objective of the Cross-Cultural Seminar held at Henley-on-Thames during the Spring of 1983 was to provide a forum for the exchange of ideas and research results on the subject. Such a forum happened to be necessary because of the increasing sophistication of management practices, because of the promising application to the field of recent developments in research, and, last but not least, because of the change of techniques, policies and decision methods warranted by the current state of uncertainty in which cross-cultural managers operate.

For the reader who is interested in a one way map through the jungle of cross-cultural management theory, methodology and application this book will be a disappointment. During the Henley seminar it became readily apparent that the state of the art had not changed a great deal since Roberts (1970) classic conclusion after a review of the field—'On looking at an elephant . . .' However in 1983 we found a rich diversity of conceptualization as well as methodology and application. As this is the case, we are interested in exposing the reader to as much of this diversity as possible. The chapters that follow represent viewpoints from many parts of the world. Traditional methodologies as well as some of the newer mapping methodologies are presented. The book deals with studies from India, Japan, Indonesia and Argentina as well as Poland, France and other parts of

Europe and the US. We have also attempted to integrate some of the traditional well known studies like Hofstede and IDE in this volume. As Laurent eloquently concluded in his chapter—'It may be that the management process in the ten countries is as much culture bound as their cooking, and that international management has to avoid the trap of international cuisine. National cultures may still offer some genuine recipes.' In other words this book represents the diverse view rather than the restaurant-chain view.

There are hundreds of cultures and subcultures of consequence that are relevant to the subject of cross-cultural management—but as we limit ourselves to those reported here, we can only hope to identify some of the factors, ideas and phenomena held in common.

Traditional management theories support the view that to understand what goes on inside the organization, one must understand what is happening outside it. The culture in which an organization operates thus must influence the practices inside it.

We wish to thank EIASM, Henley the Management College, the Institute for Management Research at the Norwegian School of Management, our fellow contributors, the publisher and all those whose efforts, support, and understanding made this book possible. We are indebted to a wide array of scholars, students and practitioners for most of the ideas presented.

Pat Joynt
Brussels, Oslo

Malcolm Warner
Henley-on-Thames

PART I

Foundations for Cross-Cultural Studies

In the first section of this book Heller introduces us to the many-faceted concept of cross-cultural studies. Not only are the definition aspects reviewed—he also takes us into the difficult domain of cooperating and financing research in this area across cultures. This first contribution lays the foundation for what will follow, and we return to some of the comments made here in the concluding chapter by Warner.

Drenth expands on Heller's introduction to cross-cultural studies and asks two central questions for both the practitioner and the researcher:

1. Can organizational characteristics be explained by cultural factors?
2. Is culture a moderator or a contingency factor between factors such as work climate, participation, etc. and organizational goals such as performance and satisfaction?

The chapter is oriented towards the discipline of organizational psychology, which has played a central role in cross-cultural research.

CHAPTER 1

Some theoretical and practical problems in multinational and cross-cultural research on organizations

Frank A. Heller

INTRODUCTION

The article presents a critical evaluation of some recent trends in so-called 'cross-cultural' research. In particular we wish to question, as did Roberts (1970) before us, whether the use of the term 'culture' has become more scientifically meaningful in organizational research in the twelve years since her article was published.

The analysis is critical of the undifferentiated use of the term 'culture' but very positive about the benefits achieved by cross-national comparative research. Various examples are given of recent comparative research with which the author was associated.[1] Cross-national research can be defended against its detractors on many grounds: it is cost effective, and leads to an important insight into the organizational issues confronting business in one's own country which can only be obtained by a comparative perspective; it helps to create international collaboration between academics and provides a natural setting for cross disciplinary research.

SOME COSTS OF CROSS-NATIONAL RESEARCH

There are a number of obvious problems with 'cross-cultural' or multinational research. It is said to be difficult to organize, expensive in time and travel, and, above all, studded with methodological pitfalls. To this list some people would add the increased possibility of frictions between individuals with different cultural backgrounds, or national teams brought up with contrasting scientific-academic traditions.

This formidable list of caveats probably explains why so little multinational research has been carried out in some areas of social science.

1. Heller & Porter 1966; Haire et al. 1966; Heller 1971, 1976; IDE 1976; Drenth et al. 1979; Rus et al. 1978; Heller & Wilpert 1979; Heller & Wilpert 1981, IDE 1981a and IDE 1981b.

We must, however, distinguish two quite distinct approaches. One, which we will call *'cross' national research* is typically carried out by one person or a team from a single country who design the project and then 'cross' over to one or more other countries to replicate the study.[3] What we will call *'multi' national research* is typically carried out by different individuals or teams in each country, led or coordinated to achieve comparability. Within these two different models there are several important variations relating to who takes initiatives, who funds the research, and what, if any, leadership style is applied in relation to the research. The range of options and some of the problems relating to them have been well described in a recent article (Fourcade & Wilpert 1977).

In my own experience there is certainly a cost to be paid for multinational research. It takes longer to launch, it creates additional problems of communications, and multinational meetings are expensive. Standardizing methodologies requires patience, some ingenuity and perseverance. Even with these angelic qualities, it is unrealistic to expect exactly the same degree of homogeneity as would be achieved by a single investigator working on his own or with a carefully trained assistant. However, in a large scale national project, with several senior collaborators plus associated field staff, quite similar problems of standardization can be found (Vallier 1972).

It must also be accepted that so far little experimentation with multinational methodologies has taken place. Most of them are unadapted replications of conventional questionnaire and interview methods.[4] The use of variations of Group Feed-back Analysis (Heller 1969, 1973) has, we believe, taken a tentative but useful step towards the development of an adaptation to multi- and cross-national research requirements.

BENEFITS FROM CROSS-NATIONAL RESEARCH

With so many organizational, scientific, cost and personal difficulties to contend with, are there any countervailing benefits to be set against them?

We believe there are five. We will describe each without implying any hierarchy of importance. In the first place, any increase in project cost due to meetings and the need for additional coordination is balanced by what can be described as the 'multiplier effect' if a semi-autonomous model of organization is adopted. Under such a model,

3. Sometimes it is possible to carry out cross-national research by staying in one country and covering different national or ethnic groups that happen to be living in a given place.

4. The well-designed cross and multinational research using questionnaires has adopted careful checks on the quality of translation and its cultural as well as linguistic adaptation (Merrit & Rokkan 1966).

each participating country team raises all or at least some of the finance needed for its own work.[5] This enables any given investment by team A (Country A) to profit from the sample, findings, experience, etc. of the other teams. In the case of one twelve-country research (IDE 1976, IDE 1981) it means that for an investment of 'x' amount of money, something like 11 'x' additional material, etc. becomes available. In terms of sample size, this means that in our case, instead of having 11 organizations on average we have 134.

Secondly there is an extension of the value of 'comparativ research'. Instead of having investigated 11 organizations in two industrial sectors in one country, we have 134 organizations in two sectors in 12 countries, so that a country comparison becomes possible, yielding potentially valuable insight into the range of variability of the phenomena under investigation. A sample of 134 also enabled us to subdivide organizations by size and skill-complexity, giving two additional dimensions, which a single-country sample could not have yielded. Furthermore, any single-country result, even if well established, may be quite misleading in the wider world context. Bass (1965) has pointed to this difficulty by arguing that: 'often what we regard as the only way, turns out merely to be the American way' (Bass 1965, p. 230).

A third aspect of multinational work is the relative ease with which genuine interdisciplinary advantages are capable of being achieved without the soul-searching strain of deliberately introducing different disciplines as part of a carefully prepared plan. In my experience, planned interdisciplinary work has a tendency to get bogged down in definitional territorial defensiveness; that is to say, skirmishes from prepared positions from which retreat is equivalent to defeat. In our experience multination teams usually contain members whose training and professional allegiance belongs to a variety of disciplines but nobody labels them, so that their different experiences can be absorbed painlessly.

A fourth plus point for this kind of research is a consequence of the increasing mobility and complexity of 20th-century life. In the 18th or 19th century only colonialism or idle[6] curiosity required country comparisons on a scientific basis. Today, people, organizations, and even Governments take on responsibilities across many frontiers. The European Economic Community, for instance, is groping its way towards a minimum framework of standardization of laws, structures, and perhaps even human conditions.[7] How much communality is desirable or feasible? How much similarity or difference exists

5. In addition, overhead and 'international coordinating expenses' may have to be funded.

6. We do not mean this in a derogatory sense. By 'idle' we mean intellectual academic curiosity without the pressure of needing answers to combat urgent problems.

7. The International Labour Organization has operated in this field for several decades.

already? The multinational company, the multinational manager, and the ubiquitous civil servant meet many problems which we do not easily understand without some comparative research (North et al. 1963, Rokkan 1970, Davis 1971).

Finally, some people maintain that collaboration and open trust develop more easily in work between national centres than within a single country. If this were so, a number of reasons or speculations could be advanced (Rapoport 1964). I will desist from such an exercise except to say that even with free and open collaboration between different teams, we have found it useful to agree on a written social contract. Such a document requires colleagues to adhere to a minimum format of acknowledgements of the contribution in work and finance that everybody has made. It may also stipulate the language(s), ownership of data, the conditions under which publications are made and the safeguards for the use of material from other countries. When many teams collaborate, it is important that one does not pre-empt the right of others by premature publication, and it may be reasonable to allow each country to make the initial interpretation of any between-country comparison. Once the material is published, the canons of academic freedom will of course prevail.

It would be wrong to champion any particular format of research. Circumstances require different approaches. There can, however, be little doubt that circumstances in the latter part of the 20th century and beyond are likely to lead to some questions that require answers in a multinational context (Trist 1976). Given that this is so, the question of feasibility and cost of this kind of research becomes important.

The article describes advantages and disadvantages of different approaches to cross and multinational research. While the evidence and arguments are based on personal experience rather than scientific data, a case is made out for the hypothesis that most of the extra problems and costs associated with this kind of research are fairly well balanced by countervailing benefits. These benefits have to be examined and subjected to tests.

In the meantime, decisions about people and organizations have to be made, many of them in an international context. Can social science research offer useful data to policy makers at the micro and macro level? Our experience suggests that a reasonable optimism is not out of place.

HOW TO APPROACH 'CULTURE'

One should approach culture the way one would an aggressive patient —without prejudice but with a resolute intention not to be bowled over or hoodwinked into prescribing either a placebo or the patient's own pet medicine. Caution is needed because of the extraordinary multifarious use to which this term has been put in the past. Resolution is essential because the concept has attracted a large and possibly growing following among devotees who are more easily offended than put off by reasoned argument.

Cultural topics have often attracted literary writers like Salvadore de Madariaga (1931) or case-study-oriented social scientists like David Granick (1960, 1962), or Geoffrey Gorer (1948, 1949). Some cross-cultural comparisons have had socio-political motives (Servan-Schreiber 1967). Systematic cross-cultural research on organizations and the behaviour and attitudes of its members is of relatively recent origin. The topic attracted very little attention before 1960 (Harbison and Myers 1959), but a survey of the comparative research literature 1962–1967 discovered about 500 moderately relevant publications (Roberts 1967).[8] Most of the comparative work up to now has consisted of samples from two or three countries, and this is, of course, quite insufficient for making broad generalizations about groupings based on similarities or differences.

There are good reasons for the reluctance of researchers to enter this area of scientific enquiry. Apart from the obvious expense in time and money, there are profound and, some will argue, intractable methodological problems which have to be faced. Merritt (1975) has described the dilemma graphically:

> Scholars performing comparative analysis are frequently like the well-known millipede who was asked one day how he was able to coordinate his many legs and feet so as to walk. The millipede responded, 'That's easy!' But the more he thought about how to answer the question, that is, the more he tried to conceptualize what came naturally to him, the more he became tongue-tied and, worse, foot-tied, with the consequences that he never walked any more after that. Comparative researchers, too, sometimes perform interesting and significant work but then, once having asked themselves whether this work is *really* comparative, and then generalizing their question to ask, 'What *is* comparative research, anyway?' spend the rest of their intellectual lives arguing about epistemology and the philosophy of science.

While a growing volume of literature has addressed itself to the methodological and theoretical problems, they have not been solved (Schweitzer 1975, Triandis 1972, Rokkan 1968, Landsberger 1970, Przeworski and Teune 1970, Schleuck 1966, Brislin et al. 1973).

The problem is often confined to the connotations evoked by the term 'culture'. Every now and again one comes across some writing where each sentence would make as much sense without the term 'culture' as with it. It is then that one suspects being in the presence of a devotee with whom arguments would take a Wittgensteinian turn. That is to say words would pass each other by 'windschief'.

The word culture was adapted in French from the Latin *cultura* which is related to the Latin *cultus*, cult or worship. In ordinary language the major meaning of the term[9] is closely associated to

---

8. Not all, of course, are cross national, but the methodological problems are similar.
9. According to the Shorter Oxford English Dictionary.

socially elitist concepts like refinement of mind, tastes and manners based on superior education and upbringing. It has also been identified with the intellectual side of civilization, particularly in its German spelling. In Europe before the Second World War the term 'Kultur' was used extensively to support arguments on the social and racial superiority of some groups over others. Even in England and in the present day, culture is a term which the average working man and woman would associate with 'them' rather than 'us'. It could also be claimed that the plethora of studies in the interwar years on 'National Character' are the precursors of what was later called cross-cultural. Much of the writing on national character emanated from nationalism and had as its barely disguised motive the description of superior and inferior traits (Hamilton Fife 1940). It is possible that the predecessor of studies on national character was the notion of a 'Group Mind' so ably described by McDougall (1920). Notions about 'collective representation', 'collective soul', or 'collective consciousness' were feverishly debated but empirical evidence was not easily adduced.

It is worth mentioning these problems from the recent past to prepare us for the fact that they have not entirely disappeared in some current work. Even social scientists have used culture in a bewildering range of meanings, starting with the anthropological definition of Taylor (1871) 'as a complex whole which includes knowledge, belief, art, morals, law, custom and any other capabilities and habits acquired by man as a member of society'. Sociologists have given the term a slightly narrower scope by concentrating on ideational, symbolic and evaluative elements, that is to say 'ideas and beliefs, expressive symbols or value patterns' (Parsons 1951). The purpose was to distinguish culture from society and social structure but the concept is difficult to operationalize. Psychologists tend to keep to the original layman's use of the term as an elitist category (Warren 1934) unless they set out to measure it by questionnaires. It can then be defined as subjective culture, that is to say a 'group's way of perceiving its social environment' (Triandis 1972). Curle (1947) defines culture as 'a cluster of socially determined attitudes and behaviour patterns grouped and elaborated round structurally defined roles and relationships'. Although the author did not intend it, this definition could be used to describe differences between social classes within a country more easily than differences between larger geographic entities. To make matters even more difficult, the term culture has been used to describe the social climate of a single manufacturing unit (Jaques 1951).

In comparative research on organizations, culture is rarely isolated as a defined category and separated from other variables as an integral part of the research design. It is more usually treated as a residual entity and as an afterthought. This problem has been scathingly analysed in a seminal article by Roberts (1970), who reviewed 526 publications and found that only 54% based their arguments about culture on empirical data. She came to the conclusion that even where data was available, the conceptualization was usually descriptive, vague, and ignored the impact of alternative factors like technology or structure which probably accounted for a larger percentage variation of the dependent variable.

Explanations for cross-country differences vary and some authors are content to describe the existence of differences without offering reasons for them. We will argue, however, that if significant country or societal differences were to emerge repeatedly in different studies, causal explanations should be sought in the form of measurable independent variables. Major candidates for such analysis are child-rearing practices, educational systems, socio-structural factors like class and religious practices, economic factors and legal-political systems. (See for instance Ajiferuke & Boddewyn 1970.)

It is worth mentioning these problems from the recent past to prepare us for the fact that they have not entirely disappeared in some current work.

CLEAR AND UNCLEAR FINDINGS

One of the earliest, best known and largest cross-national studies of managerial attitudes assembled samples from 14 countries (Haire et al. 1966). The authors grouped their results into four clusters: (i) Nordic European (Denmark, Germany, Norway, Sweden), (ii) Latin European (Belgium, France, Italy, Spain), (iii) Anglo-American (England and USA) and (iv) Developing countries (Argentina, Chile, India). Japan did not fit into any of the clusters.

More recently, somewhat similar country clusters have emerged from a research on a large multinational high technology company, which, from time to time, conducts surveys on its employees in about 40 countries. Some of these results have been analysed by Hofstede (1976, 1977, 1980). One of Hofstede's measures is called a Power Distance Index (PDI) based on three questions.[10] He finds that this measure correlates with the Gross National Economic Product of the employee's country and with its geographic location. The countries that are closer to the equator have larger PDI scores than the more nordic countries. His ranking of countries on the PDI index can also be arranged into two broad clusters not very different from the Haire et al. clusters described above. Hofstede's first group includes: Nordic countries (Denmark, Sweden, Norway, Finland), Germanic countries (Austria, Switzerland, Germany, Netherlands), and Anglo-American countries (New Zealand, Ireland, UK, Australia, Canada and USA).

---

10. The three questions relate to (i) greater or less perceived fear to disagree with superiors, (ii) subordinates' perception of their boss's decision-making behaviour, and (iii) subordinates' dependence or counter-dependence needs.

The second broad cluster is made up of Latin European and Mediterranean countries (Italy, Spain, Greece, Portugal, Belgium, Turkey and France).

In a very good recent book on comparative organization study, Lammers and Hickson (1979) put forward a theoretical argument based on a division into two main country clusters and supported by evidence from a variety of studies, including Hofstede's. The authors define culture as the 'pattern of norms and roles embedded in certain paramount values as professed by organization participants'. The theory devises two culture cluster categories, dividing bureaucratic values into a Latin and an Anglo-Saxon type. The Latin bureaucracy is characterized by centralization, a large number of hierarchical levels, rigid stratification, high bureaucratic control, low power distribution, low morale, low cooperativeness, and a preference for routine rather than innovative decisions. The Anglo-Saxon bureaucracy is pictured as having the reverse of these characteristics.

Since the conclusions of Lammers and Hickson seem to fit a number of different research projects which they review, they feel entitled to argue for the existence of broad culture clusters.

However, not all cross-national or multinational research reproduces these findings. In an earlier research, Hickson et al. (1974), working with 70 manufacturing organizations in three countries, conclude that, irrespective of country, consistent relationships exist between variables of organization context (size, dependence, technology) and measures of structure (formalization, specialization, autonomy). These findings, they argue, support the culture-free hypothesis by demonstrating that many relationships are stable across societies.[11]

In an eight-country comparative study of managerial attitudes and decision-making behaviour, Heller and Wilpert (1979, 1981) find a variety of significant country differences but no consistent culture pattern. The eight countries include France and Spain as well as Israel, the USA, UK, Germany, Sweden and the Netherlands. A number of statistical methods were used to test for country effects. Neither the two Latin nor the Anglo-German countries show characteristic profiles on leadership style or on attitude to their jobs, skills, environmental pressures or job satisfaction. Nevertheless, interesting differences between countries were found on most of these variables, for instance on the extent of centralized versus decentralized decision styles. However, contrary to the culture cluster thesis, French as well as Swedish top managers used decentralized styles, while British and American managers used more centralized methods (Heller and Wilpert 1979).

11. However, since the three countries in this research were North American, British and Canadian, the lack of difference could be attributed to the absence of Latin or Asiatic countries.

Similar non culture cluster findings are reported from a 12 country study on managerial objectives (Bass and Eldridge 1973) and from a large cross national comparison of managerial values of over 2,500 respondents in 6 countries (England 1975). In the study of values, organizational context seemed to be an important predictor, union leaders were quite different from managers, company size and career success were important factors. There was a surprising similarity in value systems of managers from such different countries as the USA, Japan, Korea, India and Australia.

It seems that it is too early to draw firm conclusions in relation to the culture-free versus the culture-based thesis, but this does not prevent us from obtaining theoretically, as well as empirically, interesting ideas from comparative research. A recent two country study can be used to illustrate the importance of comparing organizational data in different locations. Gallie (1978) examined Robert Blauner's thesis that automation creates a number of conditions that are more favourable to the worker than mass production industry. Joan Woodward had also come to believe that automation leads to a high degree of social integration. However, some French marxists put forward strong arguments in opposition to these conclusions. Gallie designed his study to compare two closely matched and highly automated companies, one in France and the other in England. He produces very convincing evidence that both the Blauner and French marxist theses could not be sustained on a generalistic basis. It seems that identical advanced automation technology is associated with high social integration in one country and low social integration in the other. Moreover, the value of this finding is independent of any cultural explanation. Gallie concludes that the reason for the difference between the French and English workers in identical petrol refineries was due to the different pattern of trade unionism and the different managerial systems in the two countries.[12] As a consequence, it seems that Blauner's widely discussed thesis depends on circumstances which only comparative research can challenge. In many circumstances country comparisons will be the most appropriate method for such a task.

A HYPOTHESIS ABOUT 'CULTURE' FINDINGS IN ORGANIZATIONAL RESEARCH

Although we have only reviewed a selection of cross and multi-country projects, the diversity of findings requires an explanation which future research in this field could test.

I would like to put forward the suggestion that culture responses are

12. There are, of course, people who would be prepared to argue that these two explanations are 'cultural'. We are back to the issue of defining culture and avoiding putting this label on any findings that show country differences (rather than on a previously agreed variable).

at least in part a function of the format used for the stimulus question. Fairly broad general questions, not relating to specific identifiable current behaviour, have tended to predominate in research studies that have found fairly clear culture differences. The Haire et al. (1966) research used deliberately broad questions, for instance: 'The average human being prefers to be directed, wishes to avoid responsibility and has relatively little ambition.' Hofstede's Power Distance Index consists of three questions, one of which asks subordinates whether 'employees in general are afraid to disagree with superiors'. In contrast, questions in the Heller and Wilpert research were very specific and concentrated on aspects of their day-to-day behaviour. For instance, managers were asked which of five alternative decision styles they used on twelve different specific tasks. They were also asked to describe the skills needed for their own job on twelve specific alternative skill categories. The Bass and Eldridge research on objectives also used carefully described situations referring to choices between specified tasks. Each participant was asked to consider himself to be a member of a management team in a firm that had shown a profit. He was then required to decide whether or not to spend $225,000 to eliminate a safety hazard, etc.

It would seem possible that the difference between research projects that produce culture clusters and those that do not, is due to the form of question used. The more general and broad question format may attract responses that are anchored in something analogous to a group's collective unconscious or to their early upbringing and family imbibed values. When the stimulus question refers to identifiable and specific situations, familiar to the respondent, the answers will tend to be descriptive of that situation and will attract less of the free floating group-determined values and preferences.

However, it is possible to think of specific situations which are deeply anchored in culturally determined values, for instance religious practices or some rituals even in modern bureaucratic organizations. Future research should therefore look into the question format as well as at the capacity of a given situational anchorage to attract cultural values. Such an approach would induce researchers to predefine what they mean by 'culture' and why they expect to get similar responses from certain groups of countries. Furthermore, once a 'cultural' variable is identified, it may be preferable to use a term that describes this particular factor. For instance, if bureaucracy in some countries is characterized by centralization, low power distribution, low cooperativeness and high control, then a term like 'centralization–control' would describe the phenomenon as well as, or better than, the term Latin bureaucratic culture. This would avoid evoking the elitist and racially discriminatory image of the term 'culture' or 'Kultur' to which we referred earlier in this paper. The more specific descriptive labelling would also make it easier to integrate later findings that size or other

FOUNDATIONS FOR CROSS-CULTURAL STUDIES

contingencies predict centralization–control in bureaucratic organizations, even in non-Latin countries.

REFERENCES

Ajiferuke, M. and Boddewyn, J. (1970), Socio-Economic Indicators in Comparative
Management. *A.S.Q.,* 15, 453–458.
Bass, B. and Eldridge, L. (1973), Accelerated Managers' Objectives in Twelve
Countries, *Industrial Relations,* 12, 158–171.
Brislin, R., Lonner, W. and Thorndike, R. (1973), *Cross Cultural Research Methods.*
New York: Wiley.
Curle, A. (1947), Transitional Communities and Social Re-Connection: A follow-up
study of the Civil Resettlement of British Prisoners of War Part 1. *Human Relations,* 1,
42–68.
Davis, S. (1971), *Comparative Management: Organizational and Cultural Perspectives.*
Englewood Cliffs, New Jersey: Prentice Hall.
De Madariaga, S. (1931), *Englishmen, Frenchmen, Spaniards: An essay in comparative
psychology.* Oxford University Press.
Drenth, P. J. D., Koopman, P. L., Rus, V., Odar, M., Heller, F. A., Brown, A. (1979),
Participative Decision Making in Organizations: A three country comparative study.
Mimeographed. Tavistock Institute of Human Relations.
Dore, R. (1973), *British Factory—Japanese Factory.* London: George Allen & Unwin.
England, G. (1975), *The Manager and his Values: An international perspective from the
U.S.A., Japan, Korea, India and Australia.* Cambridge, Mass.: Ballinger Publishing Co.
Fourcade, J-M. and Wilpert, B. (1977), *Group Dynamics and Management Problems of
an International Interdisciplinary Research Team.* Mimeographed. International Insti-
tute of Management, Berlin.
Gallie, D. (1978), *In Search of the New Working Class: Automation and social
Integration within capitalist enterprise.* Cambridge University Press.
Gorer, G. (1948), *The Americans.* London: Cresset Press.
Gorer, G. (1949), *The People of Great Russia.* London: Cresset Press.
Granick, D. (1960), *The Red Executive.* London: Macmillan.
Granick, D. (1962), *The European Executive.* London: Weidenfeld & Nicolson.
Hamilton Fyfe, H. (1940), *The Illusion of National Character.* Watts. (Thinkers
Library).
Harbison, J. and Myers, C. A. (1959), *Management in the International World: An
international analysis.* New York: McGraw Hill.
Heller, F. A. (1969), Group Feedback Analysis: A method of field research.
Psychological Bulletin, 72, 2, 108–117.
Heller, F. A. (1971), *Managerial Decision Making: A study of leadership styles and
power sharing among senior managers.* London: Tavistock Publications.
Heller, F. A. (1973), Group Feedback Analysis: A method of field research in a
multinational setting. In Graves, D. (Ed.), *Management Research: A cross cultural
perspective.* Amsterdam: Elsevier Scientific Publishing Co.
Heller, F. A. (1976), The Decision Process: An analysis of power-sharing at senior
organizational levels. In Dubin, R. (Ed.), *Handbook of Work, Organization and
Society.* Chicago: Rand McNally.
Heller, F. A., Porter, L. W. (1966), Perceptions of managerial needs and skills in two
national samples. *Occupational Psychology,* 40, 1–13. Also in Weinshall, T. D. (Ed.)
(1977), *Culture and Management.* Middlesex: Penguin Books.
Heller, F. A. and Wilpert, B. (1979), Managerial Decision Making: An international
comparison. In: England, G. W., Negandhi, A. R. and Wilpert, B. (Eds.), *Functioning
Organizations in Cross Cultural Perspective.* Kent, Ohio: Kent State University Press.
Heller, F. A. and Wilpert, B. (1981), *Competence and Power in Managerial Decision
Making.* Wiley International.

Hickson, D. J., Hinings, C. R., McMillan, C. J. M. and Schwitter, J. P. (1974), The Culture-Free Context of Organization Structure: A Tri-national Comparison. *Sociology,* 8, 59–80.

Hofstede, G. (1976), *Measuring Hierarchical Power Distance in Thirty Seven Countries.* Working paper 76–32 Brussels European Institute for Advanced Studies in Management.

Hofstede, G. (1977), *Cultural Determinants of the Exercise of Power in a Hierarchy.* Mimographed. European Institute for Advanced Studies in Management. Working Paper 77–8.

Hofstede, G. (1980) *Cultures Consequenses,* Sage Publications, California.

I.D.E.—International Research Group (1976), Industrial Democracy in Europe. *Social Science Information,* 15, 177–203.

I.D.E. Industrial Democracy in Europe Research Group (1981), *European Industrial,* Clarendon Press, Oxford.

Jaques, E. (1951), *The Changing Culture of a Factory.* London: Tavistock Publications.

Lammers, C. J. and Hickson, D. J. (1979), *Organizations Alike and Unlike.* Mimeographed. To be published as a book in 1979.

Landsberger, H. A. (Ed.) (1970), *Comparative Perspectives on Formal Organizations.* Boston: Little, Brown & Co.

McDougall, W. (1920), *The Group Mind.* Cambridge University Press.

Merritt, R. L. and Rokkan, S. (Eds.), (1966), *Comparing Nations: The use of quantitative data in cross-national research.* New Haven, Connecticut, Yale University Press.

North, R., Holsti, O., Zaninovich, G. and Zimmers, D. (1963), *Content Analysis: A handbook with applications for the study of international crisis.* Northwestern University Press.

Parsons, T. (1951), *The Social System,* Glencoe, Illinois.

Przeworski, A. and Teune, H. (1970), *The Logic of Comparative Social Enquiry.* New York: Wiley.

Rapoport, R. N. (1964), Some Notes on Para-Technical Factors in Cross Cultural Consultation. *Human Organization,* vol. 23, No. 1. Spring 1964, 5–10.

Roberts, K. (1967), *International Research Related to Organizational Behavior: An annotated bibliography.* Published Graduate School of Business, Stanford University.

Roberts, K. (1970), On Looking at an Elephant: An evaluation of cross-cultural research related to organizations. *Psychological Bulletin,* 74, 327–350.

Rokkan, S. (Ed.) (1968), *Comparative Research across Cultures and Nations.* The Hague: Monton.

Rus, V., Heller, F. and Drenth, P. (1978), *Contingency Power in Long Term Decision Making.* World Congress of Sociology, Uppsala, August 1978.

Schleuck, E. K. (1966), Cross-National Comparisons Using Aggregate Data: Some substantive and methodological problems. In: Merritt, R. and Rokkan, S. (Eds.), *Comparing Nations: The use of quantitative data in cross-national research.* New Haven, Conn.: Yale University Press.

Schweitzer, T. (1975), *Data Quality and Data Quality Control in Cross-Cultural Studies.* Paper to I.I.M. Conference on Problems of Cross Cultural Comparative Research. 28–30 Nov. 1975.

Servan-Schreiber, J. J. (1967), *The American Challenge.* Atheneum.

Taylor, E. B. (1971), *Primitive Culture,* Vol. 1.

Triandis, H. (1972), *The Analysis of Subjective Culture.* New York: Wiley.

Trist, E. (1976), Towards a Post Industrial Culture. In: Dubin, R. (Ed.), *Handbook of Work, Organization and Society.* Chicago: Rand McNally.

Vallier, J. (Ed.) (1972), *Comparative Methods in Sociology.* Berkeley: University of California Press.

Warren, H. C. (Ed.) (1934), *Dictionary of Psychology.* Boston: Houghton Mifflin & Co.

CHAPTER 2

Cross-cultural organizational psychology: Challenges and limitations*

Pieter J. D. Drenth

INTRODUCTION

Socialization is the process by which an individual develops his actual behaviour, influenced by what is customary and acceptable according to the standards of his group (Child 1954). Within the total set of social stimuli a great number have an accidental and unsystematic nature. A subset however is shared by the reference group, is persistent over generations, and is adaptive to changes in the physical world and social environment. One can speak of 'behaviour patterns acquired and transmitted by symbols, constituting the distinctive achievements of human groups' (Brislin et al. 1973) or, somewhat more restricted, of 'patterns of roles and norms embedded in certain paramount values' (Kroeber & Parsons 1958). It will be understood that in these specifications we refer to the concept of 'culture'. The social environment, therefore, plays a predominant role in the shaping of human behaviour, and important persons and institutions act as social agents in the socialization process, by making use of their reinforcement power.

With increasing industrialization more and more people spend most of their working life in work organizations of one or another form. Of course there are large differences in the way the organization influences the attitudes and behaviour of members, ranging from the alienated orientation of the Western worker in a mass production industry (Sheppard & Herrick 1972), to the care and provision of the large Japanese work organizations which extend to a good deal of the leisure time and family as well (Murayama 1977; Dore 1973). It is obvious that the study of interactions between organizations and their structural characteristics, on the one hand, and human behaviour, on the other, may yield interesting insight into the nature and determinants of the latter. In fact, the study of this interaction is the task of what is called *organizational psychology*.

*First published in: S. H. Irvine and J. W. Berry, *Human Assessment and Cultural Factors*, Plenum Press, 1983, New York.

Organizational psychology deals with two main questions: What are the effects of organizational characteristics and processes on human attitudes and behaviour, and which conditions have an influence on these relationships? This second broad question deals with contingencies, and implies yet another, more specific question: Under what conditions do certain organizational characteristics lead to effective performance or to organizational commitment and under what conditions do they not? Many of these contingent factors are inherent in the organization itself, such as technology, type of product, size, and formal aspects (centralization, formalization, differentiation, specialization). Other contingency factors are related to the individual or the group (age, sex, social economic class, education, mobilization). Again others may stem from the broader physical or social environment, such as geographical conditions, political regime, level of employment, and prevailing value systems to mention but a few.

CROSS-CULTURAL ORGANIZATIONAL PSYCHOLOGY

In the introduction it was shown that both culture and organizations have a determining influence on human behaviour. The crux becomes, then, how these two sets of determinants may interrelate, may influence each other or may be jointly dependent on other factors. Cross-cultural organizational psychology has set itself the task of studying this particular issue.

The two main questions of organizational psychology which we presented in the introduction can, in cross-cultural perspective, be specified more precisely. Can organizational characteristics, which (co)determine human behaviour in organizations, be *explained* by cultural factors? Of course, this question begs two others: Do organizations differ cross-culturally, and can these differences be explained in terms of cultural determinants? It is indeed important to know whether organizational styles affect the performance and reactions of its members, but it is always more important to know whether these different styles originate in the traditional norms and values of the culture itself.

The second broad question could be put as follows: Are the relationships between such organizational factors as work climate, participative style, degree of formalization on the one hand, and performance, satisfaction, commitment of organizational members on the other, contingent upon cultural variables? Here culture has become a moderator or contingent factor in the relationship between organizational aspects and human behaviour. With these two questions we will concern ourselves in this chapter.

The question whether organizations are culture-bound is not identical to the question whether organizations are culturally determined. The former refers to whether or not organizations differ across

FOUNDATIONS FOR CROSS-CULTURAL STUDIES

cultures, and the latter to the explanation of these differences in terms of cultural factors. Culture can indeed influence organizations and their characteristics; and there are two ways through which such an influence can be imagined.

The first way is through *political* and *legal agencies*. It can be argued that there is a mutual interaction between beliefs and values on the one hand and legal norms on the other. In fact one may state that legal norms bring under legal regulations some defined pattern of behaviours which until the formulation of the law were regulated by customary morals, folkways, mores or any other social control mechanism.

Secondly the organization can be affected by cultural factors through its participants. The first and probably most important group of participants is *management*. It will be clear that managers who set up, manage and often change an organization inscribe in the organization their preferences and premises. However, other participants also may be mentioned. Organizations are also shaped by attitudes and behaviour of the *employees* and the shop floor *workers*. They bring in norms from outside and have a direct (through representation and direct influence) or indirect (through the formation of informal organizations and informal lines of communication) impact on the structure and behaviour of the organization.

It necessarily follows that cross-cultural research on attitudes, values and roles of managers and/or workers must be of interest to the cross-cultural organizational psychologist. They are hypothetical determinants within any organization which, in its turn, influences the behaviour of the members again.

Various writers suggest that, even if differences in organizational characteristics between cultures do exist at present, this will be a declining if not disappearing phenomenon. The reason is that with increasing industrialization the impact of cultural differences on organizations will become smaller and smaller, and the influence of economic and technological factors will become stronger. This point of view is described as the 'convergence hypothesis'. Organizations will become more and more alike, and cultural differences will fade away (see also Cole 1973; Form 1979; Negandhi 1979). Groenendijk (1981) argues, however, that this convergence hypothesis is, first, very difficult to verify, and that the validation evidence which has been brought forward is not always sufficiently convincing. Furthermore, he continues, the evidence for the convergence hypothesis depends strongly on the definition of 'culture.'

METHODOLOGICAL PROBLEMS

In spite of their significance cross-cultural studies on organizations are rather recent. Before the 1960s the topic attracted very little attention.

One of the first was by Udy, who in the late fifties started a study of organizations in traditional societies, with a special eye on the impact of the social structures on the formal aspects of the organization (Udy 1970). Another leading organizational sociologist compared French with Russian and American organizations in the beginning of the sixties (Crozier 1963).

The reluctance of organizational psychologists to move into the cross-cultural field is not without reason. Cross-cultural or cross-national research in general may have its difficulties, both theoretically and practically. Cross-cultural organizational psychology, however, is facing a number of extra difficulties which will be discussed briefly.

First, the problem of the conceptual, functional and score equivalence of measures is more pertinent in organizational psychology than in the other fields of comparative research, such as experimental psychology or the measurement of personality and intelligence. A basic difficulty is that in organizational psychology constructs are mostly quite complex and abstract (with an exception, of course, of attitudinal measures). The logical distance between the construct and operational levels is usually quite large. This means that in comparative organizational psychology, although the measures often are factual and observable, the criteria for functional equivalence which Poortinga defined (Poortinga 1975) are much more difficult to meet than in comparative 'individual' psychology. (Even there they seem to be met only at the very basic level of psychological or experimental variables such as perception and reaction time.) For the measures of the complex and multi-causal concepts in organizational psychology (centralization, communication, formalization, mechanization, Price 1972), it will be extremely difficult to demonstrate functional and score equivalence (see also Przeworski & Teune 1970).

A second problem is a pragmatic but not less important one, a rationale for the sampling of countries and the sampling of organizations within countries. In an ideal case the selection of countries is made on the basis of a theory or the problem in question. This can be a representative sample of countries or the total set of countries within a certain domain (Western Europe or Latin America). It can also be one of the two options discussed by Przeworski and Teune (1970): the most similar systems design (countries differ only on the independent variable) or the most different systems design (countries differ as much as possible so as to check the theory under the most 'unfavourable' conditions). However, pragmatic factors such as availability of financial and personal resources, and the accessibility of organizations in the respective countries, will hinder such an ideal selection.

Moreover, the sampling of organization types within the country is often operationally difficult. Very often the research is time consuming and costly for the organization, and the desired permission is not easily obtained. More complications arise if a definition of 'organization' is to be kept uniform in various countries. Company structures, their financial and organizational embeddedness in larger holdings or umbrella organizations may vary extensively across countries. This often renders tendentious the comparability of the unit of analysis and reduces sampling to a purposive level. Even if the organization is the unit of analysis the variable 'organization' can transcend classification by 'country'. For example, in an interesting study Hofstede (1977, 1979a, 1979b) compared organization behaviour in a large number of countries with respect to four characteristics. In this study, all companies belonged to the same large multinational corporation, thereby introducing cluster sampling as a further complication. Generalizability over countries, therefore, may be tempered with lack of generalizability over companies. Likewise the samples studied by Haire et al. (1966) and Bass (1977) are not random or representative. A pragmatic, purposive compromise is generally the best one can do, as McMillan et al. (1973) point out.

A third methodological difficulty has to do with the level of aggregation, which in organizational studies may be higher than the level of individual data. Two problems should be brought forward at this point. The first concerns the number of observations at different levels. The higher the level of aggregation the lower the number of units of analysis. The number of organizations which has been reached in the IDE study (IDE 1981)—134—is really rare in cross-cultural organizational psychology. But at the individual level the N was 7832!

Furthermore, there is the classical difficulty of ecological correlations (Robinson 1950). It can be argued that it may not be justified to make inferences about relationships between variables at an individual level on the basis of correlational data based upon groups as units. If, for example, it is found that there is a correlation between degree of union membership and works council membership at an organizational level, it may be incorrect to conclude that this relationship exists for individuals. It may be true that union members do not tend to be member of works' councils (individual level), but that in organizations with a high degree of unionization the unorganized workers are more active in work councils (organizational level). At the same time a correlation at an individual level may disappear at a higher level of analysis since the individual variables may be cancelled out, being similarly distributed in all organizations. This is the Durkheimian type of fallacy (Blalock 1961). In general, as Scheuch (1966) shows, ecological correlations are higher than individual correlations even if the phenomena covary equally at the two levels. This is because in the process of averaging a good deal of the error variance existent at the individual level is being eliminated.

In the fourth place we may mention the problem of collinearity making the interpretation of the findings often difficult. Ideally one selects in the various countries samples of organizations which are as

---

much alike as possible. In that case the country differences are the only explaining variable for possible differences in organizational behaviour or performance. This ideal is never reached. National samples of organizations are often less comparable for other reasons as well, such as technological, economic, composition of the work force (male/female ratio), educational level, degree of unionization, and the like. Some people may argue that the latter factors (educational level, unionization, male/female ratio) are substantial parts of culture indeed, and that these differences should not be explained away or eliminated by stressing the matching criterion too much.

This last observation is correct. But it should be possible to identify and analyse these factors so as to study what is behind the factual conclusion that there are national differences. Or, in the words of Przeworski and Teune (1970), explanation means replacement of system names with variables, or countries with national characteristics. We will return to this point later.

APPARENT SHORTCOMINGS

Not only is cross-cultural organizational psychology rather recent, what has been achieved also suffers from a number of weaknesses. First, it can be said that most of the comparative work has been built upon samples from a restricted (very often only two) number of countries. Examples are the replication of the Lawrence and Lorsch study in Germany (Ruldi and Lawrence 1970), the execution of the Aston study in France (Benguigui 1979), and the many applications of Tannenbaum's control graph in another country (Tannenbaum and Cooke 1979). This restriction makes it difficult, if not impossible, to generalize the cross-cultural value of the theories.

Another restriction of much cross-cultural research in work organizations is that it is mainly concerned with individual reactions and attitudes of organizational members. Examples are the cross national study of managerial attitudes in 14 countries by Haire et al. (1966), the comparative study in managerial objectives (Bass and Eldridge 1973), managerial attitudes (Hofstede 1973), managerial values (Hofstede 1976, England 1975), psychological needs among managers (Redding 1976), work goals among employees (Ronen 1979), decision making styles (Heller and Wilpert 1981), and the like. For a review of some earlier work see Roberts (1970) and Barrett and Bass (1976).

It may even be concluded that these studies do not belong to cross-cultural organizational psychology as is defined in this chapter. The role of the organization in these studies is restricted to being the system in which the people, whose attitudes or behaviour patterns are compared, are working. The organization per se is not the subject of study either as determinant, or as moderator, or even as intervening variable in understanding the organizational behaviour of people.

Moreover, many studies like these suffer also from a basic theoretical weakness. Often the differences which are found are explained in terms of 'culture'. It can never be clear, from such limited designs, what the real cause of the differences might be. Since culture is defined as a pattern of beliefs, norms and roles, the explanation of the differences in attitudes in terms of culture runs the risk of being tautological in nature. Roberts (1970) has argued that the search for differences in traits among cultures is futile as an explanatory device. She advocated replacing the search for culture traits in phenotypical variables with the search for a set of genotypical variables that can be used to explain other variables.

Part of the more recent work in cross-cultural organizational psychology does not direct itself to individuals but to organizations as such. One example is the 'internationalization' of the Aston studies on organizational indices, in which Canadian and American results were compared with the original British data (McMillan et al. 1973). A second, Tannenbaum's cross-national research in organizations on the basis of his previous work, in which he developed and operationalized the concept of 'power distribution' and 'total amount of power' in organizations (Tannenbaum 1968); in this comparative study, five countries were included (Tannenbaum et al. 1974). This study in its turn was extended by a recent multi-country study coordinated through the Vienna Centre (Tannenbaum and Rozgonyi, in press). Also, the work of Hofstede deserves mention. Two of his measures, the Power Distance Index, and the Role Orientation Index, have been used at the organizational level, and form the basis for grouping of a number of clusters of countries (Hofstede 1979). Finally, we will mention the study carried out by an international research group of which the present author is a member, studying the impact of formal participative systems on actual involvement and participation in organizations in eleven European countries plus Israel (IDE 1976, 1979, 1981a, 1981b). Where the unit of analysis is the organization instead of individual responses the situation is different. If one deals with supra-national structural variables, which have a factual character and can be observed or derived from objective or recorded data the danger of a tautological fallacy is less eminent.

Of course, what has been said before also applies to the study of cross-cultural differences in organizations. Even if one finds cultural (often national) differences in organizational characteristics, it is not necessarily the 'culture' that is responsible for these differences. The researcher is still faced with ruling out other explanatory factors within the national context, such as economic conditions, level of national development, level of employment, type of product, etc. Clearly, not all *national* differences are caused by *cultural* factors, and the researcher is expected to take the next step of trying to make it plausible that it is the cultural factor indeed which is responsible for the differences. This has very seldom been done, and the reasons for it are quite understandable. One can never rule out all (even plausible) explanations, one can never rule out alternative explanations completely, and, moreover, it is sometimes very difficult to define an alternative interpretation as non-cultural, or unrelated to cultural factors (unionization, educational level, political structure).

CULTURE AND ORGANIZATIONAL DIFFERENCES

What *kinds* of culture-bound differences between organizations can be identified? The simplest level concerns the *presence or absence* of a certain characteristic or organizational feature. Whether or not there is a work council in organizations, whether or not there is a workers' representative on the Board of Directors, whether or not there exists child labour, and so on, are all examples of organizational differences between countries, which may be influenced by cultural factors.

Next there is the *difference in degree* in a particular organizational trait or characteristic. Lammers and Hickson (1979), who discuss various examples of these kinds of differences, mention the difference in formalization between American and British firms. In British firms one is less inclined to install and follow formal rules than the American firms, although similar forms of governance exist in both countries.

In our own study (IDE 1981) we found differences between countries regarding the relative value of representative and direct participation to be in general far greater than those determined by organizational variables such as production type, size or hierarchical level. In Table 1 the regression coefficients for these four independent variables are indicated.

Table 1: Prediction of Attitudes towards Representative and Direct Participation

Dependent variables	Independent variables			
	Country[a]	Sector[b]	Size	Level[c]
Effects of Representative Participation	.27[d]	—	.07	.04
Evaluation of Representative Participation	.29	—	.06	.07
Interest in Representative Participation	.24	—	—	.17
Effects of Direct Participation	.32	.05	—	.16
Rating of Direct Participation	.21	.10	—	.35

[a]12 countries
[b]service vs. metal industry
[c]hierarchical levels in the organization
[d]adjusted beta coefficients, i.e., adjusted for the effect of the other three variables.

Source: IDE International Research Group, 1981a, ch. 8.

Przeworski and Teune (1979) do not find these types of trait differences all that interesting. They attach more importance to differences in patterns of relationships. 'Systems differ not when the frequency of

FOUNDATIONS FOR CROSS-CULTURAL STUDIES

particular characteristics differ, but when patterns of relationships among variables differ.' With that distinction in mind, attention may be given to differences in *patterns* of characteristics which may be determined by culture. Of course, a typical pattern does not have to coincide with a country, and there could be types of patterns, which typify certain clusters of countries. A type in this respect is a certain configuration of covarying variables.

Accordingly, Lammers and Hickson (1979) make a rather strong case for three types of organizations.

A *classic bureaucracy* is typified by a high degree of centralization and bureaucratic control, pronounced stratification, many conflicts and little innovativeness. This type of organization is believed to be found more frequently in Latin countries (Italy, Spain, France and the Walloon part of Belgium). Lammers and Hickson guess that many Eastern European organizations also conform to this type, particularly where rigid state control of industry occurs. More liberal regimes foster the Anglo-Saxon type, a more *flexible bureaucracy*. This is found in North Western Europe (Scandinavia, Germany, Netherlands) and Great Britain and the USA. In such organizations one finds more decentralization of authority, less rigid stratification and less bureaucratic control, higher morale and cooperativeness, and a stronger orientation towards innovation. Third World organizations are typified by what is called the *traditional organization*: little specialization, little formalization, strong centralization and rigid stratification, rather low morale, a conflict orientation and little innovativeness. Of course, American subsidiaries in Third-World countries accord well with the Anglo-Saxon type.

With some minor deviations these clusters do not differ very much from other attempts to classify countries in terms of organizational characteristics by Haire et al. (1966) and Hofstede (1979). An empirical test of the theory may be given by our own research (IDE 1981a), where an attempt has been made to identify country clusters and profiles. Neither by use of a taxonomic 'blind' technique, nor by a more *a priori* and deductive approach based on the clusters which have been distinguished in textbook taxonomies, has a consistent pattern emerged. Only on a restricted number of variables a different pattern of Latin versus Nordic–Anglo-Saxon could be demonstrated (see fig. 1).

Some reasons for this lack of confirmation in our attempt to cross-validate the cluster-hypothesis are discussed in IDE (1981a, pp. 277–279). One of the possible explanations put forward is that clear-cut cultural differences are associated with fairly broad general issues; and these general issues cannot be identified in specific behaviour. Such difficulties are functions of predominantly questionnaire-based research as opposed to the more specific decision oriented approach of the IDE study.

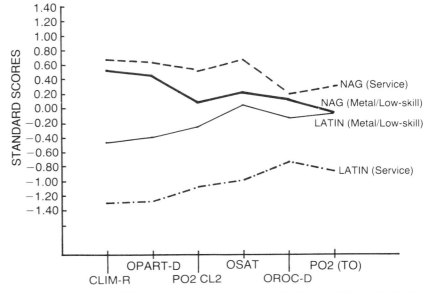

Fig. 1. Country cluster differences in the service sector and high–low skill samples in the metal sector companies (standard scores: Latin and Nordic–Anglo-German) (cf. IDE 1981a, ch. 10).

CLIM R   = Quality of Management–Employee Relations
OPART–D = Rating the Consequences of Direct Participation
PO2 CL2   = Involvement Score on short-term decisions
OSAT   = General Satisfaction
OROC–D   = Rating of Consequences of Direct Participation
PO2(TO)   = Participation score on all types of decision

The fourth aspect of organizational differences which may be caused or influenced by culture concerns *relational differences*. In this form there are different patterns of relationships in different countries. Here culture is a moderator, or contingent factor in a relationship between two or more organizational variables. For example, general work dissatisfaction or dissatisfaction with specific work aspects (security, pay) may lead to collective actions including strikes. This causal relationship is found in a much lesser degree in Yugoslavia than in Great Britain (IDE 1981b). Peruvian workers tend to react positively to close supervision and pressure for production, whereas North American workers show a negative reaction towards this leadership style (Williams, Whyte and Green 1966). Presthus (1961) shows on the basis of his study in Turkey that typical bureaucratic features of organizations, such as specialization, division of labour and hierarchical structure in countries that do not adhere to Western values, may lead to inefficiency and ineffectiveness, in contrast to

FOUNDATIONS FOR CROSS-CULTURAL STUDIES

Western organizations, where productivity is enhanced. In Britain the correlation between size of the organization and decentralization is stronger than in Germany (Child and Kieser 1979). For a decentralization overview of the relationships between organizational context and structure variables, see Hickson et al. (1979).

In all these examples it may very well be that cultural factors (such as value of authority, value of achievement, value of cooperation) are responsible for these differences. As Lammers and Hickson state:

> In general it can be said that cultural factors may affect the sign of certain correlations if values, norms, and role prescriptions entail opposite beliefs or attitudes about what constitutes a 'natural', 'normal' or even 'rational' reaction on the part of organizational participants (1979, p. 408).

Of course, it has to be demonstrated. The controversy between defenders of the cultural explanation and the defenders of the non-cultural explanation (technology, economy) will continue to exist for some time to come, and will be difficult to resolve for the pragmatic, theoretical and methodological reasons, already discussed. It remains, however, an interesting and challenging mission for the cross-cultural organizational psychologist, since it promises to increase insight in the determinants of human behaviour in organizations.

IS IT CULTURE?

In an attempt to go beyond the more descriptive level of analysis of country differences has been made by the IDE International Research team (see the last chapter of IDE 1981b). In the empirical study it was found that substantial differences between countries existed in the legal framework governing worker participation in different types of decisions. For an overall ranking of the twelve countries see the first four columns of Table 2.

An interesting question was how to explain these differences. Basically three alternative explanations could be brought forward: an 'economic', a 'cultural', and a 'structural' explanation.

The reasoning behind the economic explanation is that only in times of affluence do managers and their representatives think that they can 'afford' participation, assuming that participation is a costly affair. Additionally, a more advanced technology (in the richer countries) might require more involvement and contributions of shop-floor personnel in decision making. In analyses over countries, two economic indices have been used for the relative affluence of the country: an index of the economic growth (rapid versus slow, or with periods of stagnation), and wealth (relative ranking in terms of GPD per capita in 1975).

The *cultural* explanation would assume the participative legislation to be a consequence of certain model attitudes and values about co-operativeness, equalization of power and influence which exist in the

Table 2: Relative Standing of Twelve Countries as to Degree of Prescribed Involvement of Workers or their Representatives in Decision Making in Enterprises, and Relative Strength of Twelve Countries with respect to Conditions Favourable to de jure Participation (1947–1975)

Country	Direct involvement of workers[a]	Involvement of repr. bodies[a]	Board representation[b]	Overall standing[c]	Strength of unions[d]	Strength of management[d]	Econ. growth[e]	Wealth[f]	Cooperativeness of ISR[f]	Econ. equality[f]	Political democracy[f]
Yugoslavia	1	1	1	A	?	?	1	3	1	1	?
Germany	4	2	1	A	1	1	1	1	1	2	3
Sweden	5	3	1	A	1	1	1	1	1	1	1
Norway	2	11	1	B	1	1	1	1	2	3	1
Netherlands	10	5	2	C	2	2	1	2	1	2	2
France	8	4	2	C	2	2	1	2	2	3	1
Belgium	6	7	3	D	2	2	1	2	2	2	2
Finland	3	10	1	D	2	1	1	2	2	2	1
Denmark	9	8	3	D	1	3	1	3	3	1	3
Israel	12	6	3	D	2	2	2	1	3	3	2
Italy	7	9	3	E	2	3	2	3	3	3	3
Great Britain	11	12	3	E	2	3	2	3	3	1	2

[a] relative ranking
[b] right of appointment=1
no board participation=3
in between=2
[c] weighted combination of three variables
[d] 1=strong, 2=average, 3=weak
[e] 1=rapid, 2=slow/stagnation
[f] relative ranking 1–3

Source: IDE International Research Group 1981b, p. 255/266.

country. Three indices have been used to quantify this attitudinal complex: political democracy (relative ranking in terms of an index of 'democratic history'), economic equality (relative ranking in terms of inequality of income distribution in the mid 1960s), and 'cooperativeness of the industrial relations system' (relative ranking in terms of days lost per 1000 employed due to strikes in the period 1967–1976).

The *structural* explanation reasons that an elaborate system of formal participation will be developed and reinforced only if both parties, unions and employers, have a sufficiently strong position. A combination of strong unions and management is conducive to a high degree of prescribed involvement in enterprise policy and decision making. The strength of unions' and employers' organizations was estimated on the basis of an analysis of the industrial relations system in the various countries.

An empirical comparison of the different alternative explanations is presented in Table 2 (right part) in which the relative strength of the various conditions, favourable to *de jure* participation, is indicated. No *single* explanatory factor can be held responsible for the variance in *de jure* participation; and the 'cultural' explanation seems the weakest. Neither the degree of political democracy, nor the sorting for economic equality, is related to the overall ranking of countries. The only aspect which seems to be related is the degree of cooperativeness. The economic explanation seems to have some validity, especially as far as the economic growth factor goes. The prediction that equally strong labour and management in a country would be a favourable condition for the promotion of formal systems of participation finds strong support in the data.

Summarizing, one might conclude that a system with strong labour and management, economic growth and prosperity, and attitudes favouring cooperation rather than polarization and contentiousness may foster the development of a system of formal participation in a country. 'Real' culture factors hardly play a role. One may even argue that the variable 'cooperativeness of the IRS' might be a consequence rather than a determinant of the participative legislative system, in which case only the economic and the structural explanations prevail.

This study is discussed in some detail to show that notwithstanding the complexity and the high level of abstraction of the phenomenon, it is possible to look behind the data that simply indicate that there are differences in organizational characteristics between countries, and to try to determine the relative strength of the various competing explanatory factors, some of which we always thought to be cultural in origin.

SUMMARY AND CONCLUSION

In this paper attention has been paid to the importance of the study of cross-cultural organizational psychology for the understanding of human behaviour. Differences in cultural attitudes and value systems may affect human behaviour in organizations in various ways (see fig. 2).

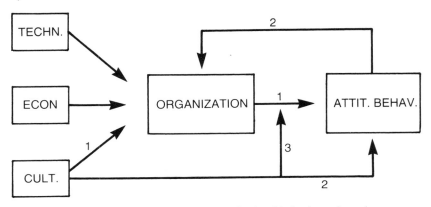

Figure 2. Model of influence of culture on organizational behaviour of members.

In the first place culture may have a direct influence upon the organization (in addition to economic and technological determinants), whereas the organization in turn influences individual behaviour (line 1 in Fig. 2). In the second place cultural factors may influence attitudes, role perceptions and values of the organizational members, which in their turn shape the organization. This again has an influence on the actual behaviour of the various (groups) of participants (line 2 in Fig. 2). In the third place cultural factors may mediate or moderate between organizational features and individual behaviour or attitudes (line 3 in Fig. 2).

It was shown that the study of cross-cultural organizational differences has its specific difficulties and pitfalls. It was stressed that the mere establishment of cultural or national differences in organizational traits, or rather patterns or relationships of organizational characteristics, is not sufficient. One should take one step further and try to explore whether it is really the cultural factor which is responsible for these differences.

If properly done, the study of cross-cultural organizational psychology may contribute more broadly to our understanding of attitudes, reactions and behaviour of people in organizations.

REFERENCES

Barrett, G. V., and Bass, B. M. Cross-cultural issues in industrial and organizational psychology. In Dunnette (Ed.), *Handbook of Industrial and Organizational Psychology.* Chicago: Rand McNally, 1976.
Bass, B. M. Utility of managerial self-planning on a simulated production task with

FOUNDATIONS FOR CROSS-CULTURAL STUDIES

replications in twelve countries. *Journal of Applied Psychology,* 1977, **62**, 506–509.

Bass, B. M., and Eldridge, L. Accelerated managers' objectives in twelve countries. *Industrial Relations,* 1973, **12**.

Benguigui, G. l'Evaluation de la bureaucratisation des enterprises. *Sociologie de Travail,* 1970, **12**, 140–151.

Blalock, H. M. *Causal Inferences in Non-Experimental Research.* Chapel Hill: University of North Carolina Press, 1961.

Brislin, R. W., Lonner, W. J., and Thorndike, R. M. *Cross-Cultural Research Methods.* New York: Wiley, 1973.

Child, I. L. Socialization. In G. Lindzey (Ed.), *Handbook of Social Psychology* (II). Cambridge: Addison-Wesley, 1954, pp. 655–692.

Child, J., and Kieser, A. Organization and managerial roles in British and West German companies: An examination of the culture-free thesis. In Lammers, C. J., and Hickson, D. J. (Eds.), *Organizations Alike and Unlike.* London: Routledge & Kegan Paul, 1979.

Cole, R. E. Functional alternatives and economic development: An empirical example of permanent employment in Japan. *American Sociological Review,* 1973, **38**, 424–438.

Crozier, M. *Le Phénomène bureaucratique.* Paris: Editions du Seuil, 1973.

Dore, R. *British Factory—Japanese Factory.* London: Allen & Unwin, 1973.

Duijker, H. C. J. Nomenclatuur en systematiek der psychologie. *Nederlands Tijdschrift voor de Psychologie,* 1959, **14**, 176–217.

England, G. W. *The Manager and his Values: An International Perspective from the USA, Japan, Korea, India and Australia.* Cambridge: Ballinger, 1975.

Form, W. Comparative industrial sociology and the convergence hypothesis. *Annual Review of Sociology,* 1979, **5**, 1–25.

Groenendijk, G. B. *De Kunst van het Vergelijken.* Amsterdam: Free University, 1981.

Haire, M., Ghiselli, E. E., and Porter, L. W. *Managerial Thinking, an International Study.* New York: Wiley, 1966.

Heller, F. A., and Wilpert, B. *Competence and Power in Managerial Decision Making.* New York: Wiley, 1981.

Hickson, D. J., McMillan, Ch. J., Asumi, K., and Horvath, D. Grounds for comparative organization theory: Quick sand or hard core? In Lammers, C. J., and Hickson, D. J. (Eds.), *Organizations Alike and Unlike.* London: Routledge & Kegan Paul, 1979, pp. 25–41.

Hofstede, G. H. The importance of being Dutch: Nationalists en beroepsverschillen in werkorientatie. In Drenth, P. J. D., Willems, P. J., and Wolff, Ch. J. de (Eds.), *Arbeids—en Organisatiepsychologie.* Deventer: Kluwer, 1973, pp. 334–349.

Hofstede, G. H. Nationality and espoused values of managers. *Journal of Applied Psychology,* 1976, **61**, 148–155.

Hofstede, G. H. Cultural elements in the exercise of power. In Poortinga, Y. H. (Ed.), *Basic Problems in Cross-Cultural Psychology.* Amsterdam/Lisse: Swets & Zeitlinger, 1977.

Hofstede, G. H. Hierarchical power distance in forty countries. In Lammers, C. J., and Hickson, D. J. (Eds.), *Organizations Alike and Unlike.* London: Routledge & Kegan Paul, 1979a.

Hofstede, G. H. Value systems in forty countries: Interpretation, validation and consequences for theory. In Eckensberger, L., Lonner, W., and Poortinga, Y. H. (Eds.), *Cross-Cultural Contributions to Psychology.* Lisse: Swets & Zeitlinger B.V., 1979b.

IDE–International Research Group. Industrial democracy in Europe. *Social Science Information,* 1976, **15**, 177–203.

IDE–International Research Group. Participation: Formal rules, influence and involvement. *Industrial Relations,* 1979, **18**, 273–294.

IDE–International Research Group. *Industrial Democracy in Europe.* Oxford: Oxford University Press, 1980a.

IDE–International Research Group. *Industrial Relations in Europe.* Oxford: Oxford University Press, 1980b.

Kroeber, A. L., and Parsons, T. The concepts of culture and a social system. *American Sociological Review*, 1958, **23**, 582–583.

Lammers, C. J., and Hickson, D. J. (Eds.). *Organizations Alike and Unlike*. London: Routledge & Kegan Paul, 1979.

Marcson, S. (Ed.). *Automation, Alienation and Anomie*. New York: Harper, 1970.

McMillan, C. J., Hickson, D. J., Hinings, C. R., and Schneck, R. E. The structure of work organizations across societies. *Academy of Management Journal*, 1973, **16**, 555–569.

Murayama, M. The oriental paradigm in business value systems. In Poortinga, Y. *Basic Problems in Cross-Cultural Psychology*. Lisse: Swets & Zeitlinger, 1977, pp. 353–360.

Negandhi, A. R. Convergence in organizational practices: An empirical study of industrial enterprise in developing countries. In Lammers, C. J., and Hickson, D. J. (Eds.), *Organizations Alike and Unlike*. London: Routledge & Kegan Paul, 1979.

Poortinga, Y. H. Limitations on intercultural comparison of psychological data. *Nederlands Tijdschrift voor de Psychologie*, 1975, **30**, 23–39.

Presthus, R. Weberian versus welfare bureaucracy in traditional society. *Administrative Science Quarterly*, 1961.

Price, J. L. *Handbook of Organizational Measurement*. Lexington: Heath and Co., 1979.

Przeworski, A., and Teune, H. *The Logic of Comparative Social Inquiry*. New York: John Wiley, 1970.

Redding, S. G. Some perceptions of psychological needs among managers in South-East Asia. In Poortinga, Y. H. (Ed.), *Basic Problems in Cross-Cultural Psychology*. Amsterdam/Lisse: Swets & Zeitlinger, 1977.

Roberts, K. H. On looking at an elephant. *Psychological Bulletin*, 1970, **74**, 327–350.

Robinson, W. S. Ecological correlations and the behaviour of individuals. *American Sociological Review*, 1950, **15**.

Ronen, S. Cross-national study of employees' work goals. *International Review of Applied Psychology*, 1979, **28**, 1–11.

Scheuch, E. K. Cross-national comparisons using aggregate data: Some substantive and methodological problems. In Merritt, R., and Rokkan, S. (Eds.), *Comparing Nations: The Use of Quantitative Data in Cross-National Research*. New Haven: Yale University Press, 1966.

Segall, M. H. *Cross-Cultural Psychology*. Monterely: Brooks/Cole, 1979.

Sheppard, H. L., and Herrick, N. Q. *Where Have all the Robots Gone? Workers' Dissatisfaction in the 70's*. New York: Free Press, 1979.

Tannenbaum, A. S. *Control in Organizations*. New York: McGraw-Hill, 1968.

Tannenbaum, A. S., and Cooke, R. A. Organizational control: A review of studies employed in the control graph method. In Lammers, C. J., and Hickson, D. J. (Eds.), *Organizations Alike and Unlike*. London: Routledge & Kegan Paul, 1979.

Tannenbaum, A. S., Kavcics, B., Rosner, M., Vianello, M., and Weiser, G. *Hierarchy in Organizations*. San Francisco: Jossey-Bass, 1974.

Tannenbaum, A. S., and Rozgonyi, T. (Eds.). *Authority and Reward in Organizations*. Oxford: Pergamon Press (in press).

Udy, S. H. *Work in Traditional and Modern Society*. Singlewood Cliffs: Prentice Hall, 1970.

Williams, L. K., Whyte, W. F., and Green, Ch. S. Do cultural differences affect workers' attitudes? *Industrial Relations*, 1966, **9**, 105–117.

PART II

Research on Cross-Cultural Management

André Laurent's work with executives at INSEAD, a European management institute in France, is an interesting study of managerial ideologies from several European cultures: Denmark, Great Britain, Netherlands, Germany, Sweden, Switzerland, France, Italy as well as the USA. The results provide an illustration of nationally bounded collective *maps* about organizations which cast serious doubts on the universality of management and organizational knowledge and praxis. Joynt integrates both macro and micro concepts in a behavioural analysis of organizational behaviour in four countries. Using the map approach for analysis the results show the need for more research and study on the aspects of cultures impact on organizational behaviour.

Anant Negandhi moves us into an area that has received almost no attention in much of the cross-cultural work. His work includes results from six developing countries: Argentina, Brazil, India, Philippines, Taiwan and Uruguay. Negandhi also reviewed a second study, which sought to evaluate the impact of technology and socio-economic systems upon work attitudes and behaviour. Two countries, India and the USA, were examined in detail from this nine-country study. Pjotr Hesseling examines a central third-world hypothesis—the transformation of instrumental rationality towards institutional and societal rationality in knowledge cycles. Indonesia is the focus for this interesting work.

No modern text is complete without alluding to the Japanese competitive edge. Andreas Falkenberg attempts to answer the 'why' and the 'how' of this central issue in cross-cultural management. We conclude the second part with the Obtój–Joynt contribution, which studies organization innovation using ten cases from Poland.

It is impossible in a book of this size to include all countries and all aspects of cross-cultural management; however, we feel the above can give the reader a realistic view of the depth and breadth of the issues involved at the conceptual level as well as with methodology and application.

CHAPTER 3

The cultural diversity of Western conceptions of management

André Laurent

BACKGROUND

In the last few years, I have been looking at the process of managing as an implementation process by which managers translate into behaviour some of their basic, implicit beliefs about effective action in organizations. This interest emerged while I was attempting to introduce managers to alternative models of managing and organizing. I realized that any attempt to communicate alternative ideas about the process of management was headed for failure if it could not in some way first address the implicit management gospel that managers carried in their heads. This became a growing conviction a few years ago when I was, for instance, trying to communicate to groups of French managers the potential interest of matrix organization design (Laurent 1981). The idea of reporting to two bosses was so alien to these managers that mere consideration of such organizing principles was an impossible, useless exercise. What was needed first was a thorough examination and probing of the holy principle of the single chain of command and the managers' recognition that this was a strong element of their own belief system rather than a constant element in nature.

Every manager has his own management theory, his own set of representations and preferences that in some way guide his potential behaviour in organizations; and it is critical for managers, management researchers, and educators to identify and understand these implicit theories of management better. This conviction that every manager has his own management gospel provided the initial ground for the research reported here, research that was not originally designed to be comparative.

In order to elicit managers' implicit theories of management, I had developed a questionnaire proposing 56 different statements about the

First publication: *Int. Studies of Man. & Org.*, Vol. XIII, No. 1–2, pp. 75–96. M. E. Sharpe, Inc., 1983.

management of organizations. A five-point opinion scale was attached to each statement to record the respondent's degree of agreement or disagreement with those statements. Owing to the bilingual setting in which the survey was to be administered, the questionnaire was developed in both English and French simultaneously rather than formally translated from one language into the other. A great deal of care was taken to avoid words, expressions, or sentence constructions that could not communicate fairly equivalent meaning in both languages.

The questionnaire was initially administered to a group of 60 upper-middle-level managers from various companies attending an executive development program at INSEAD, a European management institute located in France. This first group was composed of 40 French managers and 20 managers from several other European countries.

The original idea was simply to use the recorded opinions of the managers as an input in the pedagogical process. The objective was to explore and discuss the participants' implicit theories of management.

Since I was aware of the work conducted by my colleague Geert Hofstede, who was, at the time, analyzing his bank of comparative survey data from the Hermes multinational corporation (Hofstede 1980a), I decided to compare the results of the group of 40 French managers with those of the 20 non-French managers. The differences in opinion between these two *ad hoc* cultural groups appeared to be so great on so many items of the questionnaire that they could not be ignored.

These results led to the main working hypothesis of this subsequent research study, namely, that *the national origin of European managers significantly affects their views of what proper management should be.* National culture seems to act as a strong determinant of managerial ideology. The objective of the research thus became to assess and identify some of the national differences in concepts of management.

RESEARCH METHODOLOGY

The 56-item Management Questionnaire was systematically administered to groups of upper-middle-level managers attending the various INSEAD executive development programs between 1977 and 1979. The managers came from a large number of different enterprises and from a variety of Western countries. So as not to influence the responses, the data were always collected before beginning a program. Most of the questionnaires were administered in their English version to respondents of all nationalities, all of whom were fluent in English. For a few French-speaking programs, the French version was used.

The first part of this report summarizes the results obtained with 817 respondents from 10 Western countries (9 European countries and the United States). National sample size varies from a low of 32 for Italy to a high of 219 for France. Within each national sample there is some variance in terms of function, educational background, age, types of companies, etc. The only common characteristic of the respondents is their participation in management-education programs attracting upper-middle-level managers from a large number of business firms. The data-collection strategy was designed to randomize, as much as possible, all variables except nationality. Attempts at controlling other sources of variance in the data are presented in the second part of this report.

Statistical analysis of the data was performed by computing 'ecological' correlations among country mean scores across the 56 items. This approach of ecological factor analysis, which has been used and advocated by Hofstede (1980a, Chap. 2), considers the group—national culture, in the present case—as the unit of analysis. Thus, correlations are run among country scores, not individual scores, in an attempt to identify groups of questions in which the distribution of scores for the various countries shows similar patterns from low to high agreement across the clustered questions. These groups of questions or indices suggest factors or dimensions that may meaningfully differentiate national cultures in terms of their managerial ideologies.

Four indices or dimensions emerged from the statistical analysis. Three of them cluster three questions each; one of them clusters four questions. The four dimensions have been labeled: organizations as political systems (Table 1), organizations as authority systems (Table 2), organizations as role-formalization systems (Table 3), and organizations as hierarchical-relationship systems (Table 4). Ecological correlations among country mean scores computed across the 56 items and leading toward the selection of these four dimensions are presented in Table 5.

The four dimensions or indices do not pretend to be exhaustive. They have been selected strictly on the basis of the high level of statistical association among countries, the number of items they cluster, and the conceptual meaning of the clustered items.

The indices represent attempts to capture a structure of *collective* managerial ideologies that meaningfully differentiates national cultures. They do not account for individual ways of thinking within a given culture. Indeed, whereas correlations among country scores are very high across the clustered items within a given index, correlations among individual scores for a given country within the same index have proved to be remarkably low.[1] Once again, the purpose here is not to analyze the structure of individual opinions, but to compare countries.

Although statistical analysis was performed initially on country

1. A. Laurent (1980) 'Dimensions Culturelles des Conceptions de Management. Une Analyse Comparative Internationale'. Working Paper 80–82. Fontainebleau: European Institute for Business Administration (INSEAD), February 1980.

mean scores from five-point opinion scales, the results are presented here in terms of percent average agreement scores ('strongly agree' and 'tend to agree' responses) and percent average disagreement scores ('strongly disagree' and 'tend to disagree' responses) for ease of reading and interpretation. Each table thus presents the percentage of managers agreeing or disagreeing with each statement and their percent average score across the clustered questions (last row of the table) for each country. This last measure indicates the country score or position on the index. In each table, countries are ordered from left to right according to their increasing degree of identification with the measured dimension.

RESULTS

Organizations as Political Systems (Table 1)

The dimensions 'organizations as political systems' clusters three items dealing, respectively, with the political role played by managers in society (item No. 40), their perception of power motivation within the organization (item No. 49), and an assessment of the degree to which organizational structures are clearly defined in the minds of the individuals involved (item No. 33). In countries such as France and Italy, where managers report a stronger perception of their political role in society, they also emphasize the importance of power motivation within the organization and report a fairly hazy notion of organizational structure. Danish and British managers, on the other hand, express a significantly lower political orientation, both within and outside the organization, and a clearer notion of organizational structure.

These results may provide some insight into the extent to which managers from different countries tend to interpret their organizational experience in power terms. Clearly, the political orientation of Italian (index score 66) and French managers (index score 62) appears much stronger than the political orientation of Danish (index score 26) and British managers (index score 32). Furthermore, these findings indicate an interesting association at the country level between a lower inclination toward political behavior and a greater perceived clarity of structure (in Denmark and Great Britain) versus a greater inclination toward political behavior and a greater perceived haziness of structure (in Italy and France).

I should like to suggest at this point that it may not be by accident that the contrasting results demonstrated by the British and the French managers seem to parallel to a considerable extent the contrasting perspectives on organizations taken a decade ago by mainstream schools of organizational sociology on each side of the Channel. While the British Aston School researchers were conducting their rational analyses of structural characteristics of organizations, French socio-

Table 1: Organizations as Political Systems

772 Managers from nine countries*	Denmark	Great Britain	Netherlands	Germany	Sweden	USA	Switzerland	France	Italy
Sample size	54	190	42	72	50	50	63	219	32
% Agreement with: 40. Through their professional activity, managers play an important political role in society	32	40	45	47	54	52	65	76	74
% Agreement with: 49. Most managers seem to be more motivated by obtaining power than by achieving objectives	25	32	26	29	42	36	51	56	63
% Disagreement with: 33. Most managers have a clear notion of what we call an organizational structure	22	23	36	31	30	42	38	53	61
% Average agreement/disagreement	26	32	36	36	42	43	51	62	66

*Belgium has been excluded from this table because of its indecision rate, more than 20% for 2 items (40 & 33).

logists were describing organizations as sets of games and power strategies played by actors seeking to maintain some uncertainty around their function so as to play even more power games. Organizations were certainly perceived and defined far more as political systems by the latter than by the former. Thus, cultural differentiation may affect not only managers' implicit concepts of organizations but also researchers' explicit theories. Organization and management theory may be as much culturally bounded as the actual processes of organizing and managing (Brossard and Maurice 1974; Derossi 1978; Hofstede 1980b, 1981).

In summary, this index suggests some important effects on organizational behavior of cultural differences in the political outlook of managers in neighboring Western countries.

Organizations as Authority Systems (Table 2)

'Organizations as authority systems' groups three questions dealing with a conception of hierarchical structure as being designed to specify authority relationships (item No. 14), a perception of authority crisis in organizations (item No. 52), and an image of the manager as a negotiator (item No. 43). It differentiates three country clusters of managers' perception of organizations as authority systems. Latin countries such as Belgium, Italy, and France, at the upper end of the continuum (index score 61 to 65), present a sharp contrast to countries such as the United States, Switzerland, and Germany at the lower end (index score 30 to 34), and the remaining four countries fall in the middle (index score 46 to 49).

The belief that 'The main reason for having a hierarchical structure is so that everyone knows who has authority over whom' is associated across countries with the perception that 'Today there seems to be an authority crisis in organizations' and the expectation that 'The manager of tomorrow will be, in the main, a negotiator'. However, national culture strongly affects the popularity of such conceptions. For instance, organizations are seen significantly more frequently as authority systems by French managers (65 percent average agreement rate across items) than by American managers (30 percent average agreement rate).

French, Italian, and Belgian managers report a more personal and social concept of authority that regulates relationships among individuals in organizations. American, Swiss, and German managers seem to report a more rational and instrumental view of authority that regulates interaction among tasks or functions. For the former, authority appears to be more a property of the individual; for the latter, it appears to be more an attribute of the role or function.

This index reveals important national variations in managers' views of authority in organizations that are likely to influence their behavior.

Table 2: Organizations as Authority Systems

817 Managers from ten countries	USA	Switzerland	Germany	Denmark	Sweden	Great Britain	Netherlands	Belgium	Italy	France
Sample size	50	63	72	54	50	190	42	45	32	219
% Agreement with: 14. The main reason for having a hierarchical structure is so that everyone knows who has authority over whom	18	25	24	35	26	38	38	36	50	45
% Agreement with: 52. Today there seems to be an authority crisis in organizations	22	29	26	40	46	43	38	64	69	64
% Agreement with: 43. The manager of tomorrow will be, in the main, a negotiator	50	41	52	63	66	61	71	84	66	86
% Average agreement	30	32	34	46	46	48	49	61	61	65

Organizations as Role-Formalization Systems (Table 3)

The three items clustered in 'organizations as role-formalization systems' all focus on the relative importance of defining and specifying the functions and roles of organizational members. They stress the values of clarity and efficiency that can be obtained by implementing such organizational devices as detailed job descriptions, well-defined functions, and precisely defined roles. Here the results seem essentially to indicate a relatively lower insistence on the need for role formalization in Sweden, the United States, and the Netherlands (index score 57 to 67) than in the remaining seven countries (index score 80 to 85).

Hence, there may be national variations in the degree of formalization, often considered an important structural characteristic of organizations, that is judged desirable.

Organizations as Hierarchical-Relationship Systems (Table 4)

The last index, 'organizations as hierarchical-relationship systems', which groups four questions, shows sharp differences in management attitudes toward organizational relationships as one moves from Northern Europe and the United States on the lower end of the continuum to the Latin countries of Europe on the higher end.

Across countries, the dream of eliminating conflict from organizations is associated with the belief that a manager should definitely know more than his subordinates and that organizations should not be upset by such practices as bypassing or having to report to two bosses.

As suggested elsewhere (Laurent, 1981), an index such as this one can provide some assessment of the feasibility of new organizational arrangements—such as the matrix structure—that deviate from more classic hierarchical forms. Indeed, in matrix-type organizations, as opposed to more classic hierarchies, potential conflicts of interest about resources tend to surface more, bosses can no longer pretend to have answers to most of their subordinates' questions, bypassing of authority lines becomes more of a way of life, and, obviously, some managers have to report to two or more bosses.

Thus, the contrasting results obtained from Swedish managers (index score 25) and Italian managers (index score 66) suggest that matrix-type organizational arrangements might have better prospects in Sweden than in Italy. National variations in conceiving organizations as hierarchical relationship systems may affect the structuring of organizations in different countries and have implications for the transfer of organizational forms across cultures.

LIMITATIONS OF THE FINDINGS

The four dimensions reported above that seem to differentiate national cultures in terms of their managerial ideologies represent one

Table 3: Organizations as Role Formalization Systems

817 Managers from ten countries	Sweden	USA	Netherlands	Denmark	Great Britain	France	Belgium	Italy	Germany	Switzerland
Sample size	50	50	42	54	190	219	45	32	72	63
% Agreement with: 1. When the respective roles of the members of a department become complex, detailed job descriptions are a useful way of clarifying	56	76	71	87	86	87	89	90	89	91
% Agreement with: 13. The more complex a department's activities, the more important it is for each individual's functions to be well-defined	66	69	79	85	85	83	84	94	93	94
% Disagreement with: 38. Most managers would achieve better results if their roles were less precisely defined	50	54	52	67	68	72	71	69	73	71
% Average agreement/disagreement	57	66	67	80	80	81	81	84	85	85

Table 4: Organizations as Hierarchical Relationship Systems

817 Managers from ten countries	Sweden	USA	Netherlands	Great Britain	Denmark	Switzerland	Germany	Belgium	France	Italy
Sample size	50	50	42	190	54	63	72	45	219	32
% Agreement with: 19. Most organizations would be better off if conflict could be eliminated forever	4	6	17	13	19	18	16	27	24	41
% Agreement with: 24. It is important for a manager to have at hand precise answers to most of the questions that his subordinates may raise about their work	10	18	17	27	23	38	46	44	53	66
% Disagreement with: 2. In order to have efficient work relationships, it is often necessary to bypass the hierarchical line	22	32	39	31	37	41	46	42	42	75
% Agreement with: 8. An organizational structure in which certain subordinates have two direct bosses should be avoided at all costs	64	54	60	74	69	76	79	84	83	81
% Average agreement/disagreement	25	28	33	36	37	43	47	50	50	66

Table 5: Ecological Correlations*

	Index I (politics)			Index II (authority)	
Items	49	33	Items	52	43
40	0.73	−0.85	14	0.86	0.69
49		−0.89	52		0.88

	Index III (formalization)				Index IV (hierarchy)		
Items	13	38	Items	24	2	8
1	0.95	−0.91	19	0.88	−0.90	0.82
13		−0.83	24		−0.87	0.80
			2			−0.64

*Pearson r among country mean scores. Country mean scores per item were computed for each of the ten national samples on the basis of the managers' responses to the five-point opinion scale attached to every questionnaire item.

attempt at mapping some of the cultural differences in concepts of management and organization within the Western world. Looking at organizations as symbolic systems of social representation, this research elicits findings that emphasize the need to recognize and identify cultural specificity as a critical element in the texture of organizations. Furthermore, the reported cultural diversity poses significant challenges for both management theory and practice and seriously questions claims of universality in both.

These findings have important limitations, however.

First, they reflect the limitations of the questionnaire itself. Another researcher with different interests would have devised different questions and would have obtained other dimensions of differentiation among cultures.

Second, these findings probably reflect the French cultural identity of the author through the questions he thought of and included in the list in the first place. Indeed, it may not be accidental that whereas the positions of other countries tend to vary from index to index, the position of the Latin countries, including France, is on the high-score side of all four indices. Thus, the research findings indicate that French managers, more than managers from non-Latin countries, tend to view organizations as political, authority, role-formalization, and hierarchical-relationship systems.

From this perspective, the findings provide clearer indications about Latin countries such as France than about others in the sample. They reveal the widest gap in conceptions of management between the Latin cluster (France, Belgium, Italy) and the Nordic cluster of America and Europe (United States and Sweden). Would a British questionnaire designer have elicited dimensions illustrating the same gap? Even though Hofstede's work (1980a) partly eliminates such questions by inter-correlating the results of various independent comparative studies, and in spite of attempts by multicultural teams of researchers to design research tools jointly, the methodological challenge persists.

A third limitation of the findings stems from the limited number of countries represented in the sample. Similar data subsequently collected from Japan and Indonesia do indicate the Western bias of some of the dimensions. For instance, Japanese managers obtain both high and low scores on questionnaire items regrouped in the same Western index, thus challenging the validity of the ecological factor. The validity of the four dimensions is therefore restricted to the ten Western countries represented in the initial sample.

Finally, one may seriously wonder whether the *ad hoc* sampling method of surveying relatively small groups of managers attending executive development programs at INSEAD is valid for making inference about national cultures. Since legitimate questions could be raised concerning the representativeness of the population surveyed in the initial study, several subsequent studies were conducted to assess the validity of the preliminary results.

REPLICATIONS OF THE STUDY

A partial replication of the original survey was initially obtained by administering the same Management Questionnaire to a much younger population of British and French MBA students at INSEAD. The results, reported elsewhere (Laurent 1981), confirmed, on a preliminary index, the differences observed between British and French experienced managers.

Another partial replication was performed with a group of 55 French MBA students from ISA, a French business school. Their index scores are reported in Table 6, along with the index scores of the experienced French managers from the initial survey. The scores of these French MBA students run parallel to the scores of the experienced French managers, with a tendency toward perceiving organizations even more as role-formalization and hierarchical-relationship systems than the managers.

Table 6: Index Scores of French MBA Students and French Experienced Managers

Subjects	Index I (politics)	Index II (authority)	Index III (formalization)	Index IV (hierarchy)
55 French MBA students (ISA)	61	64	90	66
219 French experienced managers (INSEAD)	62	65	81	50

Fuller replication was then obtained in two, large, US-based, multinational companies. Since the initial results had been obtained from *ad hoc* samples of managers in executive programs, the question arose of whether similar differences in management and organizational concepts would persist within the potentially homogenizing, corporate culture of a single multinational company, or whether the multinational culture would be sufficiently strong and pervasive to swamp national differences.

NATIONAL VERSUS MULTINATIONAL CULTURES

The MNC-A Study

In order to test the above hypothesis, carefully matched national samples of managers were selected from a large, US-based, multinational, chemical firm (MNC-A) with subsidiaries in France, Germany, and Great Britain. Every attempt was made through sampling to control for all conceivable sources of variance other than nationality. A description of sample characteristics is presented in Table 7.

Table 7: MNC-A Study—Survey Sample Characteristics

Characteristics	France	Germany	Great Britain
Sample size	48	39	56
Percentage of response rate	80	91	97
Average age	42	43	40
Average number of years of work experience	17	18	18
Average number of years of service with company	15	15	14
Average number of years lived abroad	2.5	1	1.5
Percentage of respondents working in primarily line position	70	65	59
Percentage of respondents working in primarily staff position	30	35	41
Percentage of respondents with higher education at university level	91	81	85
Percentage of respondents with major professional experience in technical fields (production, engineering, maintenance, etc.)	60	58	59
Percentage of respondents with major professional experience in marketing	18	25	23
Percentage of respondents with major professional experience in administration	22	17	18

Index scores are reported for the three national groups in Table 8, along with the index scores obtained by the *ad hoc* INSEAD national samples from the original study. Although a few variations—perhaps due to corporate culture—did appear, the results clearly indicated the consistent and pervasive effects of national cultures for the three countries involved. The average distance among the three countries' scores across the four indices remained essentially the same (INSEAD sample = 13.3; MNC-A sample = 13.0), as did the average range of the country scores across the four indices (INSEAD sample=20; MNC-A sample=19.5).

Actually, when the results were analyzed not only across the 13 questions that constitute the 4 indices but across the totality of the 56 questions initially asked in the survey, it was found that:

— the range of MNC-A country averages (variance of the country means) was 28 percent greater than the range of INSEAD country averages;

— the MNC-A country averages were more widely spread than the INSEAD country averages on 41 of the 56 questions answered (73 percent).

A homogenizing effect of a large multinational corporation toward standardization of managerial concepts across national cultures was certainly not found in these data. If anything, the opposite hypothesis could be advanced.

The MNC-B study

Finally, another replication of these findings was obtained within another large American multinational company in the office-equipment industry (MNC-B). This time a different research strategy was used. A small *ad hoc* group of 30 large account managers from the 10 Western countries represented in the INSEAD study was surveyed with a condensed questionnaire containing only the 13 questions that constitute the 4 indices. 'National' sample sizes were a low 2 for the United States, Sweden, Denmark, Belgium, and Italy; a medium 3 for Germany and the Netherlands; 4 for France and Switzerland; and a high 6 for Great Britain. Minute sample sizes were, however, compensated for by a very high degree of occupational homogeneity among respondents and a very strong company culture.

Results from opposite clusters of countries on each of the four indices are presented for this group of respondents in Table 9. They demonstrate once again an intriguing overall stability of the national patterns of managerial ideologies, given the very tight conditions of the research design. The average distance among clustered countries' scores across the four indices again remained the same (INSEAD sample=26.5; MNC-B sample=26.0). There was no indication of any reduction in cultural differences in management concepts within MNC-B.

CONCLUSIONS

The findings summarized here provide an illustration of nationally bounded collective mental maps about organizations that seem to resist convergence effects from increased professionalization of management and intensity of international business. Neighboring Western nations seem to be forming fairly differentiated images of organiza-

Table 8: Index Scores of MNC-A and INSEAD Managers

	Index I (politics)		
	Great Britain	Germany	France
MNC-A managers	24	33	45
INSEAD managers	32	36	62

	Index II (authority)		
	Germany	Great Britain	France
MNC-A managers	38	42	53
INSEAD managers	34	48	65

	Index III (formalization)		
	Great Britain	France	Germany
MNC-A managers	71	88	88
INSEAD managers	80	81	85

	Index IV (hierarchy)		
	Great Britain	Germany	France
MNC-A managers	29	45	54
INSEAD managers	36	47	50

Table 9: Index Scores of MNC-B and INSEAD Managers for Opposite Clusters of Countries

	Index I (politics)	
	Denmark+Great Britain+Netherlands+Germany	France+Italy
MNC-B managers	33	56
INSEAD managers	33	64

	Index II (authority)	
	USA+Switzerland+Germany	Belgium+Italy+France
MNC-B managers	30	69
INSEAD managers	32	62

	Index III (formalization)	
	Sweden+USA+Netherlands	Denmark+Great Britain+France+Belgium+Italy+Germany+Switzerland
MNC-B managers	57	78
INSEAD managers	63	82

	Index IV (hierarchy)	
	Sweden+USA+Netherlands	Belgium+France+Italy
MNC-B managers	32	53
INSEAD managers	29	55

tions and their management. This attempt to use a comparative phenomenological approach to the study of organizations seems to elicit findings that cast serious doubt on the universality of management and organizational knowledge and praxis.

It may very well be that the management process in these ten Western countries is as much culture bound as their cooking, and that international management has to avoid the trap of international cuisine. National cultures may still offer some genuine recipes.

REFERENCES

Brossard, M., and Maurice, M. (1974) 'Existe-t-il un modèle universel des structures d'organisation?' *Sociologie du Travail,* No. 4, pp, 402–426. (English translation: 'Is There a Universal Model of Organization Structure?' *International Studies of Management & Organization,* 1976, VI(3), pp. 11–45.)

Derossi, F. (1978) 'The Crisis in Managerial Roles in Italy.' *International Studies of Management & Organization,* VIII(3), pp. 64–99.

Hofstede, G. (1980a) *Culture's Consequences: International Differences in Work-related Values.* Beverley Hills, Calif.: Sage Publications.

Hofstede, G. (1980b) 'Motivation, Leadership and Organization: Do American Theories Apply Abroad?' *Organizational Dynamics,* Summer, pp. 42–63.

Hofstede, G. (1981) 'Culture and Organizations'. *International Studies of Management & Organization,* X(4), pp. 15–41.

Laurent, A. (1981) 'Matrix Organizations and Latin Cultures. A Note on the Use of Comparative Research Data in Management Education.' *International Studies of Management & Organization,* X(4), pp. 101–114.

CHAPTER 4

Cross-cultural management: The cultural context of micro and macro organizational variables

Pat Joynt

INTRODUCTION

The notion of culture can be defined in many ways, but features such as shared rules of appropriate behavior or norms, patterned ways of thinking, feeling, values, reacting and expectations emerge in most definitions. Hofstede (1980, p. 13) defines culture as 'collective programming of the mind', and reserves the word for describing entire societies. Subcultures are used for groups within societies, and this chapter will adopt this frame of reference. Perhaps, the most complete definition of culture comes from Kluckholm (1951, p. 86):

> Culture consists in patterned ways of thinking, feeling and reacting, acquired and transmitted mainly by symbols, constituting the distinctive achievements of human groups, including their embodiments in artifacts; the essential core of culture consists of traditional ideas and especially their attached values. In many ways, culture could be described as the personality of society.[1]

The concern of this study is with micro and macro organizational management variables measured within societies. This area has also been labelled comparative management (Nath 1975; Negandhi 1975; Weinshall 1977). Two theories have tended to emerge from this literature—the convergency or culture-free theories, which imply similarity, and the contingency theories, which imply uniqueness (see chapter 2).

Recent research and literature (England and Lee 1974; Walle 1977; Schein 1980; Knudsen 1982) on the analysis of social groups point to the existence of a 'management subculture' in organizations. 'There is reason to believe that actual management behavior is based on norms that result in strategies for unilateral control of organizational events. People who become managers do so when they show evidence of having accepted the norms of management culture' (Knudsen 1982, p. 1). While others (Hofstede 1980) have often implied a management

---

1. The reader is also encouraged to review chapters 1 and 2 for a more detailed definition of culture.

subculture in their work, the above suggests this should be formally accounted for in a research design.

The concern in the context of this study is with the cross-cultural or comparative management studies that have emerged as a more or less natural outgrowth of empiric work in one country where the methodologies and concepts are then applied to another country. Integration between organization theory (research within one country) and cross-cultural management (research in several countries) is needed because of the convergence of overall findings from these two approaches. Negandhi (1975) concludes that this integration is 'conceptually and methodologically' desirable because:

1. Both theories use the principle of equifinality.
2. There is no universal applicability in both theories.
3. Objective measures are often used in developed countries, and subjective judgment (emotions, religious beliefs) is used in developing countries.
4. There are similarities and differences among managers around the world. Differences can sometimes be explained by using cultural factors.

Negandhi (1975, pp. 338–339) goes on to define the present state of the art:

> Until such time as these general systems concepts (size, technology, workflow, leadership style, strategy, structure, behavioural patterns and effectiveness) are fully developed and operationalized, the so-called midrange approach, contingency theory, seems to be providing a realistic means of utilizing some of the salient attributes of the systems concept for the study of complex organizations.

Weinshall (1977), Roberts et al. (1977) and Sorge (1979) make a strong argument for the need to study the relationship between culture and management. Also, Richman (1977) states that the debate between those who believe that efficient and effective management is based on universal principles, practices and general know-how which can and should be transferred to other countries, and those who advocate that management is essentially culture-bound, will probably be intensified as a result of current cross-cultural and international research activity. Roberts (1977) reviewed 526 publications in 26 substantive areas. Her subtitle seems a most appropriate summary of the field—*On looking at an elephant: an evaluation of cross-cultural research related to organizations.*

A REVIEW OF MICRO AND MACRO CROSS-CULTURAL MANAGEMENT RESEARCH

Rather than identify and use a single work, a group of studies will be reviewed in the area of cross-cultural management. The rationale for this approach is, for the most part, based on the present interest in the area, however, there is little evidence of a single theory being most significant. Early studies in the area include explorative and descriptive analyses by Farmer and Richman (1964), Harbison and Myers (1959) and Haire et al. (1966). The more recent studies include Negandhi (1971), Miller and Simonetti (1971), Cummings et al. (1972), Granick (1972), England (1975), Horovitz (1977), Weinshall (1977), Warner (1977), Sorge (1979) and Hofstede (1980). While much of the recent research remains explorative, some degree of agreement on variables and methods of analysis seems to be emerging. Miller and Simonetti (1971, p. 87) summarized the state of the science as:

> despite increased interest in the effect of the social environment upon management and the individual, little agreement exists as to the relative strength of internal and external factors or as to which forces are the most important. This resultant state of flux is due to the broad scope of the environment, the lack of homogeneity in research methods and the introspective nature of the forces studied.

Richman (1965, 1977) identifies some of the problems in this perspective:

1. Lack of clarity and consistency in defining and using such critical terms as principles, culture bound and management philosophy.
2. Confusion between normative, descriptive and predictive elements of management theory.
3. Absence of basic theoretical conceptual framework within which to hypothesize that certain cultural factors do in fact generally and significantly tend to influence the performance of management.
4. The lack of developmental research.

Three studies from the literature, Granick (1973), England (1975) and Hofstede (1980) deserve a methodological review because of their similarities to the present study. England used a Personal Values Questionnaire (PVQ) consisting of 88 questions that was administered over a period of ten years to large samples of managers from the United States, Japan, Korea, India and Australia. Statistical analyses included mean dispersions for each country and significant differences between countries. Granick (1973) used a linear approximation with a general regression model by first specifying the model and then testing it, using a group of interviews and objective data collected by the main researcher. The dependent variable was managerial effectiveness of the national industrial system. The independent variables included: competence of management, quality of planning, decentralization, risk, achievement, negative effects of centralization, coordination and quality of decisions.

Hofstede (1980) collected data from 40 countries, using a large multinational corporation (HERMES), with a large questionnaire in 20 languages. The country scores from HERMES were evaluated using four dimensions (power distance, uncertainty avoidance, individualism and masculinity), and scores were by rank or correlation statistics. Translations of the questionnaire involved a trial test period by personnel in HERMES.

In addition to the above several writers have tried to describe the major trends in comparative and cross-cultural research. Negandhi (1975), Nath (1974/75) and Cummings (1974/75) reviewed comparative management work, and attempted to evaluate the possibilities of linking comparative management with organization theory. Negandhi (1975) and Nath (1974/75) divide the comparative work into four major approaches. The first approach can be identified as the *economic development approach*. It is best exemplified by the work of Harbison and Myers (1959). Four stages of economic development were postulated, beginning with an agrarian-feudalistic system and concluding with an industrial democratic state.

The second approach is called the *environmental approach*, and can best be exemplified by the work of Farmer and Richman (1964). While the authors did not operationalize their variables, they did identify major external factors such as social, cultural, legal, political, educational and economic conditions. This approach has been criticized for an overemphasis on environmental factors (Boddewyn 1966).

The third approach can be identified as the *behavioral approach*, and is a reaction to the environmental emphasis of the second approach. It is based on the hypothesis that there are significant differences among cultures in terms of value systems, beliefs, attitudes and management practices (chapters 1 and 2).

The most recent approach can be labelled the *macro-micro approach*. It utilizes the open systems model in conceptualizing both macro and micro variables. According to Nath (1974/75), the organization environment focuses on such variables as size, technology, organizational climate and the human and capital resources of the firm. The task environment includes distributors, suppliers, employees, consumers, stockholders, government and community. A final layer called the societal environment was identified earlier by Farmer and Richman (1964).

This final approach closely approximates the micro and macro hypotheses which are the essence of this study. Is there a difference between comparative management and organization theory? Nath (1974/75) and Negandhi (1975) would argue that there is a difference, as the titles of their articles seem to imply—'. . . linking the two' and '. . a marriage needed', but Cummings (1974/75, p. 128) argues that there is no difference between the two, namely, that organization theory is equal to comparative management:

. . . then OT=CM. This line of reasoning leads me to question whether we should be searching for links (with the underlying assumption of difference between areas). Perhaps more fruitful strategies would be to:
1. Commit ourselves to careful, rigorous and intensive theoretical development.
2. Focus our best efforts and encourage our best researchers to focus their talents on developing the foundations of an empirical discipline, namely, the canons of scientific methodology, the fundamentals of reliability and validity, and the dogged pursuit of data with a generous dose of caution toward generalization.

In the context of this study the following are relevant conclusions from the above review of cross-cultural and comparative management. First, the discipline is, perhaps, more complex than organization theory, as it exhibits a lack of theoretical agreement and the use of explorative empiricism. Second, sufficient cross-cultural work has emerged which demonstrates dissimilarities in administrative behavior to justify cross-cultural management research as being a worthwhile endeavor. It is this last argument that is most important in the context of this study. Finally, a marriage or a linkage between organization theory and cross-cultural management research is implied through this study's strategy of using operations derived from administration and organization theory. The real issue then becomes empirical control, and not a semantic debate over organization/administrative theory and comparative/cross-cultural management.

THE ADMINISTRATIVE MANAGEMENT MODEL: METHOD AND CROSS-CULTURAL ANALYSIS

The sample used in this research initially consisted of several pilot studies, followed by reports from over 200 Norwegian organization units, who were sampled between 1976 and 1983. The concept of 'organization unit' is used, since the sample boundaries often involved parts of very large organizations, or, in some cases, a group of organizations within the same technology or market. The concept of 'organization unit' is taken from notions of Simon (1952) and Indik (1968). Individuals are considered as the smallest unit of analysis, society at large is the most encompassing unit of analysis, and in between are groups, organizations and institutions. Organization unit can be considered as falling between groups and organizations. In essence, it is part of an organization. The information was obtained from a questionnaire/interview guide in Norwegian, answered by managers involved in working for a particular organization unit in Norway. While there are dangers of inferring features from one level (organizations) of properties measured at another (managers), March (1979, p. 299) argues that 'individuals can speak in answer to question-naires where organizations cannot'.

The administrative management model consists of the following key concepts taken from a review of the theory (Joynt 1980):

Figure 1: Administrative Management Model

Independent Variables	Dependent Variables
Environmental (internal and external)	ORGANIZATION:
Technology	Effectiveness
Organization structure	Efficiency
Conflict Resolution	Innovation
Communication	Satisfaction
Motivation	Profit
Leadership	Survival
Decision Making	Growth
Job Design	

A questionnaire or interview guide is used, and this guide is presently available in Norwegian, English, American, Australian, Icelandic and German. Information was collected using both interviews and the questionnaire. In Norway, the information collection is integrated into a one-year advanced course, where a report is written from the results of a survey of some twenty managers in each organization sampled. In Germany and America the questionnaire-interview technique was used with one to three members of top management in each organization. At this point, 1984, the ongoing character of the research must be emphasized.

The purpose here is to review some of the preliminary results in a cross-cultural perspective. As such, the level of rigor and sophistication will be lower than in the Norwegian work (Joynt 1980), where regression models were generated on the goals/dependent variables. Rather than looking at all the variables in all the countries, only a few central variables will be reviewed, and the statistics used will be comparative analyses of means or rank orders. The countries used are Norway, Denmark, Germany, England and the US.

ANALYSIS

In our analysis we will deal with three of the micro variables that illustrate the diversities between cultures. It is beyond the scope of this chapter to treat the entire model in detail; however, some of the micro and macro results are also shown in chapter 8.

MOTIVATION

While much of the recent work in motivation is involved with the newer process theories, the empiric emphasis is still in the area of defining desired rewards. The initial Norwegian work involved a testing of expectancy theory; however, the empirical results with the

Figure 2: Motivation Factors Map

	NORWAY	DENMARK	AMERICA	GERMANY
INDIVIDUAL ORIENTED FACTORS	2. Professional growth 3. Using own skills on the job 4. Doing something of value 6. Security 7. Challenging job 8. Pay 9. Self-realization	1. Using own skills on the job 2. Doing something of value 3. Self-realization 4. Professional growth 5. Challenging job 6. Responsibility 10. Security	1. Doing something of value 2. Self-realization 3. Professional growth 4. Responsibility 6. Promotion 7. Using own skills on the job 8. Pay 10. Security	1. Doing something of value 2. Pay 3. Challenging job 4. Free time 5. Responsibility 6. Using own skills on the job 7. Professional growth 8. Self-realization
SOCIAL ORIENTED FACTORS	1. Positive peer relationship 5. Positive supervisor relationships 10. Recognition	7. Positive peer relationship 8. Recognition 9. Positive supervisor relationships	5. Positive supervisor relationships 9. Recognition	9. Power 10. Recognition

NOTES: 1: Samples sizes (n=organization unit) varied from country to country; this is also true for Figures 3 and 4.

2: System factors were used in a questionnaire/open interview analysis and only the top ten are ranked above for each country.

Norway: n = 250
Denmark: n = 130
America: n = 14
Germany: n = 10

measuring of instrumentality and expectancy were limited, due to the nature of the measuring instruments. At the international or comparative level, only valence or 'values of desired rewards' is measured.

Figure 2 represents a summary of the motivation factors or needs for Norway, Denmark, America and Germany. The term 'map' is used here to denote the differences in territories or domains of the four countries involved. Norway has a group need, 'positive peer relationships', as the highest desired reward, while Denmark, America and Germany have the individual oriented rewards of 'using own skills on the job' and 'doing something of value' first. Both Denmark and America have individually oriented rewards as primary (with Denmark, the first six have an individual orientation, and with the US, five of the first six have an individual orientation).

Another interesting aspect of the individual/groups/organization dichotomy is the ranking of peer relationships and supervisor relationships. In the US only, positive supervisor relationships emerged in the top ten rewards. In both Denmark and Norway, the value of peer relationships was emphasized above positive supervisor relationships. These results tend to reflect the group value emphasis in Scandinavian countries and the individual value emphasis in America.

Promotion as a value also reflected the individual emphasis in the US. It ranked sixth in the US, and was not ranked in Denmark and Norway. Self-realization also ranked highest in the US, although Denmark also had a high ranking for this value. Analysis of the three countries tends to place Norway and the US farthest apart, with Denmark in the middle.

JOB DESIGN

The new Norwegian work environment act (1977) and the Hackman Oldham (1975) model were used in this part of the analysis. Figure 3 illustrates the broad agreement found among the four cultures. Autonomy defined as 'the opportunity for independent thought and action' was ranked highest in all four countries. Variety, which was defined as 'the opportunity to do a number of different things', was ranked second in the Scandinavian cultures, and third in the US. The only significant difference was feedback, which was ranked second in the US and last in the Scandinavian cultures. Feedback was defined as 'opportunity to find out how well I am doing my job', and is often associated with the opportunity for promotion, which was also high in the US and low in Scandinavia as a desired reward.

The results here tend to illustrate the broad agreement that has emerged in recent years in the area of job design. While the Scandinavian emphasis has been on work groups and the American emphasis on individuals, the overall concept of job design defined in terms of autonomy, variety, significance and, to a lesser degree, variety and feedback, seems to describe the domains in this area.

Figure 3: Job Design Map

Norway	Denmark	America	Germany
1. Autonomy	1. Autonomy	1. Autonomy	1. Autonomy
2. Variety	2. Variety	2. Feedback	2. Variety
3. Job identity	3. Job identity	3. Variety	3. Job identity
4. Task significance	4. Task significance	3. Significance Job identity not measured	4. Task significance
5. Feedback	5. Feedback		5. Feedback

LEADERSHIP

Leadership is one of the most controversial and complex issues in the organizational theories and practices of today. The model used here has its origins in Thorsrud's and Emery's early work on socio-techno theory, in the Ohio State two factor theory of leadership as well as in the University of Michigan research studies. At Michigan, Bowers and Seashore (1966) identified four types of outlook or orientation leaders might have: support, interaction facilitation, goal emphasis and work facilitation. These orientations can be combined with the Ohio State model, which emphasizes production and personnel orientations as well as the Thorsrud and Emery work, which is the pioneering work in Europe, as shown below:

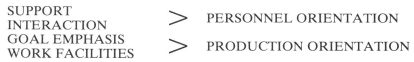

SUPPORT
INTERACTION   >   PERSONNEL ORIENTATION
GOAL EMPHASIS
WORK FACILITIES   >   PRODUCTION ORIENTATION

The new behavioral approaches attempt to emphasize a mixture of the two orientations rather than one alone. Many see this as an integration of the earlier scientific management and production approach to management and the newer human relation approach. The results shown in Figure 4 illustrate the differences in the social and task or technology emphasis in the countries Norway, Denmark, America and Germany. Germany and America tend to have both a heavy technical or task emphasis as well as a social emphasis, while Norway tends to stress the task emphasis. Denmark falls between the groups on the leadership map, as well as in the actual map of the four countries. Interviews with Danish managers tended to show that the Danes felt a need to adjust to both their neighbors, with the result being a middle ground. This area of the research shows much promise for the future. However, the results may be *very* misleading, due to the fact that a questionnaire/interview method was used to seek information on leadership attitudes. The recent legislation in Scandinavia may have tended to 'bias' the answers in an undesired direction. In other words, the legislation may have resulted in a type of negative halo effect.

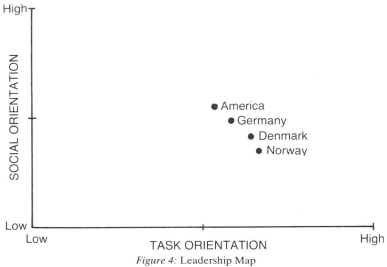

Figure 4: Leadership Map

Recent reviews in the study of cross-cultural management as well as the results of this study, strongly suggest the importance of this discipline for management. In the future, 'cultural maps' may help managers to better accommodate the differences between cultures. Many of the tentative conclusions expressed in this study require much more attention, especially in an international context. As with the manager, the scientist's job is never done.

CONCLUSIONS

The writer again wishes to emphasize both the tentative and ongoing nature of these results. The results are also only a small portion of the information being gathered in the four countries. Types of internal and external environments as well as technology(ies), communication patterns, conflict resolution methods and key organization structure variables are also being studied; in addition other countries are also being sampled. We have emphasized the micro variables in this chapter since much of the other work in Part II has a macro emphasis.

During the present century the theme of internationalization has become an important influence in the management thinking of the world. Few researchers and practitioners of today will question the

RESEARCH ON CROSS-CULTURAL MANAGEMENT

utility of using culture as a key variable in the study of organizations. The many books on Japanese management, European management and American management are an attest to this. The approaches and methodologies vary from the traditional one person's view in a book to numerous tables and figures that summarize and compare the results of economic and attitudinal information. Much of this work needs a more critical interpretation in terms of both the methodology and the type of analysis used. Indeed, the abstract words used to describe management and organization may vary enough between cultures to make comparisons very tentative in nature. The cultural bias in the abstract model or framework used may be disfunctional rather than functional in many respects.

As an example of the above, the writer found that extensive time was required during the trial testing phase of the questionnaire or interview guide in each language. Substantial differences were found between the 'English' and 'American' versions, and a no response rate is very high on some of the questions using the German version. Much of the previous cross-cultural work has been done using only one language, or one theory, and this may be a serious problem taken in the light of the experience here.

This work is limited by the four cultures reported and the cultures fall into the traditional category of Western Countries. The variations may have been greater if other cultures were considered.

REFERENCES

Adler, N. J. Special Issue on Cross-Cultural Management, *International Studies of Management and Organization,* Winter 1982–83, spring 1983.

Boddewyn, J. *Comparative Management and Marketing,* Glenview: Scott-Foresman, 1969.

Bowers, D. G., and Seashore, S. E. Predicting Organizational Effectiveness with a Four-Factor Theory of Leadership, *Administrative Science Quarterly,* Vol. 11, No. 2, 1966.

Cummings, L. L. Personality, Bargaining Style and Payoff in Bilateral Monopoly Bargaining among European Managers, University of Wisconsin, Madison. Monograph, 1972.

Cummings, L. L. Comparative Management and Organization Theory, *Organization and Administrative Sciences,* 1974/75.

England, G. W., and Lee, R. The Relationship between Managerial Values and Managerial Success in the United States, Japan, India, and Australia, *Journal of Applied Psychology,* 1974.

Farmer, R., and Richman, B. A Model for Research in Comparative Management, *California Management Review,* Vol. 4, No. 2, Winter 1964.

Granick, D. *Managerial Comparisons of Four Developed Countries: France, Britain, United States and Russia,* Cambridge, Mass., The MIT Press, 1972. (Revised 1979.)

Hackman, J. R., and Oldham, G. R. Development of the Job Diagnostic Survey, *Journal of Applied Psychology,* 1975.

Haire, M. et al. *Managerial Thinking, An International Study,* Wiley, New York, 1966.

Harbison and Myers, *Management in the Industrialized World: An International Approach,* McGraw-Hill Book Co., New York, 1959.

Hofstede, G. *Culture's Consequences,* Sage Publications, California, 1980.

Horovitz, J. Comparative Management and Control Practices, EIBA Conference, Sweden, 1977.

Indik, B. P. *People, Groups and Organization,* New York, Teachers' College Press, 1968.

Joynt, P. *Contingency Models for Administrative Behavior,* Ann Arbor, 1980.

Kluckholm, C. The Study of Culture in Lerner, D., and Lassvell (Eds.). *The Policy Sciences,* Stanford University Press, 1951.

Knudsen, K. Management Subcultures: Research and Change, *Journal of Management Development,* 1982.

March, C. Problems with Surveys: Methods or Epistemology?, *Sociology,* 1979, 13 (2).

Miller, S. W., and Simonetto, J. L. Culture and Management: Some Conceptual Considerations, Working Paper, Kent State, 1971.

Nath, R. Comparative Management and Organization Theory: Linking the Two, *Organization and Administrative Sciences,* 5, (4), 1974/75.

Negandhi, A. R. Comparative Management and Organization Theory: A Marriage Needed, *Academy of Management Journal,* 18, 1975.

Negandhi, A. R. (Ed.) Special issue on Cross-Cultural Management, *Journal of International Business Studies,* Fall, 1983.

Negandhi, A. R., and Prasad, S. B. *Comparative Management,* New York, Meredith Corp., 1971.

Richman, B. M. Significance of Cultural Variables in Weinshall, T. D. (Ed.), *Culture and Management,* London, Penguin, 1977 and 1965.

Roberts et al. On Looking at an Elephant: An Evaluation of Cross-Cultural Research Related to Organizations in Weinshall, 1977.

Simon, H. A. Comments on the Theory of Organization, *American Political Science Review,* 1952.

Sorge, A. *Culture and Organization.* Berlin, International Institute of Management, 1979.

Schein, E. *Career Dynamics,* Prentice Hall, London, 1980.

Walle, A. Lederutvikling-medlemskap i krise? *Bedriftsøkonomen,* 1977.

Warner, M. *Organizational Choice and Constraint: Approaches to the Sociology of Enterprise Behavior,* Farnborough, Saxon House, 1977.

Weinshall, T. D. (Ed.). *Culture and Management,* London: Penguin, 1977.

CHAPTER 5

Management in the third world

Anant R. Negandhi

INTRODUCTION

The title of this chapter connotes the third world or the so-called developing countries as being homogeneous in their management as well as in their socio-economic, political, legal, and cultural environments. It may need very little argument to prove that such is not the case. The third-world countries, in many aspects, are more heterogeneous in their environments and socio-cultural heritage than many of the industrialized countries. For example, the countries in South East and West Asia predominantly reflect the cultural heritage emanating from Bhuddist, Confucian, or Hindu philosophies, while those in South and Central America share the Christian religion and philosophy (Catholicism), although in terms of the economic and industrial developments, they may all look alike. In terms of economic well-being and standard of living among the developing countries, the oil-rich countries in the Mid-East are far superior to those possessing little oil or no oil at all, although the former countries are much less developed politically, socially, and economically than the latter ones.

Given such heterogeneity in their socio-economic political developments as well as in their cultural milieu, it is useless to talk or write about the third-world countries as a single entity. In other words, to avoid a sweeping generalization concerning the management system in the 100 odd countries, classified as third-world countries, we need not only selectivity and specificity of the topics and the countries but also must have some sort of theoretical or conceptual paradigm to compare and contrast managerial systems of the third-world countries with the industrialized countries. Accordingly, the chapter will discuss and analyze the specific managerial practices, such as planning, control, manpower management, leadership, and directing in a few selected countries like Argentina, Brazil, India, Philippines, Taiwan, and Uruguay with the following conceptual paradigms in mind.

First published in: *Advances in International Comparative Management,* VAI Press, Greenwich, 1983.

Conceptual Paradigms

Two interrelated conceptual paradigms are utilized to analyze the managerial systems in developing countries. These are:

(1) The issue of applicability and transferability of advanced management know-how and practices* of industrialized countries to the developing countries.

(2) The impact of the socio-cultural variables on management practices.

Briefly, the rationale for the applicability and transferability of advanced management know-how and practices rests on the premise that such know-how and practices augment and hasten the industrial and economic development processes in the developing countries, while the issue of the impact of socio-cultural factors on management practices pinpoints the difficulties inherent in transferring advanced management practices to the developing countries.[1]

Whether one believes in these issues or not and considers them relevant and valid under present circumstances, in my opinion, they do provide some systematic way of comparing and contrasting management practices in the developing countries with the industrially-developed world.

The Definition of Advanced Management Know-How and Skills

Although many authors have argued for the transfer of managerial practices and skills from developed countries to underdeveloped ones, few have attempted to provide the operational meaning of such terms. For the purpose of this chapter, we have adopted the definition proposed by AIESBC-International. They have defined managerial skills as 'the special capabilities that make a manager what he is. The capacity to collect, process, and evaluate information; the ability to distinguish the alternatives and make a decision; and the resourcefulness in communicating to others the reasons behind his decisions and actions.'[2]

Translated into operational terms this may involve the following:

1. Systematic and detailed long-range planning of goals and a means of reaching these goals.
2. Greater involvement of member participants in decision-making, both in the planning process and general organizational activities.
3. Objective measurements of achievements against targeted goals.
4. Explanation of deviations between achievements and targeted goals.
5. Exercising the leadership that will contribute most in increasing employee-satisfaction in work and productivity.
6. Establishing selection, training, and promotion procedures which will not only be 'equitable and just', but also more conducive to higher productivity.

RESEARCH ON CROSS-CULTURAL MANAGEMENT

7. Solicitation of employee cooperation at all levels in achieving the firm's objectives or goals.
8. Utilization of techniques and methods, such as cost accounting, quality control, and budgeting, which will enable the firm to reduce costs.

This list is by no means all inclusive. It only outlines the major facets of managerial practices which are more conducive to higher productivity.

Impact of Socio-Cultural Factors

During the last 20 years or so, much has been written on the impact of socio-cultural variables on management practices and effectiveness. In spite of the voluminous writings, there is as yet no clear-cut answer to the specific impact of the socio-cultural factors on management. Accordingly, the issues of applicability, transferability, and utility of advanced management know-how and practices have remained cloudy, if not controversial. It is beyond the scope of this chapter to discuss the subject in detail. However, to provide some perspective on this issue, we will briefly summarize a few of the important cross-cultural management studies.

Brief Review of Cross-Cultural Studies

1. The employees in Brazil preferred participative-democratic style of leadership while in Japan employees preferred more authoritarian leaders. Overall, IBM employees in some 45 countries preferred consultative-type leadership.[3]
2. In terms of managerial attitudes and behavior, there seems to be a cultural cluster of developing countries which are not related in terms of culture as much as in those of economic growth.[4]
3. There are definite culture differences in supervisory preferences and style. India has been found an authoritarian country as compared with the other countries.[5] Morale and productivity were higher under authoritarian than under democratic leadership in India; the results in the United States show opposite effects.[6]
4. Managers projected their own judgments onto others, and they saw differences in a very specific way. For example, Indian managers projected their values mostly upon others and were also least accurate in rating other colleagues. But they did not disparage others. In contrast, the British managers projected almost as much as the Indian managers but did negate others. The Danish, Norwegian, Italian, and Spanish were similar in both empathy and projection, but the Danish and Spanish were higher on negation than Italian and Norwegian managers.[7]
5. There seems a significant difference between managers from various countries both in their problem-solving and their listing

of corporate objectives. Tentative data indicate that the economic factors seem to be of more importance than the cultural variables in this regard. For example, Indian and Columbian managers put less emphasis on meeting competition than do the American, British, and Dutch managers. In general, managers in developed countries lay stress upon objectives of growth and competition; while their counterparts in developing countries are satisfied with the usual maintenance of their operations.[8]

6. Managers from developed countries give the poor performer less than average money in terms of increments as against the manager from the developing countries who did not differentiate salary increments between poor and average performers.[9]

7. Indian managers prefer high risk and ideal outcomes while American managers prefer moderate risk with moderate outcome.[10]

8. In terms of the value systems, the majority of the managers in each country are pragmatically oriented. Although there are similarities in the managers' orientation, G. W. England has advanced the thesis that the cultural factors do make a difference in the managers' orientations.[11]

9. Average level of achievement in a nation is a predictor of subsequent economic growth.[12]

10. More democratic supervisory style is associated with greater growth in GNP and per capita income.[13]

11. Anglo-Americans tend to regard work as an important end in itself; while the concept of work as an end in itself is largely alien to the Mexican culture.[14]

12. Utilization of scientific method is second nature to the US managers. Mexican managers hold no such regard and respect for scientific method.[15]

13. Whereas US managers can be characterized as being 'pro-delegation', Mexican managers can be characterized as being 'anti-delegation'. Participative management embodies a threat to the Mexican manager's role and image as others see it, and is incompatible with his role as he himself perceives it.[16]

More recently, Hofstede, in his study of a single large multinational company (nevertheless a truly monumental and ambitious study), has attempted to demonstrate the strong influence of socio-cultural variables on authority distribution and the boss-subordinate relationship. Utilizing the concept of 'power-distance' between the superordinate and subordinate, he has shown that the power distance between the boss-subordinate is larger in developing countries than in developed nations.[17] (The larger the power distance, the more authoritative or autocratic the leadership style.) Table 1 shows the power distance values in selected developed and developing countries.

Table 1: Power-Distance Index Values in Selected Developed and Developing Countries

Country	Power-Distance Index* (Actual)	Country	Power-Distance Index (Actual)
Philippines	94	South Africa	49
Mexico	81	Argentina	49
Venezuela	81	USA	40
India	77	Canada	39
Singapore	74	Netherlands	38
Brazil	69	Australia	36
Hong Kong	68	West Germany	35
France	68	Great Britain	35
Columbia	67	Switzerland	34
Turkey	66	Finland	33
Belgium	65	Norway	31
Peru	64	Sweden	31
Thailand	64	Ireland	28
Chile	63	New Zealand	22
Portugal	63	Denmark	18
Greece	60	Israel	13
Iran	58	Austria	11
Taiwan	58	Mean of 39 countries	51
Spain	57	(multinational	
Pakistan	55	organization)	
Japan	54	Yugoslavia	76
Italy	50	(same industry)	

Source: Geert Hofstede, 'Hierarchical Power Distance in Forty Countries' in C. T. Lammers and D. J. Hickson, *Organizations Alike and Unlike* (London: Routledge and Kegan Paul, 1979), p. 105. Permission of the publisher gratefully acknowledged.

*Higher the index number, higher will be the power distance and autocratic relationship among the super-ordinates and subordinates.

Table 2 exhibits the causes for national differences in a hierarchical-power distance.

Based on the theory of cognition applied in cross-cultural settings, Reddings and Martyn-Johns[18] advanced and partly tested the following hypotheses through their survey of managerial beliefs in South East Asian countries:

Hypothesis 1: Oriental* companies will use either less formal planning systems, and/or planning systems with fewer variables than equivalent Western companies.

Hypothesis 2: In Oriental companies the degree of formal organization (in terms of defined differentiation of functions, integrating

*For the sake of simplicity the word 'Oriental' is used as an umbrella phrase for the context which is being studied here. It is meant to embrace Hong Kong, Singapore, Malaysia, Indonesia, Thailand, the Philippines (and originally, South Vietnam). Japan is omitted from the list because of its special cultural nature and because of the degree of Westernization which has taken place there, but some of the ideas are still held to apply there.

Table 2: Origins of National Differences in a Hierarchical-Power Distance

Large Power-Distance Index	Small Power-Distance Index
Tropical and subtropical climates	Moderate to cold climates
Survival and population growth less dependent on man's intervention with nature	Survival and population growth more dependent on man's intervention with nature
Less need for technology	More need for technology
Historical events: divided inheritance law	Historical events: integral inheritance law
More traditional agriculture, less modern industry, less urbanization	Less traditional agriculture, more modern industry, more urbanization
Less need for education of lower strata	More need for education of lower strata (literacy, mass communication)
Less social mobility and weak development of educated middle class	Greater social mobility and strong development of educated middle class
Less national wealth	Greater national wealth
Wealth concentrated in hands of small elite	Wealth more widely distributed
Political power held by oligarchy or military	Political power based on system of representation
Little popular resistance to integration into a large state; large size of population	Strong will to be independent; smaller size of population
Historical events: occupation, colonialism, imperialism	Historical events: independence, federalism, negotiation
Centralization of political power	Less centralization of political power
Slower population increase	Faster population increase
More static society	Technological momentum of change
Children dependent on parents and elders	Children learn things which elders never learned: less dependent
Teachers are omniscient. Teaching is one-way	Some teaching is two-way

Source: Geert Hofstede, 'Hierarchical Power Distance in Forty Countries' in C. T. Lammers and D. J. Hickson, *Organizations Alike and Unlike* (London: Routledge and Kegan Paul, 1979), p. 111. Permission of the publisher gratefully acknowledged.

control mechanisms, and co-ordinating processes) will be less than in an equivalent Western company.

Hypothesis 3: In Oriental companies the staffing function will be less programmed and will contain less formal training than in equivalent Western companies.

Hypothesis 4: Oriental managers make promotion decisions using less objective data than equivalent Western managers.

Hypothesis 5: The style of leadership employed by Oriental managers will rely less on interpersonal confrontations with subordinates than would be the case with Western managers, and in order to compensate, different social structures and norms will operate to facilitate control.

Hypothesis 6: Managerial decisions in Oriental companies will take greater account of effects on the relative status of other people, than in Western companies.

Hypothesis 7: The control of performance in Oriental companies will be less formal, using less information and a shorter time span of discretion than the Western equivalent.

Hypothesis 8: Oriental managers will display less precision and less urgency in matters of time such as timekeeping, scheduling, and completion of programs than Western equivalents.

To summarize, the review of cross-cultural management studies indicates the following:

1. There is no one-way of doing things. The principle of equifinality applies to the functioning of social as well as business organizations. Managers may achieve given objectives through various methods.

2. There is no universal applicability of either authoritarian or participating-democratic management styles. In general, the United States can best be characterized as democratic-participative management style, while Germany, France, and most of the developing countries are authoritarian in their management style. Authoritarian style is not necessarily dysfunctional in developing countries. This may be perhaps the 'right type' of leadership.

3. More objective measures are brought to bear in making managerial decisions with respect to compensation, objectives, goal-settings, etc., in the developed countries; while much subjective judgment (emotions, religious beliefs) enters into the decision-making processes in developing countries. '

4. There are enough similarities and differences among the managers around the world. Similarities are explained in terms of industrialization or industrial sub-culture. Differences are explained in terms of cultural variables. Cultural factors are considered as the most important influencing variables.[19]

We shall return later in this paper to argue against the cultural imperative hypothesis. Preceding this discussion, however, we shall attempt to provide some realistic perspectives on the actual management practices utilized in selected developing countries. The following two large-scale, cross-cultural studies were undertaken by the author and his colleagues during the period of 1967 to 1978.

RESULTS OF THE TWO CROSS-CULTURAL STUDIES

Transferring Advanced Management Practices

In the first study reported below, our concern was to examine the applicability and transferability of advanced management practices and know-how from industrialized nations to developing countries. The study was undertaken in six developing countries, namely: Argentina, Brazil, India, Philippines, Taiwan, and Uruguay. It was a comparative study of American subsidiaries and comparable local companies in those countries.

Space limitations preclude us from discussing in detail the findings of the study. The interested reader is urged to refer to the previously published work of the author and his colleagues.[20]

In this chapter attempts are made to summarize the main findings of our study. In so doing, we first provide the overall profiles of organizational practices and effectiveness of US subsidiaries and comparable local firms in the six developing countries studied. Second, we will highlight the regional differences (Latin American countries versus Far Eastern countries) in practices and effectiveness; third, we will discuss the impact of socio-cultural factors on practices and effectiveness.

The data were collected from 56 American subsidiaries, 55 comparable local companies in three Latin American countries—Argentina, Brazil, and Uruguay—three Far Eastern countries—India, the Philippines, and Taiwan—and 15 US parent companies in the USA. The latter data are being used for comparative purposes.

Structured and non-structured interview guides were prepared. Altogether, eight investigators conducted interviews with top, middle, and supervisory personnel as well as employees at operative levels in the six countries. Some interviewers were nationals of the country in question and others were fluent in the language of the country. Some interviews were repeated for clarification. A 40-page interview guide was used to collect specific information. (For interview guide and operationalization of variables see Negandhi, 1975, pp. 274–308.)

PROFILES OF US SUBSIDIARIES AND LOCAL FIRMS

The profile of management practices and effectiveness outlined below includes the firm's orientation toward planning, policy-making, control devices, leadership style, manpower management practices, management effectiveness. The detailed data on which the following conclusions are based can be found in our previously published work (Negandhi 1975).

US Subsidiary

Long-range planning with a time horizon ranging from five to ten years was common practice in the US subsidiaries in the six developing countries. The typical US subsidiary also formulated its long-range plans in considerable detail and involved all levels of managerial, technical, and supervisory personnel in the planning process. The policy-making task was taken quite seriously by this type of firm. Efforts were made to use *major policies* effectively, both as guidelines and as instruments for overall control to achieve the firm's objectives. Major policies were made by top-level executives but, in their formulation, all levels of managerial and technical personnel were consulted and their views considered. These policies were generally concentrated in the areas of pricing, personnel selection, plant investment, and salary and wage standards.

Employee training, employee relations, purchasing, acquisition, and expansion received much less emphasis, however. *Other control devices* used by the US subsidiary included cost and budgetary controls, quality control, the maintenance of equipment, and setting of work standards for blue-collar, supervisory, clerical, and managerial personnel. Such techniques as periodic management audit systems, however, were only used by a few of the US subsidiaries.

The US subsidiary was organized on the basis of major business functions (for example production, sales, accounting, and finance). A typical firm had five to seven departments. Specialized staff personnel were found frequently. Service and maintenance departments were well organized.

Authority definition was clear for each position in the organization. *The degree of decentralization* in decision-making was greater in the US subsidiaries than in the local firms. Attitudes of executives in the US subsidiaries regarding decentralization were only partially consistent with their practices.[21]

The *leadership style* used in the US subsidiary can best be characterized as democratic or consultative. Executives of the US subsidiary manifested a great deal of trust and confidence in their subordinates. The attitudes of the executive of the US subsidiary were not totally consistent with their leadership styles.

Manpower management practices were well developed. The personnel department was organized as a separate unit with a specialized, trained personnel manager. Manpower management policies were formally stated. Such personnel techniques as job evaluation, development of selection and promotion criteria for managerial and technical personnel, and training programs for the blue-collar employees were widely utilized. However, there was not much sophistication in compensation and motivational techniques and practices.

Managerial effectiveness, in terms of handling human resources, was found 'excellent' in some aspects and 'poor' in others. For example, while the typical US subsidiary did not find it difficult to attain high employee morale, it experienced some difficulties in motivating its employees. Particularly, absenteeism was a problem. Employee productivity was average and scrap loss was higher as compared to the US parent companies.

With regard to high-level manpower, the US subsidiary was able to attract and retain trained managerial and technical personnel and was able to achieve cooperative departmental relationships. It was also able to effectively utilize its high-level manpower and adapt and respond to environmental changes without much difficulty. By and large, the US subsidiary made good profits and was expanding its sales considerably (three- to five-fold on average).

The local firm

The planning orientation of a typical local firm can best be characterized as being medium- to short-range. The typical firm in this category planned for a horizon of one or two years. The resulting plans were less comprehensive and detailed. Review procedures, as well as strict adherence to planned targets, were taken less seriously than in the US subsidiary. There was relatively less participation of other echelons of managers in the planning activities.

Policy-making was less formalized and generally not documented. No serious attempts were made to utilize major policies as guidelines or control mechanisms; however, some other forms of control devices were utilized. They included quality control, cost control, and maintenance of equipment.

The organizational set-up in this type of firm was not very different from that of the US subsidiary. For example, the various divisions and departments within the firm were organized on the basis of such major business functions as production, sales, and purchasing. Similar to the US subsidiary, the local firm had five to seven departments. The departmental lines were not clear-cut, however. The local firm generally did not utilize specialized staff personnel, although a service department was utilized to some extent.

Authority definition was very unclear and diffuse. *The degree of decentralization* was low as compared to the US subsidiary. *The leadership style* could best be characterized as paternalistic. Trust and confidence in subordinates was low.

Manpower management practices were least developed. The personnel department itself was not organized as a separate unit, and a qualified and trained personnel manager was not employed. No attempts were made to formulate manpower policies.

Job evaluation techniques, however, were utilized in some form or another. Some attempts were also made to formulate selection and promotion criteria. Training and development programs were poor and used only for blue-collar employees. Compensation and motivational techniques being utilized were simple and mainly monetary in nature.

Management effectiveness in the local firm was poor compared to the

US subsidiary. For example, employee morale in this firm was moderate, absenteeism high, turnover low, and productivity low.

In terms of high-level manpower, the local firm was less successful in attracting and retaining trained managerial and technical personnel. Interdepartmental relationships among different departments ranged from 'somewhat cooperative' to 'poor'. Managers of this type of firm seemed to stress optimization of the departmental goals in contrast to the firm's overall goals and objectives. Also, the typical local firm was not effectively utilizing its high-level manpower and was experiencing considerable difficulties in adapting to environmental changes. Growth in sales and profits, however, was average in this type of firm.

Summing up

This overall profile of management practices and effectiveness of the US subsidiary and the local firm is outlined in Table 3, in a very abbreviated form.

Table 3: Profiles of Management Practices and Effectiveness of the US Subsidiary and the Local Firm

Elements of management practices and effectiveness	US subsidiary	Local firm
1 Recruitment of potential managers	Formally and systematically done. Open-minded on all potential sources for managerial personnel	Done on ad hoc basis. Restricted to small group of family members or relatives and friends
2 Recruitment of middle and senior managers	Formally and systematically done. Provided opportunity for advancement within the firm	Done on ad hoc basis. No systematic attempt at providing opportunity for advancement within the firm
3 Management education	Formally done. Regularly used outside training courses or personnel	Done on irregular or ad hoc basis
4 Attitudes toward management development	Visualized as necessary element in company's growth and survival	Considered as unnecessary expense
5 Treatment of existing management	Continuous evaluation. Ready to demote or fire second-rate and promote young and qualified	Little or no evaluation. Adherence to seniority.
6 Delegation by senior management	Delegate authority to subordinates	Unwilling to delegate authority
7 Management structure	Decentralized: individual positions are well defined and specified. Organization charts and manuals used	Centralized: individual positions not well defined; authority line diffused. Organization charts not widely used
8 Management communication	Free flow of communication encouraged and demanded	A great deal of secrecy and hoarding of information at all levels

Table 3—continued

Elements of management practices and effectiveness	US subsidiary	Local firm
9 Use of management consultants	Used frequently	Not used
10 Interfirm comparison at home and overseas	Done on regular basis	Not done at all or done on ad hoc basis
11 Market share	Constant awareness of market share	Not much concern
12 Objective of firm	Growth and profits	Profits
13 Assessment of performance	Measured in terms of growth, long-term potential, human resources, profits, assets, and sales	Measured in terms of short-term profits
14 Diversification	Considered as desired objectives	Undertaken as necessary evil
15 Future of firm	Evaluated on long-term basis	Evaluated on short-term or medium-term basis
16 Long-range planning	Five- or ten-year horizons. Systematic and formalized	One- or two-year horizons. Done on ad hoc basis
17 Use of budgetary control	Used with considerable emphasis on its importance to the firm	Done haphazardly with less emphasis on its importance for the firm
18 Review of operations	Regularly undertaken with feedback mechanism well developed	Done on ad hoc basis with no feedback mechanism
19 Capital budgeting	Regularly done	Done on ad hoc basis or not done at all
20 Relationship of sales to production	Production facilities are planned on creating greater demands for the goods	Production is based on serving short-supply market conditions (seller's market)
21 Advertising and public relations	Seen as useful in creating public image of the company	Used only as a necessary evil
22 Capacity, efficiency, and productivity	Assessed on regular basis	No regular assessment
23 Plant capacity	Utilized at the fullest possible level; regular maintenance	Utilized as seems appropriate by top man without objective assessment. Irregular maintenance
24 Buying function	Conceived as managerial function	Conceived as clerical function
25 Suppliers	Conceived as partners in progress	Conceived as a necessary evil
26 Operational research techniques	Uses various techniques to optimize plant capacity	Regards various techniques as status symbols
27 Creation of positive labour relations	Conceived as management responsibility	Conceived as government/labour union responsibility
28 Assessment of good labour relations	Done on regular and systematic basis	Done on ad hoc basis
29 Grievance procedure	Carefully worked out, agreed by all parties and adhered to	Roughly drawn up and not always followed

Table 3—continued

Elements of management practices and effectiveness	US subsidiary	Local firm
30 Unions	Conceived as having constructive role to play	Conceived as nuisance
31 Workers' output	Belief that employees will give their best when treated as being responsible	Belief that employees are lazy
32 Personnel function	Conceived as top priority	Conceived as clerical chaos
33 Training and education of workforce	Conceived as necessary element of organizational activities; variety of training	Conceived as a necessary evil. Mostly on-the-job training for the blue-collar employee
34 Shortage of skilled labour and/or other labour	Not taken for granted. Action to train up semi-skilled and unskilled personnel	Acceptance of shortage of skilled employees as limiting factor
35 Method of payment	Based on objective criteria. Attempts to pay higher than market rate	Based on what they can get by with the minimum
36 Employees	Conceived as resource	Conceived as a necessary evil
37 Relationship of research department to production	Close cooperation between two units	Research department usually non-existent, or if it exists operates as separate unit
38 Problems of firm	Conceived as an opportunity to undertake cost-efficiency	Conceived as fault of others—government, labour union, competition
39 Unprofitable products	Ready to drop unless found useful for the long-range growth	Unable to find out in the first place
40 Competition	Conceived as healthy and necessary	Conceived as unfair and destructive

This overall profile of management practices and effectiveness of the US subsidiary and the local firm represents a dominant picture of the actual situation in those developing countries. However, as the sophisticated reader will recognize, such an overall profile of management practices and effectiveness covers up many significant inter-firm, inter-country, and inter-regional differences. As noted earlier, the space limitation prohibits us from providing a detailed analysis of these differences in the practices and effectiveness of US subsidiaries and the local firms in the six developing countries. For a brief review here, we will only analyze the most significant differences between these two sets of firms on a regional basis.

Regional Differences in Organizational Practices and Effectiveness

My data show that Latin American local companies engage less often than Far Eastern companies do in comprehensive long-range planning and also in the use of formalized budgetary controls. In addition the local firms studied in Argentina, Brazil, and Uruguay utilized certain advanced manpower management practices less often than similar firms in India, the Philippines, or Taiwan.

Furthermore, an interesting difference between these two regions comes to the fore when we compare the two sets of local firms with the number of hierarchical layers reported by our respondents for their companies. While only 12 percent of the local firms in Latin America claim to have more than 8 layers, 45 percent of their counterparts in the Far East report more than 8 hierarchicai echelons. One wonders if these results indicate that Latin American local firms are more decentralized than those in Far Eastern countries. However, my interviews with lower levels of personnel in these two regions suggest, first, greater degrees of authority differences and, second, authority overlap among local companies in Latin America. Thus, a 'flat' structure in those companies apparently means higher *centralization* rather than delegation of authority. US firms in Argentina, Brazil, and Uruguay appear to utilize less often formalized procedures for major policy-making and standard setting than those in India, the Philippines, and Taiwan. Moreover, our results also indicate that lower managerial and supervisory levels in Latin America participate less often in the processes of policy-making and standard-setting than their colleagues in the Far East. The same holds for participation in planning; here we also encounter evidence that there is more decentralization of decision-making in Far Eastern, than in Latin American US subsidiaries.

However, in apparent contradiction to these findings, I found that subordinates in Latin American firms perceive the leadership style of their superiors more frequently as democratic than their counterparts in Far Eastern firms. One can only speculate on such a discrepancy between these two sets of findings. Perhaps in those Far Eastern firms more actual power-sharing takes place between managers and those under their command, although at the same time, status differences are maintained. In Latin America, on the other hand, there may be less social distance between adjacent levels in the hierarchy, but also less consultation and joint decision-making.[22]

One should keep in mind that the British influence in the Far East (especially in India) on patterns of management is still rather strong, while in Latin American firms the North American style of management looms large. Many managers of American subsidiaries in the Far East, especially in India (comprising roughly 50 percent of the total sample in this region) are British-born and educated. Managers of US firms in Latin American countries, on the other hand, are usually born and raised in the US. Therefore, it is perhaps possible to distinguish between, on the one hand, an 'American' style of rather authoritative decision-making but at the same time rather status-free, informal intercourse between superiors and subordinates, and on the other hand, a 'British' style of participative management accompanied by relatively formal relations in the social sphere.

As in the case of the local companies, there also comes to the fore a difference between the US subordinates in both regions with respect to organizational effectiveness. Latin American firms on the average score lower than Far Eastern firms on such indicators as 'employee morale', 'cooperative inter-departmental relationships', 'the firm's overall objectives perceived as important', and 'executives spend their time on policy-making and future planning'.

Of course, it is tempting to ascribe all differences found between these two parts of the world in managerial practices to socio-cultural determinants. However, I would venture the hypothesis that several differences, e.g., with respect to planning, policy-making, and controls can be explained in terms of such factors as geographic distance and economic and political instability. For instance, Latin American countries are closer to the USA than those in the Far East, which makes it easier for subsidiaries in Latin America to rely more on parent companies in the USA and for parent companies to dominate their subsidiaries. Furthermore, economic and political situations in these two parts of the world differ considerably. Although price and wage spirals and subsequent inflations are serious problems confronting most of the developing countries, the level of price increase and degree of inflation in Argentina, Brazil, and Uruguay is much greater than in India, the Philippines, and Taiwan. Rampant inflation in the Latin American countries affects future planning and policy-making. In addition to economic instability, Latin American countries are plagued by revolutions, dictatorships, and 'coups d'état'. Far Eastern countries are more stable politically. Obviously, political instability takes away necessary incentives for private enterprises to look ahead and formulate specific policies for future development of company activities. Davis[23] found that this was true even in Chile, which was then more stable than other Latin American countries. In Chile, Davis argues, businessmen are more concerned with survival than with policy-making, generating profits, and developing and co-ordinating the internal functions of the organization.

THE ENVIRONMENTAL AND SOCIO-CULTURAL IMPACT ON THE ORGANIZATIONAL PRACTICES

In recent years governmental officials, industrial leaders, politicians, and economic planners in the developing countries have realized that the key to higher economic growth is higher productivity from the industrial worker. In studies of employee morale and commitment to industrial life and productivity in underdeveloped countries, however, many researchers have written pessimistically. In his study of industrial workers in India, Ornati has concluded:

Indian workers are not interested in factory work; they resist adjustment to the type of life which goes with industrial employment. In the value scheme of the majority of Indians, factory labor does not offer any avenue for the expression of their individual personalities; wage increase and promotions do not operate as stimulants to greater exertion, nor does greater exertion lead to changes in status.[24]

Commenting on the labor commitment in underdeveloped countries, Kerr and his co-researchers had this to say:

Cultural factors (such as religious and ethical valuations, the family system, class, and race) all have a bearing on commitment . . . The greater the strength of extended family, the slower the commitment of workers to industrial life.[25]

Farmer and Richman, following the work of McClelland arrived at this conclusion:

The importance of a country's view of achievement and work as a vital determinant of managerial performance and productivity efficiency must not be understated . . . Prevailing religious beliefs and cultural values, in connection with parental behavior, child-rearing practices . . . traditional Hinduism, Buddhism, Islam, and even Catholicism are not generally conducive to a high achievement drive in their orthodox followers.[26]

Myrdal's monumental study of South Asia also reveals the impact on labor efficiency of tradition, custom, value systems, and attitudes in these countries. Myrdal argues: 'in [the] absence of simultaneous changes in institutions and attitudes, the effect on labor utilization and productivity throughout the economy may still be less consequential'.[27] Similarly, scholars studying the industrial scene in Latin American countries have argued that the industrial employees in these countries are more interested in maintaining and enhancing their family status and fulfilling obligations to friends and relatives than in increasing their productivity or wages.

Zurcher, Meadow, and Zurcher, in their comparative study of Mexican, Mexican-American, and Anglo-American bank employees, found that Mexicans are more particularistic than Mexican-Americans, who are in turn more particularistic than Anglo-Americans.[28] (Particularism signified the value orientation toward institutionalized obligations of friendships; in contrast, universalism indicates a value orientation toward obligation to the society and organizations.)

More important, these authors also found that alienation from work was significantly and positively related to particularism and negatively related to job longevity, position level, satisfaction with the position, and plans to continue working in a bank.

Of course not all scholars agree with the above contention that prevailing socio-cultural factors in the Far East and Latin American regions have a negative and dominating impact on employee commitment to industrial life. A number of researchers have cast doubts on these assertions.

Morris, for example, has pointed out:

> Much of the literature tends to base interpretation on hypothetical, psychological, and sociological propositions which themselves are highly suspect. The argument typically rests on scattered fragments of evidence taken indiscriminately . . . It is impossible to generate a satisfactory analysis from this sort of melange.[29]

He goes on to say:

> The evidence from Bombay and Jamshedpur suggests that the creation of [a] disciplined industrial labor force in a newly developing society is not particularly difficult . . . The difference in worker stability cannot be accounted for by any substantial differences in the psychology of the raw labor recruited. Nor can it be attributed to dissimilarities in the traditional environment from which the workers came. If there were differences in work-force behavior, these flowed from employer policy.[30]

McMillan's research in Brazil revealed that:

> [South] Americans are under less compulsion to probe the attitude of their workers than they are in the United States . . . Enlisting the allegiance of workers is easier, and motivating employees, most Americans appear to agree, is not difficult.[31]

In his study, *Social Factors in Economic Development in Argentina*, Fillol observed:

> There is no reason to believe that Argentina workers have basically different attitudes toward their jobs from workers anywhere else in industrialized Western countries . . . Industrialists in general do not seem to have given any thought to the fact that the productivity, motivation, and cooperation of labor are primarily determined by the management which employs it and not by the more or less enlightened social and economic policies of government.[32]

Steven Piker, who based his research on Thai peasants, has argued against the influence of religion and/or the belief system (such as reliance on rate and *Karma* principles) on worldly behavior and activities of peasants. He has pointed out, for example, that although the Thai peasant's belief in *Karma* (fate) has remained strong, he is considering life-here-and-now as important, if not more so, as the life beyond. In his words: '[The Thai peasant] makes merit in the hope not of attaining *Nirvana*, but of reentering the world of humans on terms more favorable to himself . . . (this) means his being more closely placed to substantial wealth and influence.'[33]

Finally, in the most comprehensive study, Sirota and Greenwood raise considerable doubts about the prevailing thesis of the impact of socio-cultural variables on motivation. In opposition to the cross-cultural thesis, they state that such generalizations, although interesting, are 'based almost entirely on the subjective impressionistic experiences of the observers'.[34] They further state: 'Acceptance of these conclusions must therefore depend largely on faith—faith both in the observer's objectivity and in the representativeness of the anecdotal evidence he usually presents as proof of his case.'[35]

My research in the six developing countries, as well as the findings of some other writers, questions such a pessimistic outlook. For example, my interviews with more than 500 industrial employees in developing countries clearly indicate that these employees, like their counterparts in the industrialized countries, want higher wages, opportunity for advancement, job security, fair treatment, better working conditions and welfare, and a higher standard of living for their children. I did not find many employees looking to heaven and yearning for the ultimate *Nirvana*. An increasing number of scholars support this contention. Gangulli, in his study of factory workers in India, found:

> The four most important things that the workers want are sufficient and adequate income, a sense of security, an opportunity for promotion and advancement, and finally, the opportunity to learn a more interesting trade . . . In these and also in their aspirations and expectations, there does not seem to be any fundamental difference between this group and other groups of factory employees in other countries.[36]

Altimus, Richards, and Slocum,[37] in their study of Mexican and American industrial workers, found that job security, esteem, autonomy, and self-actualization needs were very much in the minds of the Mexican workers.

Deasi's study of blue-collar and white-collar employees in India revealed that both groups prefer higher wages, better fringe benefits such as provident fund (retirement), profit-sharing plans, etc., and impartial policies on promotion and reward systems.[38]

Are local companies more traditional, 'sleeper'-like,* because their managers have been raised in and are still primarily exposed to traditional culture-patterns? If the answer should be in the affirmative then, by the same token, US subsidiaries exhibit more modern, 'thruster'-like characteristics because their managers have been trained in modern, Western ways of thinking about industry and management and continue to be influenced by Western culture.

*This terminology is derived from Gater et al. study of British firms. For comparison of the results of their study with the present study, see Anant R. Negandhi, 'Convergence in Organizational Practices: An Empirical Study of Industrial Enterprises in Developing Countries', in C. J. Lammers and D. J. Hickson, *Organizations Alike and Unlike* (London: Routledge and Kegan Paul, 1979, pp. 323–345). For Gater's study see A. D. Gater et al., *Attitudes in British Management: A PEP Report* (Harmondworth: Penguin, 1964).

On the basis of my research results, I wish to challenge this cultural explanation of differences in management practices between developed and relatively underdeveloped countries. In my view, economic and political factors are far more important as determinants of managerial practices. I will illustrate my thesis by referring to the impact of external factors on planning and on decision-making. In cross-cultural management studies, the relationships among economic, political, and legal conditions, on the one hand, and *planning* in firms, on the other, have been hinted at by a number of scholars. Davis,[39] in his study of Chile, Lauterbach,[40] in a number of Latin American countries, and Lauter,[41] in Turkey, have indicated a relationship between economic-political-legal conditions and the planning function. Davis reports: 'In answer to the question "How far into the future does formal planning in your enterprise extend?" more than half of the interviewed answered: "that depends on how long it is before the next election".'[42]

Enquiring about the impact of economic, political, and legal factors on planning, we asked the executives to identify the most important environmental variables affecting their long-range planning activities. To evaluate the importance of those factors, we carried out many follow-up discussions.

A seller's market, governmental control of prices, the availability of raw materials, inflation, and the political situation were mentioned frequently by these executives. There were some differences in rank-order importance of these factors among different countries. Executives in the Latin American countries, for example, were worried about political instability and inflation, while those in the Far East showed more concern over the existence of a seller's market. Overall, my findings show that a large majority of the executives interviewed in Argentina, Brazil, India, the Philippines, Taiwan, and Uruguay indicate that the seller's-market condition in those countries makes planning less necessary for firms to achieve high profitability. In such a situation all firms make high profits regardless of their managerial practices. Approximately the same proportion of executives pointed out that governmental control on prices and the unavailability of raw materials are factors inhibiting long-range planning. Inflation, the political situation, and government attitudes toward the business community were mentioned as additional factors that discourage firms from planning for the future.

As to *decision-making*, many writers affirm that the authority structure of industrial enterprises (and, for that matter, governmental agencies and other social organizations) in developing countries is highly centralized.

In my interviews with top-, middle-, and lower-level executives in American subsidiaries and local companies in the six developing countries studied, the impact of the following factors on centralization was frequently mentioned: the owner-manager situation; the seller's-market condition; the governmental interference and controls on imports of raw materials, machinery, foreign exchange, etc.; and the lack of experience with delegation of authority.[43]

The typical mentality of an owner-manager is well expressed by an executive in Uruguay: 'I do not believe in anybody having anything to do with management except my own family. There is a clear distinction in my organization. My family is on one side, and the rest of the salaried and hourly personnel are on the other side.'

Coupled with the owner-manager situation, the seller's market provides much less incentive to the owner-manager to delegate authority to specialized and qualified employees. Under such a condition, huge profits are made regardless of cost and quality of products. However, the owner-manager takes this positive profit picture as a sign of his success as a manager or decision-maker. And why shouldn't he? After all, in a capitalist economy we preach that the primary role of the business enterprise is to 'serve' its stockholders (the owner). As a sole stockholder, the owner-manager does exactly this. His only mistake is that he has not learned to distinguish between short-run and long-term profitability. Unfortunately, the seller's market itself seems to be a 'long-term' proposition in many of the developing countries. In this matter, it is doubtful that, under a similar (seller's) market condition, the counterpart owner-manager in industrially developed countries will be able to distinguish between short-term and long-term objectives.

In my opinion, the impact of the seller's market on managerial decision-making seems greater than any other environmental cum cultural factors mentioned by other writers.

One might ask, at this stage, why employees in developing countries accept this sort of managerial behavior. Cross-cultural theorists have argued that employees *prefer* such an autocratic style.

Based on our observations in the six developing countries, we would make a decision between what is accepted and what is preferred by the employees. Lower-level subordinates accept autocratic leaders simply because that is the only way they can hold on to their jobs. If jobs were plentiful and job security was guaranteed, most employees would prefer greater autonomy. A recent extensive study by Sirota and Greenwood[44] in 25 countries appears to support these views. They found that autonomy was ranked as one of the ten goals of employees in all the countries studied. They also found differences in the rank-order of goals between professions more pronounced than between different countries in a given profession.

Even Haire, Ghiselli, and Porter,[45] who have otherwise offered a cultural explanation, found that the managerial need for autonomy was higher in Chile, Argentina, and India.

Our own observations in the six developing countries are most in line with those of Sirota and Greenwood, Haire et al. In other words, we are of the opinion that the employees in developing countries prefer participative leadership, but that the actual leadership behavior practiced seems to be autocratic and paternalistic in nature at the present time.

AUTOMOBILE AND STEEL INDUSTRY STUDY

Our overall conclusions concerning the over-emphasis on the impact of socio-cultural factors on employee motivation and satisfaction for developing countries were also borne out in our recent comparative studies in automobile and steel industries.

The study reported in this paper represents a small part of a large-scale study undertaken in nine countries. It sought to evaluate the impact of technology and socio-economic systems upon work attitudes and behavior. This chapter only examines the data collected from two countries, namely India and the USA. Samples of workers in both countries were drawn to represent relatively high and relatively low levels of technologies as utilized in the steel industry in the respective country. All work places or major job types in the selected plants were sampled. None of the samples can be said to be representative of all steel workers within the country, but the samples were, to a large extent, comparable in terms of the design for the nine nations' steel study.

The data-collection instruments (interview guides and questionnaires) were identical and the data-collection procedures were similar in the two countries.*

USE OF REFERENCE GROUP

To highlight the extent of national *versus* industrial (technology) differences, we utilized a reference group of employees in the American auto industry.† Both the instruments and the procedures for data collection were very similar for the auto industry in the US, as well as the steel industry in the US and India. The logic of our analysis and of using a reference group (in at least one country) is both simple and straightforward: (1) In the domain of content with which we are dealing, the differences must be relatively large in magnitude before they are viewed as possible significant country differences; (2) We need to be concerned with both the level of responses, and the pattern of responses in identifying significant country differences; and (3) Country differences in employee responses within the same industry must be *considerably greater* than differences in responses of employees in different industries within a country—before we have identified important national differences.‡

*For a detailed description on methodology of this nine-country study, see Spray, S. O., Adamek, R., and Negandhi, A., *United States National Report: Technology and Steelworkers* (mimeographed report), Kent State University, 1976.

†For a fuller description of the US automobile study, see: Jacob, Betty M., England, G. W., Jacob, P. E., Pratt, R. C., Whitehill, A. M., and Ahn, C., *The Automobile Worker: A Multinational Perspective Report of the United States Research Team* (mimeographed report), University of Hawaii, 1975.

‡For details on our rationale and discussion on the results, see George W. England and Anant R. Negandhi, 'National Contexts and Technology as Determinants of Employee's Perceptions', in George W. England, Anant R. Negandhi and Bernhard Wilpert, *Organizational Functioning in Cross-Cultural Perspective* (Kent: Comparative Administration Research Institute, 1979, pp. 175–198). The analysis of data and discussion of the results of this study are drawn from the above paper.

We are interested in examining, then, only relatively large differences in employee perceptions where there is reference-group support for the assertion that this appears to be an area of significant country differences. It is only these differences that merit the painstaking effort required to show that they are 'culturally or environmentally determined' differences and to trace those elements of culture and/or environment that seem to produce them.

ANALYSIS OF RESEARCH RESULTS

Concern about Public Issues

The three samples were asked about their personal concern about ten public issues. Not surprisingly, this is a content area where real national differences seem to exist. The difference in level of concern about each of the ten issues between the United States steel workers and Indian steel workers was large (both in a statistical and in a practical sense), and the pattern of responses for the two groups was quite different. The Indian sample indicated a high level of concern with only two issues: the country's economic problems and housing problems. Both issues may well reflect important and elemental needs for basic survival. In contrast, American steel workers indicate a high level of concern with a much wider range of issues. These include elemental needs as well as more collectively oriented concerns, such as youth problems, problems of war and peace, and pollution.

The contention that these are real national differences, was strengthened by the fact that the two US samples showed very similar levels of concern with each individual issue and almost identical patterns of concerns. In short, the differences between countries in level and pattern of response were large, while the intra-country differences were small.*

The importance of worker's jobs was evaluated using eight job facets. Indian steel workers attach greater importance to all eight job facets than did US steel workers, significantly so on six of the eight items. The establishment of these differences in 'work values' as representing real national differences, is severely questioned by the fact that intra-country differences between the two US samples are as large or larger than the inter-country differences on four of the eight items. Additionally, the very similar patterns of responses (relative ranking of the eight items) among the steel workers in the two countries mitigate against the conclusion that large and meaningful country differences exist in work values across the two countries.

*A relatively similar difference in concerns was found between national samples of the two countries twenty-five years ago in the pioneering work of Hadley Cantril, as reported: *The Pattern of Human Concerns*. New Brunswick, New Jersey: Rutgers University Press, 1965, Chapters 4 and 5.

The question of whether or not there are major national differences in terms of the extent to which the presence of various job facets 'explains' or predicts the level of overall or general job satisfaction, has recently attracted considerable attention.[46] The real question centers around the issue of whether there is some small subset of job facets whose presence or absence is crucial in determining one's satisfaction with his work situation, or conversely, is the determination of work satisfaction largely idiosyncratic at the level of individuals and nations. The results, then, did not support the notion that there are large and meaningful differences between Indian and American workers about what 'explains' or 'produces' general job satisfaction; indeed, the intra-country differences were more impressive than the inter-country differences. The real question posed by this data is: why are the US automobile workers so different from both groups of steel workers in terms of these relationships? An interesting question, but thus far we have not probed it further.

A lack of meaningful national differences was also observed when one examined the workers' perceptions about the factors influencing promotion. Five factors were used here. While it was clear that the level of importance attached to each of the five factors is somewhat lower for Indian workers than for either of the American samples, pattern similarities and the fact that intra-country differences are about as large as inter-country differences cautions against viewing these findings as supporting the establishment of meaningful country differences. The evidence was ambiguous at best, and to a large extent, reflects the harsh realities of economic (but not cultural) life in India.

With reference to worker satisfaction, three independently measured forms of worker satisfaction (a single item measure), satisfaction with management and company (a five-item measure), and overall satisfaction with the union (a single-item measure) were used. There were rather large differences (both in a statistical and practical sense) between Indian and American steel workers on all three measures of work-satisfaction. One would certainly be tempted to view this as an area where real national differences exist. However, when one views the reference-group results of American automobile workers, it is apparent that the within-country differences in satisfaction measures are approximately as large as the between-country differences. Thus, our reference-group analysis, as well as the pattern similarity, cautions against clear interpretation of the observed country differences as indicating meaningful national level differences.

Obviously, we are in the minority among cross-cultural management researchers in down-playing the importance of national differences in employees' commitments, aspirations, and desires. It is interesting to note, however, that several of the well documented studies undertaken in India and other developing countries seem to support our contention. For example, in a more recent study entitled *South Indian Factory Workers*, Holmström (1976) inquired as to how factory workers see their jobs. His findings are:

> ... (workers) see factory work as a citadel of security and relative prosperity, which it is; it offers regular work and promotion and predictable rewards, as against the chaos of terrifying dangers of life outside. For every one inside the citadel, there is a regiment outside trying to scale the walls. Even educated Brahmans will take unskilled, casual factory work in the hope of permanent jobs.[47]

In criticizing the socio-cultural explanation, Holmström goes on, saying that:

> The argument that Indian factory workers keep up a minimum standard of performance because they think of a job as something like the right to perform a customary service in the village *jajmaani* system may have been true in the past or in other places—not in Bangalore now. The evidence used to support that view can be explained as the result of management practices and/or the logic of the worker's situation inside the citadel, but with obligations to a number of people outside it. The factory worker is not quite an economic man minimizing risk, but much of his behavior can be explained as the pursuit of a limited number of economic and other goals, and informants can often say specifically what they are: security, higher pay, easier or more interesting work, freedom from close supervision, a pleasant atmosphere at work, respectability, a better chance for one's children, socialism, work well done as religious duty and so on.[48]

Similarly, Mandelbaum, a social anthropologist, warns us that it is a misguided notion that there are inherent contradictions between established customs and modern industrial life. Drawing from his comprehensive anthropological study of Indian villages, he states:

> ... there has been considerable cultural continuity along with the modern social change ... One of the ways of maintaining both persistence and change is through compartmentalization, the traditional mode of separating the standards of the work sphere from those of the domestic sphere.[49]

Referring to Milton Singer's study of leading industrialists in Madras, India, Mandelbaum states:

> In their household behavior, members of these families tend to observe spiritual standards much more closely than they do in their activities outside the house. These industrialists separate the two spheres of action more sharply than was done in their boyhood homes ... This device is not restricted to the industrial elite. Even the men who pull rickshaws in the streets of Lucknow (a city in India) similarly separate their standards for conduct in their work domain from those followed in their homes.[50]

To sum up, our findings indicate that national differences in worker perceptions existed only on such global issues as pollution, national economy, and housing problems, while national differences with respect to job content areas, factors influencing promotions and employees' satisfaction, preferences and willingness to participate in decision-making, were marginal at best. In other words, intra-country differences in employees' perceptions were as large or larger than the inter-country differences.

In our judgment, the literature purporting to show real national and cultural differences in employee-attitudes, behavior, and commitment are highly exaggerated. From the massive data generated during the last two decades or so, one can easily be convinced that the attitudes, beliefs, values, and need hierarchies, are vastly different in different societies. They are even different among different subgroups (ethnic and/or occupational) within a given society. We believe that many of the culture-related concepts are ill-defined, and their operational measures are poorly conceived. For example, as Ajiferuke and Boddewyn have stated: 'Culture is one of those terms that defy a single all-purpose definition, and there are almost as many meanings of culture as people using the term.'[51] It also appears that culture, although used as an independent variable in most cross-cultural management studies, has an obscure identity and often is used as a residual variable. As comparative researchers, we would argue that one should not get overly excited about observed national differences, unless they are rather large in magnitude, in an *absolute sense* and in a *relative sense*, when compared to observed differences within a given country. It is only when national differences are large in both an absolute and a relative sense, that it seems worthwhile to pursue the very difficult issues surrounding the reasons (cultural and other)—why such differences exist, and what the consequences of such differences could be. Suggestions of this type are not popular among social and behavioral scientists, who view null-hypothesis testing as the major function of their research, or for the less sophisticated 'difference detectors'. Nevertheless, we believe that this moral has considerable merit.

CONCLUDING REMARKS

Although in the two large-scale, cross-cultural studies reported here and elsewhere, we made serious efforts to understand and examine the impact of socio-cultural and environmental variables on organizational practices and effectiveness, our findings tend to underscore the similarities in management practices and their relationships to organizational effectiveness among different firms in different developing countries and among these firms and firms in developed countries. This is not to say that the environmental and socio-cultural variables do not influence management practices and effectiveness. However, our research in a number of developing and developed countries suggests, to us at least, a necessity for rethinking this issue at this stage. Although our studies revealed a considerable impact of socio-cultural variables on employee morale, interpersonal relationships, etc., it also indicated that many of the elements of management practices, such as planning, organization decision-making, controlling, etc., were both under the purview of management control and constrained only by technological and market conditions. And these technological and environmental factors are themselves becoming similar in our shrinking technological world, giving further impetus to convergence in organizational practices.

Studies also reveal that the similarities in management practices lead to similar organizational effectiveness. For example, our findings indicated that the differences in a firm's effectiveness could largely be explained by the differences in their management practices. More specifically, Spearman's rank correlation between management practices and effectiveness was 0.81; decentralization in decision-making and effectiveness was 0.91; and manpower-management practices and effectiveness was 0.63.[52]

Such relationships compel us to support the convergence thesis. In this respect, it may be appropriate to conclude this paper by quoting two of the pioneering cross-cultural management researchers, who, in our opinion, were largely instrumental in highlighting the *difference* and non-convergence thesis, and who express hope for future convergence.

First, Harbison and Myers, in studying the management development processes in twelve countries, had echoed the 'Organization building has its logic . . . which rests upon the development of management . . . and there is a general logic of management development which has applicability both to advanced and industrializing countries in the modern world.'[53] second, almost two decades ago, Farmer and Richman echoed:

> We began this book by observing differences in management between nations . . . As the general similarity of men everywhere is recognized, and as managerial and technological necessity presses all types of culture toward a common road, nations everywhere become more similar. Not all countries will arrive at the end of the trip at the same time, . . . but those who make the journey may, to their own surprise, discover that the road of others was not so different after all. Studies in comparative management at the time will be largely obsolete . . . Instead of differences, we shall find similarities, because the logic of technology and management will lead all to the same general position.[54]

To conclude, we do not contend that the studies in cross-cultural management are obsolete, but we do feel the logic of technology is taking over man's differing beliefs and value orientations. Increasingly, the road is becoming one.

NOTES

1. Negandhi, A. R. *Organization Theory in an Open System: A Study of Transferring Advanced Management Practices to Developing Nations.* New York. Dunellen Publishing Company, 1975.
2. 'International Transfer of Management Skills', *AIESEC International News Letter,* February 1968, p. 1.
3. Sirota, D., and J. M. Greenwood, 'Understand your Overseas Work Force, *Harvard Business Review*: 49: 53–60.

4. Haire, M. D., E. Ghiselli, and L. W. Porter. *Managerial Thinking: An International Study.* New York: Wiley, 1966.
5. R. D. Meade, and J. D. Whittaker, 'A Cross-Cultural Study of Authoritarianism', *Journal of Social Psychology*, LXXII (1967), pp. 3–7.
6. R. D. Meade, 'An Experimental Study of Leadership in India', *Journal of Social Psychology*, LXXII (1967), pp. 35–43.
7. G. V. Barrett, and E. C. Ryterband, 'Life Goals of United States and European Managers', in *Proceedings, XVIth International Congress of Applied Psychology* (Amsterdam: Swets & Zeitlinger, 1969), pp. 413–418.
8. M. H. R. Hoekstra, 'Corporate Objectives: A Cross-Cultural Study of Simulated Managerial Behavior', in *Proceedings, XVIth International Congress of Applied Psychology* (Amsterdam: Swets & Zeitlinger, 1969), pp. 429–435.
9. K. M. Thiagarajan, *A Cross-Cultural Study of the Relationships Between Personal Values and Managerial Behavior,* Technical Report 23, NONR N00014–67–A (Rochester, New York: University of Rochester, Management Research Center, 1968).
10. K. M. Thiagarajan, and B. M. Bass, 'Differential Preferences for Long vs. Short-Term Payoffs in India and the United States', in *Proceedings, XVIth International Congress of Applied Psychology* (Amsterdam: Swet & Zeitlinger, 1969), pp. 440–446.
11. G. W. England, 'Personal Value Systems of American Managers', *Academy of Management Journal*, X, No. 1 (1967), pp. 53–68. G. W. England, and R. Koike, 'Personal Value Systems of Japanese Managers', *Journal of Cross-Cultural Psychology*, I (1970), pp. 21–40. G. W. England, 'Personal Value System Analysis as an Aid to Understanding Organizational Behavior: A Comparative Study in Japan, Korea and the United States' (presented at Exchange Seminar on Comparative Organizations, Amsterdam, Netherlands, March 23–27, 1970).
12. D. McClelland, *The Achieving Society* (New York: D. Van Nostrand, 1961).
13. G. V. Barrett, and B. M. Bass, 'Comparative Surveys of Managerial Attitudes and Behavior', in *Comparative Management: Teaching, Research and Training,* ed. by J. Boddewyn (New York: Graduate School of Business Administration, 1970), pp. 179–207.
14. Eugene McCann, 'An Aspect of Management Philosophy in the United States and Latin America', *Academy of Management Journal*, VII, 1964, No. 2, pp. 149–152.
15. Eugene McCann, 'Anglo-American and Mexican Management Philosophies', *MSU Business Topics,* XVIII, No. 3 (1970), pp. 23–38.
16. *Ibid.*
17. Geert Hofstede, 'Hierarchical Power Distance in Forty Countries', in C. J. Lammers and D. J. Hickson, *Organizations Alike and Unlike* (London: Routledge and Kegan Paul, 1979), pp. 97–119.
18. S. G. Reading and T. A. Martyn-Johns, 'Paradigm Differences and Their Relation to Management, with Reference to South-East Asia', in G. W. England, A. R. Negandhi and B. Wilpert, *Organizational Functioning in a Cross-Cultural Perspective* (Kent: Comparative Administration Research Institute, 1979), pp. 103–125.
19. See Negandhi op. cit., pp. 1–12 and 245–272.
20. Negandhi, A. R. and S. B. Prasad (1971), *Comparative Management,* Appleton-Century-Crofts, New York.
21. Negandhi op. cit., pp. 134–135.
22. Davis, Stanley M. (1969), 'US Versus Latin America: Business and Culture', *Harvard Business Review,* Vol. 47, November–December, pp. 88–99.
23. Davis, Stanley M. (1971a), 'Authority and Control in Mexican Enterprises', in Stanley M. Davis, *Comparative Management,* Prentice-Hall, Englewood Cliffs, N.J., pp. 173–87.
24, Ornati, O. A., *Jobs and Workers in India,* Ithaca, N.J.: Cornell University Press, 1955.

25. Clark Kerr et al., *Industrialism and Industrial Man,* Cambridge, Mass.: Harvard University Press, 1960, p. 97.
26. Richard N. Farmer and Barry M. Richman, *Comparative Management and Economic Progress,* Homewood, Ill.: Richard D. Irwin, 1965, pp. 154–59.
27. Gunnar Myrdal, Asian Drama: *An Inquiry into the Poverty of Nations,* New York: The Twentieth Century Fund, 1968, p. 1, 150.
28. L. A. Zurcher, Jr., A. Meadow, and S. E. Zurcher, 'Value Orientation, Role Conflict and Alienation from Work: Cross-Cultural Study', *American Sociological Review,* 30 (August 1965), pp. 539–48.
29. Morris Davis Morris, *The Emergence of an Industrial Labor Force in India; A Study of the Bombay Cotton Mills, 1849–1947,* Berkeley, University of California Press, 1965, p. 4.
30. *Ibid.,* p. 202.
31. Claude McMillan, Jr., 'The American Businessman in Brazil', *Business Topics,* Spring 1965, reprinted in *International Dimensions of Business,* East Lansing, Mich.: Graduate School of Business Administration, Michigan State University, 1966, p. 103.
32. Fillol, *Social Factors in Economic Development in Argentina.*
33. Steven Piker, 'The Relationship of Belief Systems to Behavior in the Rural Thai Society', *Asian Survey,* 8 (May 1968), pp. 386–99.
34. David Sirota and J. M. Greenwood, 'Understand Your Overseas Work Force', *Harvard Business Review,* Vol. 49, No. 1 (January–February 1971), pp. 53–60.
35. H. C. Ganguli, 'An Enquiry into Incentives for Workers in an Engineering Factory', *Indian Journal of Social Work,* June 1954, p. 10.
36. C. Altimus, Jr. et al., 'Cross-Cultural Perspectives on Need Deficiencies of Blue-Collar Workers', *Quarterly Journal of Management Development,* 2 (June 1971), pp. 91–103.
37. K. G. Deasi, 'A Comparative Study of Motivation of Blue-Collar and White-Collar Workers', *Indian Journal of Social Work,* 38 (January 1958), pp. 380–87.
38. Davis, Stanley M. (1970), 'The Politics of Organizational Undevelopment: Chile', *Industrial and Labor Relations Review,* October, pp. 23–83.
39. Lauterbach, Albert (1966), *Enterprise in Latin America,* Ithaca, Cornell University Press.
40. Lauter, G. Peter (1970), 'Advanced Management Processes in Developing Countries: Planning in Turkey', *California Management Review,* Vol. 13, No. 3, Spring, pp. 7–12.
41. Davis, Stanley M. (1971b), 'Politics and Organizational Underdevelopment in Chile', in Stanley M. Davis, *Comparative Management,* Prentice-Hall, Englewood Cliffs, N.J., pp. 173–87.
42. Negandhi, A. R., 'Advanced Management Know-How in Underdeveloped Countries', *California Management Review,* Vol. 10, Spring 1968, pp. 53–60.
43. Sirota, David, and J. Michael Greenwood, 'Understanding Your Overseas Work Force', *Harvard Business Review,* Vol. 49, 1971, pp. 53–60.
44. Haire, M., E. E. Ghiselli and L. W. Porter, *Managerial Thinking: An International Study,* Wiley, New York, 1966, p. 94.
45. Hofstede, G., A. I. Kraut and S. H. Simonetti, 'The Development of a Core Attitude Survey Questionnaire for Internal Use', Working Paper 76–17. European Institute for Advanced Studies, Brussels, 1976.
46. Holmström, M., *South Indian Factory Workers—Their Life and Their World.* Cambridge, Cambridge University Press, pp. 137, 1976.
47. *Ibid.,* p. 40.
48. Mandelbaum, D. G., *Society in India: Change and Continuity, II.* Berkeley: University of California Press, p. 645, 1970.
49. *Ibid.*
50. Ajiferuke, M., and J. Boddewyn, 'Culture and Other "Explanatory" Variables in Comparative Management Studies', *Academy of Management Journal,* 13: p. 154, 1970.

51. Negandhi, *Organization Theory in an Open System,* op. cit., p. 268.
52. Spray, S. O., Adam, K. R. and Negandhi, A., *United States National Reports:* 'Technology and Steelworkers', Kent State University, 1976.
53. Farmer, R. N., and B. M. Richman, *Comparative Management and Economic Progress,* Irwin, Homewood, Ill., p. 400, 1965.
54. Harbison, F. H., and C. A. Myers, *Management in the Industrial World,* McGraw-Hill, New York, p. 117, 1959.

CHAPTER 6

Transfer of knowledge for economic organization: The Indonesian case

Pjotr Hesseling

INTRODUCTION

The seminar on cross-cultural management at Henley Management College was an intensive exchange of opinions and evidence between a small number of scholars around a few seminal issues. The chapters in this book present the state of the art and some promising new lines of research. The experience stimulated me to reconsider my own strategies of research intervention for development. What do we have to offer for management in the so-called Third World, if anything at all? Instead of reviewing again available empirical evidence I decided to take a more speculative and pragmatic stance. Since 1976 I have made regular, three months a year, visits to Indonesian institutes of administration and management, both in the public and private sector. As a consultant and tutor I discussed many research projects in this field with Indonesian colleagues and research candidates. It became increasingly clear that debates on convergence or divergence, the meaning of culture or promising new theories or methods in comparative organization studies were largely academic. In some situations it was possible to buy or make available an updated library of reading material. In other situations some projects could be satisfactorily completed as a thesis. Nevertheless, whatever the quality of reading lists and individual pieces of research, knowledge seemed to be stuck in isolated niches of information. There was no critical mass to review, digest or adapt collected evidence, there was no continuity of promising lines of thinking, there was a lack of internal cohesion between stages and projects. Almost every return visit needed a fresh start. Knowledge seemed to leak away.

EXPLANATIONS OF FAILURES IN TRANSFER

There are many possible explanations
(1) An old and tenacious argument blames the cultural environment. I
   am not an expert in differential psychology, but studies such as

that by Vernon (1969)[1] have convinced me that there is no solid evidence for such an explanation. Moreover, in comparing Indonesians with their Dutch counterparts intelligence does not seem to be a differentiating factor in my own experience. It seems a normal distribution.

(2) The bureaucratic fragmented structure of Indonesian universities and research institutes could offer another explanation. However, the Indonesian fragmentation in faculties and subfaculties and strict differentiation between functions, such as Research and Development on the one side and Organization and Methods on the other, looks familiar to a Dutch observer. Lack of flexibility and linkages might explain some failures but it is no complete answer (Beers 1971).[2]

(3) Indonesian researchers are as a rule underpaid. This lack of financial incentives for research work forces them to moonlight to the extent that can block their pursuing of research lines. Indeed this argument is valid in various Asian countries (S. Panitchpakdi).[3] However, it is not a completely satisfactory explanation. Also in the Dutch situation research candidates are relatively underpaid.[4] Moreover, I have met many Indonesian research candidates who were ready for a reduction in income within reasonable limits. Research is more of a vocation ('Beruf') and a long-term investment than a commercial or industrial career. There is at least no direct correlation between the research output of the higher-paid echelon and the lower-paid echelon of researchers, as far as I know.

(4) The nature of 'technical assistance' and 'development aid' programmes offers another explanation. Development economics as a subject was invented by Westerners. Basic elements of development economics derive from the economics of colonialism on the one hand (in this case Boeke and van Gelderen),[5] and from the post-war European economic rehabilitation programme (Marshall plan).[6]

Only recently have scholars from the less-developed world contributed to the conceptual framework of development economics. They argue that the alien elements which have been introduced into the subject from the outset have led practitioners into wrong paths. One has to start all over again from a more eclectic conceptual framework. Indeed, this might explain many of the futile exercises as social, cultural and economic dissimilarities abound. However, it is not the whole answer. The Japanese case in the transfer of Western scientific and technological knowledge shows a successful application (Querido).[7]

(5) Scholarship for the revered institutions of higher learning in the Western world were mostly offered as a reward to those close to the powers-that-be. This elite group had a limited commitment to

problems at the grass-root level. It has been observed that their choice of a field of research work was frequently influenced by the ease with which research materials can be gathered and the acceptance by foreign professors rather than by the urge to contribute to solving any particular social problem at home (Panitchpakdi, note 3). Indeed this might explain the lack of operational implementation of development studies. However, most societies in whatever stage of development rely for the knowledge cycle on the elite. The elite can act as a caretaker for those who deserve development skills most (Köbben).[8]

(6) Distrust in common sense and lack of appreciation of their own history and destiny has been observed as an explanation of the almost magic meaning of foreign textbooks. Formulae are quoted blindly and case studies in other societies are accepted as the ultimate truth. Indeed, the traditional reverence for a 'guru', a 'sensei' or other respected teacher has given rise to rigid programmes of thought without challenging the assumptions. However, this is a temporary learning stage and experienced members of the knowledge community in the Third World become as critical as their counterparts anywhere else.

(7) Lack of societal respect for academic knowledge as an independent source of action is another explanation. Indeed in order to be successful, academic researchers have to enter the bureaucratic polity (Girling).[9] Quotations of those in actual power are accepted as principles of action and academic knowledge is useless. It is sometimes dangerous to refer with too much emphasis to interesting lines of thought of indigenous scholars. Jealousy easily arises, and academic success can only be rewarded by positions of bureaucratic or entrepreneurial power. This seems to be the most satisfying explanation of the isolated research communities in the Third World. There is no demand for independent thought (Peres).[10] However, history teaches that traditional bureaucracy and scholarship have led to effective administration in the past. The present intellectual quality of those in power is impressive. If appropriate strategies can be found, societal acceptance of independent thought seems feasible in the near future.

(8) Evaluation of specific development projects leads in each case to a particular pattern of bureaucratic and institutional obstacles. It is easy to make a list of some twenty factors which are responsible for the stoppage of some 3000 development projects (Dir. Gen. Gandhi to the Indonesian parliament).[11] Sometimes I have tried to evaluate specific projects in which I had been involved. However, it does not seem feasible to blame a particular foreign project officer, team leader or Indonesian official for such a failure. Frequently they have left or have been replaced, and reconstruction of original intentions and cash flows is well-nigh impossible.

The failure rate is too high for accepting individual culprits as an explanation. Also in the private sector without bureaucratic obstacles failures are more frequent than successes.

Each explanation is ambivalent. Foreign Ph.D. projects are useless, yes, but many key figures have experienced the personal value. Irrelevant planning exercises deliver nominal figures of growth rates, manpower requirements, unemployment rates or accounting matrices and are not of much use in formulating action programmes, yes, but long-term planning helps to monitor critical issues over time.

Irrelevant econometric exercises, yes, but they can help to discover underlying ideas and concepts.

At this moment there seems to be an awareness of the need for radical changes in development policy. The ruling elite realises that reliance on foreign aid projects is misleading. The North–South dialogue is in a deadlock. The new generation shows increasing interest in the cultural and ideological heritage of their own country. ASEAN and the Pacific Base countries will become more central, in the coming decade, whereas Europe will be more peripheral.[12] A new thrust seems to awake in the region. This reflection, meandering between macro and micro analysis of specific events, has led me to search for a more fundamental explanation of economic growth. The central thesis is that the knowledge cycle in creating, maintaining and developing economic organization depends on the history, the socio-political climate, available human and material resources and market conditions. Without coupling this knowledge cycle with the dominant institutional and societal rationality, neither capital nor technology can be made effective. Instrumental knowledge alone of an individual decision-maker is necessary but not sufficient for effective economic organization. This central thesis is derived from a framework of energy, information and value.

ENERGY–INFORMATION–VALUE

The first article in *Management Science* starts with the sentence: 'Wherever people have gathered to pursue a common and desired end, there has been an inevitable necessity to organize minds, hands, materials and the use of time for efficient and contributive work' (H. F. Smiddy and L. Naumu).[13] Organizations are the infrastructure of each society. They have a double meaning: on the one side there is a synergy which is more than the sum of individual efforts and wishes, but on the other side there is a recalcitrant force in organizations which perpetuates social inequality and prevents natural dynamics.[14] What knowledge is needed in economic organization for delivering efficient and contributive work?

I consider energy, information and value as three hinges in explaining organizational development. The main function of management and administration is to search for an equilibrium between energy consumption, information exchange and value orientation within its territory. Because energy, information and value have a different loading over time and in different countries, management must be always appropriate (F. Schippers).[15]

In the first industrial revolution the transition from work at estates and home towards factories gave rise to 'management', in the modern sense. S. Pollard aptly describes the genesis of modern management. Everywhere management appears to have adopted itself merely to the needs of technology, discipline or financial control. 'Management' was the instrument, if not the originator, of many of the forces of rational self-interest, the ambiguities of ownership and control of firms . . . which became peculiar to Western industrial capitalism.[16] Analytical time and motion studies translated into costs were the most important contribution of a 'science of managing'. It is still a core. Recently M. Jellinek[17] explained organizational learning systems by returning to the original contributions of Frederick Windsor Taylor and Alexander Hamilton Church. Systematic soldiering and systematic use of experience emerges from an *instrumental* rationality. This management thinking assumes utility maximalization for the individual decision-maker. However, 'it is more than doubtful that circumstances characterizing the industrial revolution of Western Europe have their counterpart in developing countries today' (S. Panitchpakdi).[18] Instrumental rationality has given rise to many behavioural, economic and political theories of organization (Pfeffer 1982, pp. 41–79).[19]

In the second industrial revolution emphasis lies on information and human capital. In contrast to energy it is not physical but symbolic. Information is a representation of reality in our mind. Language is the vehicle of information. Writing and other forms of documentation have created many processes which organize, accumulate and transmit increasing amounts of information. Systems of information—clustered around principles, aspects or objects—have established sciences and disciplines. The interpretation of information is jealously protected by members of a professional clan.

Education and research require an increasing amount of time and resources for transfer, maintenance and development of available information. Endless reading lists, indoctrination of dominant theories, and a strict programme of examinations make students distrust their native common sense and curb their generous impulses.[20] The present information technology makes available a huge amount of information everywhere. In 1952 one expected some seven computers in the future, whereas millions of similar and more powerful computers are now available as personal tools. The utilization of information, however, depends on an *institutional* rationality. Not the individual decision-maker, but his environmental network of users determines the effectiveness of information in economic organization.

Highly skilled people who can process and interpret information from a particular theoretical point of view become useless as they find out that what they have learnt cannot find any application in their home situation. In an economic organization where the supply of skilled manpower is abundant, specialization might be needed to satisfy a differential demand. But in a family business run by the owner-founder, as it appears in South East Asia, specialization is inappropriate. Research degrees where candidates are forced to dig deep into one particular subject and theory might prevent people from looking at other contributing factors. From an institutional point of view individual actors are only pawns and links in a historical and cultural network. Environmental variables largely determine the effectiveness of individual knowledge. This institutional rationality is not a substitute for instrumental thinking. It is a complement (J. Pfeffer).[21]

A third industrial revolution arises from societal values. What society do we want? What is the sense of direction and destiny in a community? Values cannot be reduced to energy or information. People with equal access to energy resources and equal education or access to information might still strive for other ways of living and behavior.

There is no end of ideologies. Values in economic organization are shaped by a continuous interaction between the power holders, interest groups and managers. The resulting *societal rationality* can be defined as a search for acceptance in one's own community and society. In Dutch society there is a tight web of rules for almost every aspect of economic organization. The selection of energy sources is discussed nation-wide under the guidance of a special committee. Employment opportunities for school leavers, better balance between men and women, extra opportunities for handicapped people, regional differentiation in tax regulations, obligatory participation in every major decision and so on. Management has to interact continuously with public administration. It is not the place here to elaborate the theoretical foundation of this model. I have done it elsewhere.[22] It is here sufficient to emphasize the relevant outlines. The main function of management and administration is to search for an equilibrium between available choices of energy consumption, information exchange, and value orientation within the territory of its jurisdiction. Over time there are transformations. The rate of change in energy consumption, information exchange, and value orientation greatly varies. Moreover the differentiation between industrially developed and developing countries is enormous. Each of the levels and stages in development requires its own organizational rationality or paridigm if you like. There is no unilinear development. For the knowledge cycle there are important implications. Instrumental knowledge, what is the core of business economics and administration (Blaug,[23] see also Locke, chapter 10), can be transferred within a reasonable time. Some six years of higher education, according to Dutch traditions, provide a reasonable set of accounting principles and techniques, cash flow calculation, marketing and so on. The coupling of this instrumental knowledge with existing or new institutional networks takes more than a generation. For universities in developing countries some information is available.[24] But also a solid body of statistics, planning models or financial accounts require more than a lifetime. Societal knowledge where a common creed and identity is made operational in regulations for a nation state takes an even longer period.

The discrepancy between the level of instrumental rationality of the elite, the level of institutional rationality in family businesses, plantations and community agencies, and at the top the level of societal rationality makes the process of transfer itself ineffective. Only research, case-by-case, issue-by-issue, instrument-by-instrument, can make instrumental knowledge gradually relevant. A simple representation of this model is given in Fig. 1.

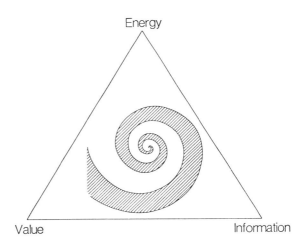

As in any general theory the value depends on testing actual fluctuations and discontinuities. I do not believe in the noble savage of Jean Jacques Rousseau, but I do assume a more balanced leadership in centuries old primitive communities. The French historians around the 'Annales' have shown that at least European medieval history is full of dramatic episodes.[25]

THE INDONESIAN SITUATION

Indonesia counts more than three thousand inhabited islands along a stretch of 6400 km. from Sabang (Acheh) to Merauke (Irian Jaya). It

RESEARCH ON CROSS-CULTURAL MANAGEMENT

covers an area of 5 million sq. km. (of which more than 2 million sq. km. are land). Indonesia is on the brink of becoming a new industrialized country and is, within the ASEAN context, a leading nation due to its rich human and natural resources.

Besides 43 state universities (including teachers colleges, IKIP), there are more than 300 private universities for human resource development which cannot yet cater for all the candidates graduating each year from the senior colleges (SMA). After a selective entrance examination for the top state universities (Perintis) the majority of candidates have to find access by extra financial expense to other universities at home or abroad. Education, upgrading and academic degrees have a high priority for the new generation ('generasi penerus'). Higher education embodies three elements: (1) education and instruction, (2) research, and (3) community service (act of 1961, Tridharma, see Koesnadi Hardjasoemantri, 1981).[26] It is frequently observed, that for managerial and administrative sciences, instruction of normative elements is emphasized (G. Hofstede 1982).[27] Recently, however, staff development, post-graduate training and research are given elaborate attention (Ito 1982).[28] It is envisaged to bring administrative and managerial sciences from the separate faculties of economics, law, social sciences and engineering into a new interfaculty.

There is still a horizontal and vertical imbalance in higher education (Ito, op. cit.), but policy intentions offer challenging opportunities for human resource development.

Natural resources are mainly utilized at the primary level with a continued emphasis on agriculture, forestry, fishing and mining. Manufacturing and construction are a minor sector of the national product (I. Palmer 1978, p. 187).[29] The increase of oil prices has given only a temporary release from foreign dependency. A growing population (from 150 million in 1982 to almost 200 million by the year 2000), an uneven distribution (two-thirds of the inhabitants living on 7 percent of the land), acute poverty for some 60 percent, an 'open door' policy with regard to foreign investment, manufacturing industry based on foreign capital and highly capital-intensive, mismanagement of oil resources and a cash-flow investment policy create 'a perfect example of a developing country whose future will depend on the strategies it adopts' (OECD 1979, p. 211).[30]

The management of human and natural resources depends on a bureaucratic polity—the armed forces, police and civil administration —rather than on political parties operating under parliamentary rules. The bureaucratic polity is the core and source of power, as Fred Riggs observed in his pioneering study of Thailand.[31] This bureaucracy is not primarily interested in 'achievement' goals, but is concerned to promote its own values: these are the values of a status society, hierarchically organized, and motivated by personal leadership and patronage rather than Weberian impersonal norms of legal-rationality. The 'casual and slipshod' and the 'arbitrary' ways in which issues are discussed and committees operate are not so much indications of inefficiency or inability to master Western methods but are rather the expression of political aims, ambitions and rivalries.

'Indecisiveness', delays, and ambiguities are tactical ploys in the struggle for power and advantage among bureaucratic interests and military functions. This power denotes access to wealth as a prerogative of office in uneasy contrast to Western professionalism.[32] Also the idea of power, e.g. in Javanese culture runs counter to Western assumptions: it is concrete, homogeneous, constant and does not raise the question of legitimacy.[33] Especially this lack of legitimacy poses ethical dilemmas for many Western observers and consultants. Democracy as it has been established in the foundation of the United Nations is a Western concept, and there is no indication that the new countries joining the U.N. and becoming gradually the majority, aim at accepting the Western concept of democracy. Only lip-service can be expected, if it fits the power game.

It seems to me that bureaucratic polity has to be accepted as the dominant mode of government and its administration in Asia. If the Indonesians, with a securer sense of their own identity and less defensive insights into their strengths and weaknesses than previously, are able to design viable strategies of managing their human and natural resources within their own traditions, these strategies may prove to be effective even without Western assumptions of legitimacy.[34] Any Western student or practitioner of Management and Administration needs to clarify these assumptions before entering the arena of action or action research in these countries.

INDONESIAN KNOWLEDGE CYCLES FOR ECONOMIC ORGANIZATION

For our purpose I will focus on the Indonesian knowledge cycles for economic organization. Five different cycles might be distinguished: proto-Indonesian, colonial, new Indonesian, neo-colonial, and ASEAN.

PROTO-INDONESIAN KNOWLEDGE

The Greeks neither described nor believed in the specialized divisions of knowledge that we are familiar with today. Instead, they firmly believed that a ruler—one selected to govern—ought to be a truly knowledgeable person.[35] European social and cultural history has followed a quite different course than Oriental history and culture, but in Indonesia also one has to discover the roots.

The concept of *pamong praja* seems a reasonable start. 'Praja' means land, people, and the economy, and 'pamong' is from 'among' which means to guide, to care for, to protect, to guard, to educate, to develop. Pamong praja means therefore 'Custodian of the Country'. It already existed in the Empire of Majapahit and was well organized under the leadership of Prime Minister Gajah Mada. This empire stretched its power to what are now Indonesia, Philippines, Thailand and Indo-China. The style of leadership can be formulated from the following principles:

1. Tan hana mangua: there is no place for double loyalty. In practice it means that one should not make a distinction between personal loyalty to the superior and organizational loyalty as existing in modern organizations.
2. Hing karsa asung tulada: in front, to give the example. In practice it means that the leader should be the example in everything that concerns the performance of job, duty, mission or work. Regularly there is an 'upacara' (ceremony), where the leader gives his message ('amanat'): explaining policies, issuing warnings and expressing his expectations.
3. Hing madya manguan karsa: to be amongst the people and from there to stimulate their ambitions/desires. In practice it means that any job, work or duties should be distributed and the authority delegated as far as possible, in such a way that every member of the group can get the opportunity to participate as actively as possible. It means also, that the ones who are not involved by the leader have a serious problem. If this problem is not solved in a personal discussion, it may be interpreted as lack of interest.
4. Tut wuri handayani: to influence society, yet at the same time following or observing the path of its development. In practice it means that the leader should trust his subordinates and let them do the job without interference. It is expected that subordinates report to their superior when problems arise and ask for advice ('penunjuk') or his blessing ('doa restu').

The roots of these leadership principles are so strong that the influence of Hinduism, Buddhism, Islam, Christianity, and modern science are only phenomenal. 'Rukun' is the basic organizational unit, meaning familially or communally being together with feelings of affection. Since the Japanese occupation one has divided people into Rukun Tetangga, the neighbourhood unit. It consists of 10–25 families. The role of the elected chairman is very important. He (or she) is not a public servant and not paid for services. There are many organizational principles embedded in the proto-Indonesian culture, such as 'gotong-royong' (mutual help), 'musyawarah' (collective decision-making, arriving at a consensus rather than agreement through voting), and 'arisan' (mutual credit arrangements). This is only a brief sketch from Indonesian sources (Atmosudirdjo, Tjondro-negoro, Mulyono).[36]

For an Indonesian expert it is too sketchy and for an outsider it might be too complex. The point is here that at the smallest unit of organization in Indonesia these patterns exist. Of course, there is variety in subcultures and regions. This is an ideal type.

The transfer of this knowledge is done through all stages of education and work. Through Wayang (shadow) plays the gist of this lifestyle and behavioural patterns is expressed and impressed with episodical evidence. Operationalization is through stories and symbols.

COLONIAL KNOWLEDGE

With the disbandment of the VOC (the Dutch East India Company) on 31 December 1799, Indonesia became 'a state' in the broad sense of the word. The VOC system before that time was based on political and trade contracts. The company's servants had only to check every time whether the bupatis and other chiefs complied with the provisions of the contracts. Armed troops and Chinese businessmen were the instruments of the VOC. Daendels, doctor of law, served in the French army under Napoleon. In 1808 he was sent by King Louis Napoleon of Holland to organize the defence system of Indonesia against a possible invasion by the English. He improved the postal services and the overall communication system, the administration of finance and the General Secretariat. In 1811 Raffles, Lieutenant-General, ruling on instructions from Lord Minto in Calcutta, wanted to by-pass the bupatis, and instructed the European administrators to deal directly with the village people. He abolished the compulsory delivery-system of export crops by the village people, and replaced it with a new land taxation system, the land-rent system, which in a modified way still exists today in Indonesia. Daendels and Raffles were the founders of the modern Administration in Indonesia. Their ideas were very advanced at that time and therefore hardly viable. There was no well-qualified administrative staff to put the regulations and instructions into operation. Van den Capellen made the first steps in Education and Training of the Indonesian Administration (1819), mainly public administration and regional languages. An Institute for Javanese linguistics was established at Surakarta in 1832, after a study at the Military School at Semarang in 1818 was felt to be inadequate.[37]

In 1843 the Royal Academy at Delft was founded. This was the start of Indology. This field of knowledge was characterized by a minimum of differentiation (LIPI I, 167, LIPI II, 368, see note 9). It had a strong legal orientation. Only three branches of specialization emerged, i.e. the studies with a dominantly literary-historical orientation, those with a dominantly socio-political orientation, and studies with a dominantly socio-economic orientation. It was in fact a European mode of pamong praja. I will not describe here the various changes in this type of education in Delft, Leyden and Utrecht. In 1942 there were 850 European civil servants who had passed this type of education.

Economic education was in this development part of the Law School in Batavia (Jakarta). From 1924–1928 J. H. Boeke was the first teacher in economics before he was appointed professor in 'Colonial Economics' at the university of Leyden. He coined the term 'economic dualism'. After Boeke, J. van Gelderen and subsequently G. H. van der Kolff held the chair in economics at the law school in Batavia. After the war the chair was briefly held by D. H. Burger, a former student of Boeke. The discussions between Boeke, van Gelderen, van der Kolff and Burger on the possibilities for Indonesian economic development have exerted a great influence on Indonesian intellectuals, particularly lawyers, who received their university education during the 1930s (LIPI, II, 227, see note 33). However, economics was only a supplement to the main courses in law. Only a handful of Indonesians could follow a full-fledged university education in economics in the Netherlands, such as at the Netherlands School of Economics in Rotterdam. People like Moh. Hatta, Aboetari, Hidajat, Saroso, and Sumitro Djojohadikasuma were among the few.

Business economics is a special case. In the Dutch tradition there were two competing schools of thought. An 'Amsterdam-school' was highly normative and deductive. Since his appointment in 1922 at the new Faculty of Trade Sciences at the University of Amsterdam, Limperg built an impressive logical structure of available partial theories. His main effort was to arrive at the 'right' norms for costs and profits. Locke's description of the German case in chapter 10, gives an excellent insight into the thinking pattern. However, Limperg tried to indoctrinate his students that it was his own theory.

He did not write a textbook. Students had to buy the lecture notes (dictaat) composed by G. D. Ribbius, but Limperg never accepted them as the 'source of truth'. After his death his daughter and some of his students who had become professors edited these notes in seven impressive volumes (1964–1968). Until the present time 'dictat' is a good Indonesian word for indicating teaching material. The competing older school was the Rotterdam tradition. Volmer, Nico Polak and Goudriaan were the key figures. They worked in a more inductive way: observe what the practising bookkeeper is doing and try to discover the logic behind the observed behaviour. For the argument here it is sufficient to say that also during recent visits to economic faculties in Indonesia questions about these schools, the 'right' concepts of price, costs and profits, and the difference between deduction and induction are prevailing. A history on the relative impact of these schools in Indonesia has not yet been written (see note 34).

NEW INDONESIAN KNOWLEDGE

Officially Indonesia became independent on 17 August 1945, but the August 1945–August 1950 period is characterized mainly by the conflicts (military and ideological) between the Indonesian Republican forces and the Dutch. From the Indonesian side it was the Independence war, from the Dutch side the Pacification war.

As Indonesian economists were scarce, it was difficult to start an appropriate Indonesian education. In the final days in 1948 the first School of Economics was established by the Dutch authorities in the city of Macassar (now Ujung Pandang). Dutch professors and lecturers made up the teaching staff. In Jakarta a separate faculty of economics was established in September 1950 as part of the Universitas Indonesia. The first dean was a professor in law, Sunorjo Kolopaking. In 1951 he was succeeded by Professor Sumitro Djojohadikusumo. He was able, through his past association with the Netherlands School of Economics, to recruit qualified Dutch professors and lecturers. In 1957 Djojosutono succeeded Sumitro. By 1970, some 1345 economists had graduated from this institution.

Gradually one tried to give a much more pragmatic bent to economic education. However, the Dutch influence was still strong. It took the student eight years to graduate as Sarjana Ekonomi (or the still used equivalent Doctorandus). In 1970 only six students had completed their study within a period of less than five years. In general there have been more graduates in business economics than graduates in any other field of specialization. Until 1970 only eight doctorates were granted. One started to build also research and management institutes connected with the economic faculty. But in general research was restricted to short-term problems with a routine character. Since the start of the First Five Year National Development Plan in 1969 (Repelita I) instant research on a contractual basis was carried out for government agencies. The relatively low salaries the staff earned made it necessary to do some moonlighting. Moreover, many became flying professors (dosen terbang) filling in the gaps in the many new faculties of economy over the country.

There is no need to describe here the gradual establishment of other economic faculties. They followed more or less the same pattern. The ten or so qualified economists in 1950 had to spread their knowledge thinly over an increasing amount of students. It could be only a textbook knowledge. Research was restricted to quick surveys (see note 35). Gradually one started to look for quality improvement and factors impeding research (e.g. LIPI, Kerangka untuk meneliti faktor, see note 2, sosial-budaja dalampenbamgunan ekonomi, 1969).[36] In 1982 a questionnaire of 58 pages on research productivity was sent to some 25,000 staff members of the Indonesian state universities. I do not know whether the large amount of data has already been processed, analysed and interpreted. In discussions about this project I suggested a case approach for analysis.

NEO-COLONIAL KNOWLEDGE

This term is not used in a pejorative sense. It indicates 'development aid' derived from knowledge in the sponsoring countries. Since 1953 increasing numbers of American professors and experts entered the scene, when Dutch public servants were beginning to leave the Indonesian public services.

Moreover dozens of faculty members and advanced students of the faculties of economics (mainly from Universitas Indonesia and from Universitas Gadja Mada, established in 1955) were sent to the United States for advanced studies in economics and business administration. The University of California at Berkeley affiliated with the Universitas Indonesia. The University of Wisconsin at Madison affiliated with the Universitas Gadja Mada. Some returned with Ph.D. degrees. Due to the Dutch–Indonesian conflict on Irian Barat at the end of the 1950s Indonesian students in the Netherlands had to leave. Many went to German universities. For public administration the major link was with the Indiana university. Also Japanese scholarships were offered as part of war damage negotiations. The scattered information on different schools of thinking in Indonesia has not yet been written.[37] My own observations suggest rather fragmented clusters of graduates around foreign universities. Because it was mainly textbook knowledge, discussions tend to be in terms of these schools and not in terms of empirical evidence or relevance to Indonesian development. Due to the typically Dutch compartmentalization of the Indonesian university structure, problems remained within a particular faculty. Cross-fertilization between faculties was difficult. Therefore Indonesian surveys on knowledge stick to the established procedures of a particular discipline. It is unfortunate, in my assessment, that for example public administration is mainly given in social faculties, and business administration in economic faculties. Transgressing the boundaries is frowned upon. However, there is a general awareness that one needs a problem-oriented approach rooted in Indonesian culture.

ASEAN KNOWLEDGE CYCLE

At this moment a new knowledge cycle seems to be gaining momentum. Historically, South East Asia has many common roots, where trade, religion and civilization have shaped a special culture. The Majapahit empire of the 15th century is an example. Today ASEAN offers a potential platform for an intellectual revival.

From an ASEAN point of view there is much more integration

between cognition (what one knows), emotion and empathy (what one feels), rationality (what one uses for reasoning), beliefs (what one accepts as truth), and institutions (how one classifies the world) than in Western Europe. In a certain sense cognitive expertise as an individual capacity is not accepted, if it does not fit the society and its institutions. ASEAN needs its own way of creating, disseminating and applying knowledge. How can one capitalize on this cross-cultural learning experience? Recently Lee Kuan Yew, the Cambridge-educated lawyer who is now the unquestioned leader of a prosperous and politically stable city-state, emphasized the role of ASEAN. At his 60th birthday party he reflected on the challenges of the next generation:

> We are on our own, responsible for our own defence and survival. We have to weave our regional net of relationships. Otherwise, economic development is impossible. The present leaders of ASEAN are in accord and harmony because they share common objectives. By the 1990s, ASEAN leaders will come from a generation that did not have this common experience. Therefore we must make these personal experiences into part of ASEAN's institutional memories so that not too much will have to be learned all over again, and at too high a cost. (*Asiaweek*, vol. 9, no. 39, Sept. 30, 1983).[38]

There have been impressive efforts to relate Indonesian management education to South East Asian roots. In 1976 I participated in a Regional Seminar on Business and Culture in South and South East Asia.[39] The business leaders and government officials there discussed in detail the opportunities. Unfortunately the proposals for follow-up meetings in Malaysia could not be fulfilled. In 1979 another seminar on the 'Konsep Manajemen Indonesia' was held in Jakarta with representatives of academic, business and government (Marbun 1980).[40] The combined experience of the five ASEAN countries seems to offer an operational platform for utilizing the pro-Asian, colonial, postwar and development aid knowledge cycles. One needs to break through the western boundaries of rationality and take the lead in one's own history of institutional learning.

PRACTICAL IMPLICATIONS

If one accepts the 'long wave' of knowledge cycles in Indonesia and South East Asia as a feasible proposition, there are a number of practical implications.

Firstly, designing an operational strategy for building up appropriate human capital. What type of economist, manager or administrator does one need in the coming decade? I would suggest that he (or she) needs: (1) to be able to discover a realistic problem, (2) to select feasible methods for solving this problem within given constraints, (3) to evaluate the strong and weak points of the solution, and (4) to indicate modes of implementation. He (or she) has to accept the culture-bound restrictions in economic thinking. This implies an integration of national public administration with (business) economics. The resulting bureaucratic economics require an entrepreneurial spirit. It looks like a paradox, but human nature is unpredictable.

Secondly, selecting small clusters of research projects, which have a high societal priority. Each of these projects needs a minimum critical mass of co-operating research fellows and a realistic time period for the stages.

In the present new Dutch policy of the Ministry of Education and Research a new instrument has been implemented; the so-called conditional financing. Within the available budget of a university projects with a minimum of five full time equivalents and a time horizon of five years (25 full time equivalents) the capacity will be reserved and guaranteed, if the projects show internal cohesion, have societal priority and fit accepted standards. The reactions of universities have not been favourable, but mainly because of too vague criteria and too much internal bureaucracy. As an instrument, however, to allocate existing research capacity for productivity within universities it has a high potential value.

If a multidisciplinary approach is seen as important, interfaculty approval in this case between public administration and business economics, is necessary. However, no instrument is able to guarantee a conducive climate for research productivity. Monitoring is more important than strict *a priori* criteria.

Reaching a critical mass in this type of 'bureaucratic business economic studies' cannot be achieved overnight. In the realities of research and development the duration of take-off stages seems always to be underestimated. Thirdly, agreeing on a bottom-up approach, where the roots of the 'pranata sosial' (the hidden social structure) can be discovered at the smallest scale. The 'rukun' seems an appropriate scale. Rather than surveying all kampungs in Jakarta, it seems better to focus on a specific, representative kampung and follow up the research outcomes over time and case-by-case.[41] Rather than surveying a large sample of villages, it seems better to study one or a few cases in detail and follow up the outcomes.[42] Rather than surveying a large number of plantations, it seems better to select a few for detailed observation.[43]

Fourthly, designing and focusing in a reiterative process rather than looking for complex methodology and impressive models. Regular tutoring sessions between research supervisor and research fellow are needed to keep the project on the track and to prevent a rigid adherence to textbook knowledge. Books such as Field Data Collection in the Social Sciences based on experiences (Agricultural Development Council, New York 1976)[44] are more important for inspiration than methodology as such. It is also necessary to prevent copying of a so-called successful thesis elsewhere. Research is a process of chase, chance and luck. It requires flexibility, courage and patience.

Fifthly, establishing extension networks to reach the target group. The majority of potential users work in small businesses and agencies.

A special translation effort is needed to present the outcomes in pragmatic and visual form with examples. Each finished report must be read and reviewed by the relevant policy makers and this means executive summaries for stimulating their interest. The traditional Ph.D. format is too heavy for utilization. This might need special skills. Vertical integration with the occupational level is essential.

Sixthly, selecting only transferable knowledge from abroad. In Fig. 2 I have made a model for classifying these areas. It is clear that one has to select a special focus for each research project.

The actual production level is the core, not the structure of the strategic apex. This implies an integration of qualitative and quantitative approaches. In economics this is still a much desired objective. It suggests also an integration of the former Indology, with its emphasis on history, adat (customary law) and languages, into social economy.[45] For implementation economic science has a too dry rationality.

Seventhly, accepting failure rates, critical issues and adaptations. Each research project is an expedition in the unknown. No planning or financing can prevent discontinuities and sudden obstacles. At the level of practical operations, such as logistics and access to field situations, the major difficulties in the practice of research tend to arise. Data get lost or unexpected information becomes available. If one has to stick to a pre-structured rigid schedule, research opportunities get lost. Frequently one observes a scanning approach where only information which fits the model is accepted as legitimate. Of course, the research fellow can meet the targets, but the outcome is an artifact of the design.

Finally, I have no intention of giving a comprehensive list of practical implications. It would require detailed discussions with practitioners. Especially the desirable integration between private and public sectors of economic organization, horizontally and vertically, is too ambitious for an outside observer. If one could arrive at a joint effort of business leaders and government officials for establishing a research centre for administration and management within the available capacity, it would be an impressive result. Originally, the Netherlands School of Economics was started by captains of industry and commerce. Gradually it has become integrated as a state university. In ASEAN there are different mixtures between private and public sectors. The ASEAN setting might provide the fertility for a new integration. The major challenge seems to break through the relics of colonial and neocolonial structures of the knowledge industry. It requires broad-based guidelines, couched in terms of a firm philosophical background culled from the indigenous culture (Panitchpakdi).[46]

It does not need new capacity but a restructuring of available capacity around priorities and a sense of common destiny. It implies an integration of academic and vocational skills at various levels.

Figure 2: Areas for Cross-National Management Development/Change/Transfer

Structure/Power	Level	Cognition	Emotion/Affection/Empathy	Rationality/Calculus/Logic	Behaviour	Performance
Democracy Bureaucratic Polity Dictatorial	Societal	CS Understanding, images (School, University Programmes)	ES Cross-cultural Tolerance (Cosmopolitan versus Local)	RS Utilization of Mix of cross-cultural styles for different tasks	BS Learning capacity + strategies (Human Resource Development)	PS Contribution of organization to world socio-economic development. Industrial Policy.
Family Firm Mono-product Multi-product Multinational Conglomerate Joint-venture	Organizational	CO Business Intelligence for Strategic Decision-Making	EO Authority and Reward Systems (Careers)	RO Capacity for adaptation of decision, control + personnel syst.	BO Organizatinal Climate and value assumptions Work objectives	PO Multinational balance in system design + performance
e.g. typology of Joan Woodward Unit–Mass Process Degree of automation, Robotization	Production System	CP Cross-cultural Operational System Knowledge (combinations)	EP Group attachment Team Loyalty	RP Capacity for planning, supervision of new operational systems	BP Interpersonal skills (social/linguistic)	PP Multicultural Leadership style and objectives for supervision
e.g. collective versus individual hierarchical versus participative	Individual	CI Cross-cultural Personal Style Knowledge	EI Security of identity Work motivation	RI Conceptual and analytical capacity styles	BI Task completion	PI Criteria for Achievement/Advancement

Is there a role for cross-cultural management studies as described in this book? Yes, I hope so. As Negandhi observed, increasingly the road is becoming unified. However, one has to start from one's own situation. From an Indonesian and ASEAN point of view the role of foreign universities and research institutes can be only complementary. A careful selection of what is transferable needs to be made given the knowledge cycles there. It seems to me impossible to leap too fast. Continuity and internal cohesion of a research community determine the speed. This research community needs to be rooted in actual economic organization and to be accepted by the national elite. From our point of view, a research and Ph.D. programme for ASEAN business and administration has been designed which follows the suggested outline and tries to link the knowledge cycles here and there. However, it is only complementary.

EPILOGUE

A rough sketch of Indonesian knowledge cycles for economic organization has been given. Knowledge cannot be transferred as capital or technology. It requires a long process of creation, adaptation, maturation and utilization at the local level. Individuals can be trained, but institutional networks need their own timing. Societal recognition takes even longer. The proposed strategy of research intervention needs more pairs of eyes to become operational. I am not calibrated to the Indonesian culture, nor am I an Indologist. It might be an advantage to be an empathic outside observer. May-be it is too naive and academic. But one needs a vision. The role of cross-cultural organization studies, to which I have devoted most of my thinking since 1960 from an industrial and university home base, will be different in the coming decade. There is no time left for massive world-wide new programmes as in the days of Harbison, Vernon or the IBM surveys. We have to start from available human capacity and build up, case-by-case, issue-by-issue, problem-by-problem, a modest and coherent set of operational rules.

One has to revitalize proto-institutional viable structures and to get rid of neo-colonial institutes, which have been built up on foreign models only. Peres aptly commented on an Asian Research Corporation as an ineffective reaction to foreign knowledge cycles. This has lead to too heavy structures of research co-ordination with minimal and discontinuous output. Of course, we have to accept conflicting ideas and paradigms along the way, but there seems to be a readiness for new challenges in ASEAN. It is to be hoped that these ideas might trigger off a more rewarding, even if not frictionless, new development effort.

NOTES

1. Philip E. Vernon, *Intelligence and Cultural Environment* (London, 1969).
2. H. W. Beers, *An American Experience in Indonesia* (Kentucky, 1971).
3. Supachai Panitchpakdi, 'Underdevelopment of Development Economics in Thailand', presented to Workshop in University of Malaya, organized by The Regional Institute of Higher Education and Development (RIHED), Singapore and The Asian Regional Team for Employment Promotion (ARTEP), Bangkok, 14–16 December 1981. This paper has inspired me very much. Dr. S. Panitchpakdi did his Ph.D. on *Educational Growth and Planning in Developing Countries* (Rotterdam, 1973). Unfortunately his other papers are in Thai. He is now director of the Bank of Thailand.
4. The present proposal for Dutch universities is to create research fellowships at a minimum level of income. Of course, if research is valued, one needs to pay the market price. Good researchers are scarce. In economics I estimate that less than 10% of the graduates are promising candidates. However, financial incentives have not yet been a guarantee for success.
5. J. H. Boeke, *Economics and Economic Policy of Dual Societies as Exemplified by Indonesia* (New York, 1974).
   J. van Gelderen, *The Recent Development of Economic Policy in the Netherlands East Indies* (London, 1939) see also: P. Hesseling, *Effective Organization Research for Development* (Oxford, 1982), pp. 130–132.
6. In April 1981 a Marshall Plan Symposium was held at the Graduate School of Management (Delft). In the summation lecture I tried to specify how to learn from the evaluation of the Marshall Plan for development. It seems that each participating European country was stimulated to search for its own identity in developing appropriate managerial and administrative skills. American consultancy and business school models and methods were tested and adapted but never completely copied.
   Moreover, the institutional component of establishing national research units was critical. A publication of revised papers is in preparation.
7. A. Querido, 'The Role of the Dutch in Japan's Scientific and Technological Development during the EDO Period', Tokyo, 2 April 1982 (in publication). The author, a professor of Medicine in Leyden university and founder of the Rotterdam Medical School, distinguishes three stages in the transfer of scientific thinking. The first stage concerns instruments and skills, the second the emergence of textbooks mainly translated and annotated, the third structured education in home universities with incremental additions.
8. A. J. F. Köbben, *De Zaakwaarnemer* (The Caretaker), Deventer, 1983.
9. J. L. S. Girling, *The Bureaucratic Polity in Modernizing Societies* (Singapore, 1981, Institute of Southeast Asian studies).
10. L. Peres, Asian Research Corporation (unpublished draft). I have only a draft paper that he gave me during discussions in Jakarta in 1979. He is a research consultant from the Australian university for UNESCO.
11. The information is based on a report in a Dutch newspaper by Hans Rolloos. I do not have the original Indonesian text of director general Gandhi's (Finance) statement to parliament.
12. *Asiaweek* (weekly, vol. 9, 1983) gives a concise description of this transformation.
13. Harold F. Smiddy and Lionel Naum, Evolution of a 'science of managing' in America, *Management Science* (no. 1, vol. 1, 1954, pp. 1–31).
14. C. J. Lammers, *Organisaties vergelijkenderwijs* (Comparing Organizations) (Utrecht, 1983, p. 481).
15. Frits Schippers, *Appropriate Management* (Singapore, 1983).
16. Sidney Pollard, *The Genesis of Modern Management,* p. 314 (Penguin, 1968).
17. M. Jellinek, *Institutional Innovation: a study of organizational learning systems* (New York, 1979).

18. See note 3.
19. Jeffrey Pfeffer, *Organizations and Organization Theory* (Boston, 1982).
20. Joan Robinson, Teaching Economics, in Joan Robinson *Collected Economic Papers,* vol. 3 (Oxford, 1965).
21. Jeffrey Pfeffer, op. cit. pp. 80–177.
22. P. Hesseling, op. cit. pp. 114–132.
23. M. Blaug, *The Methodology of Economics* (Cambridge, 1980).
24. K. W. Thompson, B. R. Fogel and H. E. Danner, *Higher Education and Social Change,* vol. I and II (New York, 1976, 1977);
    Philip G. Altbach, *Higher Education in the Third World: themes and variations* (Singapore, 1983).
25. *Annales,* Economies-Societés-Civilisations. Their 'longue durée' approach with micro observations fascinates me, but I am not an historian.
26. Koesnadi Hardjasoematri, *Study Service as a Subsystem in Indonesian Higher Education* (Leyden, Ph.D., 1981).
27. Geert Hofstede, *Culturele Problemen voor Nederlandse Managers en Deskundigen in Indonesië* (Deventer, 1982). This is a brief exploration of his Indonesian sample which has not been treated in his impressive Culture's Consequences, see other chapters.
28. Ito, Staff Development in Indonesian State Universities, Regional Institute of Higher Education and Development (Singapore, 1982).
29. I. Palmer, *The Indonesian Economy since 1965* (London, 1978).
30. OECD, *Facing the Future* (Paris, 1979).
31. Fred Riggs, *The Modernization of a Bureaucratic Polity* (Honolulu, 1966).
32. See note 9.
33. R. O.'G. Anderson, The Idea of Power in Javanese Culture, in Claire Holt (ed.), *Culture and Politics in Indonesia* (Ithaca, 1972).
34. A. R. Willner in L. W. Pye (ed.), *Cases in Comparative Politics: Asia* (Boston, 1970), pp. 242–306. Indonesia is in a state of transformation. Local newspapers and discussions with Indonesians sometimes give new insights, which do not fit the stereotypes.
35. R. F. Rich (ed.), The Knowledge Cycle (Beverley Hills, 1981) is a rich source of inspiration and references.
36. S. P. Atmosudirdjo, *A Brief History of the Education and Training of the Indonesian Administration* (EUR, Rotterdam, 1982).
    S. P. Armosudirdjo, *The Role of Indonesian Administration in the Indonesian Business World* (EUR, Rotterdam, 1983).
    Prof. Atmosudirdjo was the first director of the Indonesian Institute of Public Administration (1957). As a visiting member of our department he has been a continuous source of experience for understanding Indonesian realities.
    S. M. P. Tjondronegoro, *The Organizational Phenomenon and Planned Development in Rural Communities of Java* (Ph.D., Jakarta, 1977).
    Mulyono Gandadiputra, *A Study of the Superior-Subordinate Relations in some organizations in Jakarta* (Ph.D., Jakarta, 1978).
37. Based on Atmosudirdjo (1983).
38. The Indonesian Institute of Sciences (LIPI) did in 1972 a survey on the development and state of the main disciplines in the social sciences in Indonesia. The results have been published in two volumes (Jakarta, 1975 and 1979). The introductory chapter on higher education in the social sciences by Koentjaraningrat and Harsja W. Bachtiar gives an insight into the explosive quantitative expansion, especially in the social sciences. Law is the oldest discipline. Economics developed after the war and today is one of the most popular subjects. Here I have used especially the chapters on Economics by Thee Kian Wie and on the Science of Administration by Buchari Zainun and others. For Economics there is another survey by Adolf J. H. Enthoven, *Accounting Education in Economic Development Management* (Amsterdam, 1981), chapter XIX. For Business Administration and Management a World Bank report is

being published at the moment of writing (September 1983).

From the Dutch side Indonesian Studies have been given priority after a review under chairmanship of Piekaar (1982). The emphasis is here on language and history.

39. LIPI, The Social Sciences in Indonesia, II, 227.
40. For the Dutch scene there is one written by Wouter van Rossum (Ph.D., Amsterdam 1979). I have some comments by former Dutch economics teachers in Indonesia, but insufficient for any conclusion.
41. Thee Kian-Wie, Economics, p. 261 in LIPI, II.
42. There is a continuous search for social-cultural factors in economic development, such as the LIPI report Kerangka untuk meneliti faktor^2 sosial-budaya dalan pembangunan ekonomi (Jakarta 1969).
(Framework to study the social cultural factors in economic development) by Koentjaraningrat and Harsja W. Bachtiar. The same framework has been applied to understanding the poor quality of Indonesian research.
43. The university of origin is relevant information for every government official, because it usually determines the selection of key assistants. In daily conversations one refers to 'gangs'. However, a more eclectic approach is becoming visible.
44. Asiaweek, vol. 9, no. 39, 30 September 1983. In Singapore there are already many ASEAN-oriented activities, such as RIHED, Institute of South-east Asian Studies, and Journal of South-east Asian Studies. However, there is a careful regional balance. The secretariat general of ASEAN is in Jakarta.
45. Business and Culture in Asia and South East Asia (Jakarta, 26–31 July 1976), unpublished papers.
46. Marbun, B. N. (ed.), Konsep Manajemen Indonesia (Jakarta, 1980), The LPPM, the oldest business school in Indonesia and one of the organizers of this seminar together with the Economic Faculty of Universitas Indonesia, plans to open its own Graduate School of Business Administration in 1985. Recently a number of other private initiatives to start MBA types of education have been made either by instrumental training within available models or by more emphasis on Indonesian research. It is not a question whether Indonesian organization studies are needed, but when and at what scale. Research intervention is a long term strategy.

CHAPTER 7

The Japanese competitive edge:
Why and how?

Andreas W. Falkenberg

INTRODUCTION

The rise of Japan as an economic empire over the past 130 years presents two fundamental questions: why and how did it happen? Until the 1850s Japan was isolated and rather unknown to the rest of the world. Today its economy spans the globe and its products are being marketed in virtually every town (if not every store) throughout the world. As MITI (Ministry of International Trade and Industry) declared in 1980, the goals of the Meiji government of 1868 have been reached: namely to catch up with the West without being dominated by foreigners politically or economically. With the exception of the US occupation following World War II, Japan has maintained its independence for centuries. Given the Euro-American involvement in the other countries of the region during the last 130 years, the Japanese situation is quite unique.

It is not possible to fully explore all the variables which have contributed to Japan's success in this chapter; however, the few selected here should lend insight and give a fuller understanding of the phenomenon. First, any kind of performance requires motivation, and exceptional performance requires exceptional motivation. Second, a nation's performance requires a large extent of agreement around a useful modus operandi, which in turn is derived from the culture itself. Third, there must have been favourable institutional arrangements facilitating the development. Fourth, a leap from economic under-development to its present advanced state is facilitated by successful adaptation and learning from the countries which pioneered that process. Learning from the successes and failures of others is far less costly than it was for those who found the way initially. In summary, it will be argued that the economic performance was facilitated by an extraordinary motivation, a strong and beneficial cultural heritage, favorable institutional arrangements, successful adaptation of Western practices. Some of the more significant results are presented towards the end.

MOTIVATION

The initial contact with the West came in the 1500s in the form of Portuguese explorers and missionaries. These were later expelled and Japan went into isolation until the arrival of Commander Perry in 1853 and the subsequent dictation of the unequal treaties by the Western Powers. Japan no longer had the choice of isolation, and the Meiji restoration (enlightened rule) embarked upon an ambitious program of modernization in 1868. Engineers were hired from Europe to construct shipyards and railroads, Japanese citizens were sent to the West to bring home the latest in the technological, economic and political sciences. The primary motivating force at the time may have been the desire to avoid the fate of the neighboring countries, which were dominated and exploited by the Western colonial powers. The way to avoid this was to build a strong economy and a strong military power, modeled initially on the British example in Europe. Later, Japan did attempt to create an Empire in the British style, but never did gain the recognition of the West (Scott et al. 1980). This effort came to an abrupt end with the termination of World War II. Some argue that the current pursuit of a major world market-share is similar to that of the military pursuit during the first half of this century. Perhaps it is propelled by a drive for international recognition; in the past, a world power was measured by its colonies, which is no longer the ideal. Now technological, cultural and economic achievements are the main entry requirements to the club of leading nations, and Japan's desire and drive toward this end seem second to none.

Another motivating force is the fear of losing face which is ingrained into the culture and which should be avoided at virtually all costs. On a national level, the unequal treaties from the middle of the 19th century must have been seen as national humiliation and loss of face. This motivating force is the reverse of struggle for recognition discussed above; by making progress, one avoids the humiliation of defeat.

However, Japan did not avoid humiliation in its struggle toward acceptance. During the early parts of this century they repeatedly failed to gain the recognition of the West and were criticized for their military adventures. This culminated in a devastating national humiliation at the end of World War II.

The humiliation issue is far from absent in present-day Japan as the trade policies have come under increasing scrutiny in the West for three reasons. First, because they do seem to produce better quality products at lower prices than the Western competitors, which has caused labor unrest in the West as well as sharp reactions from many firms. Second, there is increasing evidence that the Japanese industrial policy gives an unfair advantage to Japanese companies and that some companies themselves conduct their business in a manner which may be in violation of e.g. US laws. (Technological espionage, erroneous product documentation, bribery, pricing violations, etc.) Finally, whereas we perceive the West to have a liberal, open policy with respect to imports, the Japanese are seen as protectionists. Regardless of whether the above is true or not, if the unfavourable perception becomes sufficiently strong, then the Japanese may be in for another humiliation in trade relations. Both the Japanese Government and the Japanese businesses are aware of this, and they have created a very sophisticated network of public and private lobbyists around the world promoting and marketing Japanism in order to keep the raw materials flowing and the markets for finished goods open. This brings us to Japan's fundamental dilemma—Japan needs the West for resources and as markets for their output, but we do not need Japan to the same extent. Should the trade between the West and Japan come to a standstill, the impact in Japan would far exceed the impact on the West.

This brings us to the third motivational factor, namely resources. Initially, the resource most needed was food, but as the economy grew it became increasingly evident that sustained economic growth could not be supported by the natural resources in Japan; one had to 'export or die'. If one could not gain access to the resources through military conquest, as pursued initially, then one must trade for them. The dependency on outside resources and export markets is quite considerable and is perhaps the number one motivator behind the recent rapid economic development. Table 1 contrasts the US and Japanese dependency on foreign suppliers of basic raw materials.

Table 1: Overseas Dependency on Key Resources (1978)

	Imports as a % of National Consumption		Imports as a % of World Trade	
	U.S.	Japan	U.S.	Japan
Energy	21.9	92.4	18.9	13.7
Coal	(−) 7.9	75.2	1.5	26.9
Crude oil	37.7	99.8	18.3	14.6
Natural gas	4.5	82.6	17.5	9.3
Iron ore	30.4	98.4	14.0	40.5
Copper	38.0	94.1	11.4	23.9
Lead	61.3	78.6	18.4	5.0
Zinc	67.0	62.4	26.5	8.5
Tin	100.0	98.0	31.7	19.5
Aluminium	66.5	100.0	22.9	17.6
Nickel	92.9	100.0	28.6	9.5
Lumber	2.7	66.4	18.7	21.6
Wool	27.0	100.0	2.2	17.5
Cotton	(−)118.3	100.0	0.0	16.3
Soybeans	(−) 70.3	95.7	0.0	18.4
Corn	(−) 38.5	99.9	0.1	15.6
Wheat	(−)229.5	93.8	0.0	7.7

Source: 'White Paper on International Trade, Japan 1980', J.E.T.R.O., pp. 39/40.

The struggle for international recognition, the need to avoid humiliation, and the need for foreign materials and markets are perhaps the primary driving forces behind the Japanese push towards development, and may help us to understand the 'why' part of the question posed in the title. However, there are a number of nations in which similar motivating forces may be present but which have not been able to succeed as Japan has done. This leads us to the question of how it was possible. The answer to this may lie in the unique cultural heritage of the Japanese as well as the ability to adapt developmental ideas from the West to the Japanese situation.

CULTURAL HERITAGE

Perhaps it was because of its mountainous isolation and lack of agricultural lands that the Japanese culture developed so differently from the North American value system. Life in Japan required a large portion of cooperation, since survival demanded a strong degree of interdependence. This is also reflected by the philosophy of the nature religionic genesis, which is based on the mutually supportive interdependencies of man and nature (Drucker 1981). Shortage of resources and relative isolation (society is closed to outsiders) coupled with this philosophy have made groupism and the long-term cooperative modus operandi a favored means to survival. By contrast, this was not necessary in North America. The American heritage includes ample resources, an open society as well as an anthropocentric view of man. This philosophy puts man at the center as an individual— independent and free to pursue his aims without too much responsibility to others or to nature. (See the cultural contrast model, Fig. 1.)

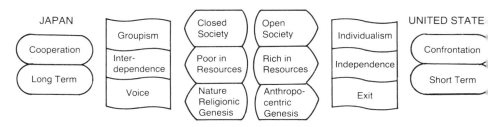

Figure 1: The Contrast Model

Social, Economic and Philosophical Basis:
1. Closed Society: Homogeneous, culturally pure, difficult for an outsider to gain acceptance.
2. Open Society: Heterogeneous, cultural variety, easy for an outsider to gain acceptance.
3. Resources, rich and poor: Self explanatory.

4. Nature Religionic Genesis: Nature as the center of things; man is subordinate to and part of the system.
5. Anthropocentric Genesis: Man is at the center, man can control his environment.

Resulting Cultural Values; dichotomies: Individualism versus Groupism
Independence versus Interdependence
Exit versus Voice

Reinforced Problem Resolution Modes: Long Term Cooperation versus Short Term Confrontation

—Falkenberg (1982)

This rather unique value system has facilitated the much heralded Japanese management style, which has proven to be quite capable of coping with the rapid changes of the last several decades. Some of these traits are listed in Table 2.

Table 2: Organizational Characteristics

— Job security by life-long employment for some 35% of the work force
— Consensus decision-making in which the implementation of major decisions is facilitated through involvement on the part of those affected by the decisions during the strategy formulation stage
— A vertical godfather system (oyabun/kobun) in which a senior in the organization looks after a junior
— A group performance orientation rather than a focus on individual achievements
— An emphasis on the harmony of the group
— A fear of being put in an embarrassing situation vis-à-vis others, loss of face, due to lack of performance
— A focus on long-term survival, perhaps through gaining a market-share, as opposed to short-term profits
— A fierce loyalty to the organization and to Japan often resulting in rejection of foreign goods and employers
— An emphasis on developing generalists rather than specialists allows a broader understanding for all
— A more cooperative relationship between unions and management
— Firms seem to have stronger commitment to the overall welfare of the employees
— Encouragement of mutual dependence in the organization

These contrasts boil down to a more cooperative interdependent emphasis than what is typically found in Western organizations, and many of these traits have their roots in the unique culture and are therefore not easily transferrable to other cultures. It should also be emphasized, however, that elements of these traits are present in most cultures, but perhaps not to the same extent nor in the same magnitude.

INSTITUTIONAL ARRANGEMENTS

Until the Meiji restoration, the Japanese society was rather feudal. Some democratic changes took place prior to World War II, but the main dosage of democracy came during the American Occupation following the war. The changes dictated by the Americans were aimed at preventing a repetition of what led up to the war, as well as at laying the foundation for an independent and democratic Japan. Some of the changes included voting rights for women, land reform, economic decentralization of the Zaibatsu, strengthening of the educational system, and the creation of labor unions. These initiatives also served to decentralize sovereignty—from those who were in control prior to the War to the people itself. Germany and Japan are perhaps the only two countries that have had democracy thrust upon them, and both have seen remarkable progress since that event. It may be that a good measure of freedom and democracy is a prerequisite for economic performance. Clearly, several of the countries with a natural resource endowment much superior to that of Japan are far behind in economic development and behind on the road toward decentralization of sovereignty, notably Brazil, Argentina, Chile, the Philippines and others. If this hypothesis is true, then the road to international competitiveness, increased GNP and economic efficiency may go through increased sovereignty for the people. Examples from Scandinavia, Israel, Germany, Japan and the US and Canada indicate that this may be true, especially when contrasted with the autocratic and feudal governments.

It is also worth noting that the relationship between business and government is rather unique. Whereas the US seems to have a

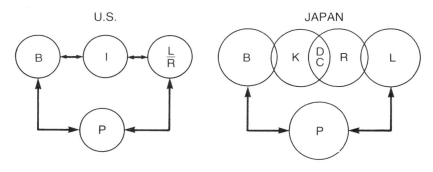

Figure 2

Where:
    B=Business
    I=Intermediaries
    L=Lawmakers
    R=Regulators
    P=Public

Where:
    B=Business
    K=Keidanren
      (Business Federation)
    D–C=Deliberative
      Councils
    R=Regulators
      (MITI/MOF)
    L=Lawmakers (DIET)
    P=Public

confrontive tradition between business and government, the Japanese system seems to be more cooperative. Fig. 2 depicts these relationships.

In the American system there are some 92,000 intermediaries whose livelihood depends on prolonging and widening the conflicts between business and government (Reich 1980). In a balanced system of opposing powers, the forces tend to neutralize one another and the resulting policies are largely perceived as fair. In Japan however, there is a formalized and intimate relationship between the major institutions. Business interests, represented by Keidanren, meet with the major regulating agencies in Deliberative Councils to seek to influence and unite around an industrial policy good for Japan. The lawmakers tend to accept the advice of regulators following the consultation with business, and a unified industrial policy may evolve. This rather unique institutional arrangement facilitates a degree of economic coordination unknown in the West during peace time, and has probably been one of the variables responsible for the recent economic performance.

TECHNOLOGY, ECONOMICS AND INDUSTRIAL POLICY

Since 1868, the government of Japan has served as an agent for technological and economic change. From the early building of railroads and shipyards with the help of British engineers to the current drive toward the development of the next generation of computers, the government has facilitated and subsidized, if not paid directly for, the acquisition and later the development of the latest technology of the time. The government, mainly through MITI and MOF (Ministry of Finance) has cooperated extensively with industry and sought to develop an industrial policy which would benefit the growth of the Japanese economy. Following World War II, the government played an active part in promoting the heavy industries initially and later the high tech consumer goods industry. MITI was not always right of course and did discourage expansion in the automobile industry in the early sixties.

It is interesting to note that the industries that were targeted for development were those which have been considered as having high barriers to entry and therefore subject to scrutiny by antitrust enforcement agencies in e.g. the US. The targeted industries include automobiles, aircraft, photographic supplies, steel, drugs, tractors, computers, copying equipment, heavy duty electrical equipment and shipbuilding. Perhaps the barriers were not as high as was at first believed. There were also restrictions on sales of goods to Japan. Whereas iron, coal, oil and forest products are easily sold, finished goods are subject to a maze of rules and regulations. At one time, the only way many European and American firms could do business in

Japan was to license Japanese companies to produce their products. Other options, such as exporting, production in Japan, and joint ventures were virtually unavailable. Many Western firms now regret their licensing agreements with Japanese corporations, who, they allege, have taken the technology, made minor improvements, and now compete with the new versions world-wide, which was not intended by the spirit of the agreements.

Whereas the average tariffs are fairly low in Japan, there are several other obstacles put in the way of free trade by the Japanese officials. Until recently, for example, no automobiles were allowed into Japan without a careful one-by-one inspection of the cars. This is of course both expensive, cumbersome, and time-consuming and resulted in numerous petty adjustments. The VW Golf (Rabbit) was the first car that was accepted on a model wide basis and not subjected to such harassment in the early 1980s.

It should also be noted that as Japan has caught up with the West, further improvements will be harder to make. The Europeans and the North Americans have been willing teachers and the Japanese have been excellent students. However, new technologies come only after much investment of time and money, so the cost of further improvements will now be as high for the Japanese as it is (and has been) for the West.

Some of the policies and practices that have facilitated the recent growth include:
— A foresighted industrial policy which encouraged new industries and discouraged old outdated ones through subtle pressures from the MOF channeled through the banks and their willingness to lend to 'favorable' projects. (Window guidance)
— Availability of low cost loans faciliated by deposits of tax revenue which required no interest payments, thereby reducing the cost of funds for the major banks. The availability of investment funds is also facilitated by an unusually high personal savings rate. This is in part due to general frugality, low level of general social security support, and a payment system which includes large semi-annual bonuses, which are often saved or invested.
— The government support of facilitating agencies abroad to stimulate trade and create a favorable political climate for Japan's foreign trade: a national marketing task force with a global mission.
— Massive investment in new production facilities, leaving the average age of the US capital stock older than that of the Japanese. In 1972 it was 6.3 years vs. 10 years, in 1978, 7.3 years vs. 9.4 years respectively. This means that both nations have rebuilt several times following World War II. An 80/20 debt equity ratio which allows lower cost of capital and a more active role to be played by the banks (e.g. Sumitomo bank's assistance to Toyo Kogyo following the market failure of the rotary engine).

RESULTS

The results of these and other practices are quite impressive and there is perhaps a lesson for other industrialized nations in the tables which follow.

Table 3 contains estimates of the sales volume per employee for the major US and Japanese companies. This is commonly regarded as a good measure of productivity. A word of caution is appropriate, however. It is not clear that all the companies listed perform similar tasks in the same legal unit. For example, Toyota as listed may be the part of the overall conglomerate that assembles cars, whereas GM may include fabrication and assembly. It is virtually impossible to ensure 100% comparability; yet the differences are so large and persistent from one industry to the next that one must consider the challenge serious.

Table 3: Sales Volume per Employee for major US and Japanese Corporations (1980)

Automotive				
	General Motors	$ 77,387	Toyota	$354,338
	Ford	$ 86,903	Nissan	$251,654
	Chrysler	$ 99,645	Honda	$303,635
	AMC	$109,088	Toyo Kogyo	$180,073
Steel				
	US Steel	$ 83,725	Nippon Steel	$198,937
	Bethlehem Steel	$ 75,653	Sumitomo Metal	$211,195
	Armco	$ 94,759	Kawasaki Steel	$158,862
Electrical Equipment				
	RCA	$ 60,214	Nippon Electric	$136,028
	GE	$ 62,102	Matsushita	$202,155
	Westinghouse	$ 58,499	Sony	$278,945
Pharmaceuticals				
	Johnson & Johnson	$ 65,096	Eisai	$132,229
	Bristol Meyers	$ 90,469	Daiichi Seiyaku	$ 99,263
	Pfizer	$ 73,520	Nippon Shinglalan	$140,749
	Eli Lilly	$ 91,064	Sankyo	$122,591
Chemicals				
	DuPont	$100,444	Mitsubishi Chem.	$452,250
	Dow Chemical	$180,771	Sumitomo Chem.	$316,700
	Union Carbide	$ 86,093	Showa Denko	$425,735
	Monsanto	$106,537	Asahi Chem.	$204,966

Compiled from the following sources:
  (1) Japan Company handbook, 2nd half 1979 (employees)
  (2) Business Week, July 06, 1981, pp. 60–75 (US employees/sales)
  (3) Business Week, July 20, 1981, pp. 115–118 (Japan sales)
  (4) Japanese annual reports

A popular myth has been that the Japanese workers are paid much less than the US workers. This may be the case of the sheltered US workers but not in trades subject to a competitive labor market. Table 4 compares US and Japanese earnings in 1979.

Table 4: Earnings Comparison (1979)

	US[1]	Japan[2]
Overall average	11,440	15,838
Mining	18,980	15,261
Manufacturing	13,988	14,972
Transportation		
Communication	16,952	{ 15,132
Public Utilities		18,760
Wholesale trade	12.896	} 15,403
Retail trade	7,228	
Finance & insurance	9,984	22,753
Steel	21,674	
Automobiles	18,866	
Chemicals	15,787	
Electronics	15,163	

Sources:
(1) *Statistical Abstract of the US* (SAUS) 1980, p. 421, based on gross weekly earning×52, current $.
(2) *Statistical Survey of Japan's Economy*, 1980, p. 61, 'average monthly cash earnings of regular workers (male)' multiplied by 12, exchange rate used: 1$=¥219.
Note: There is some question as to the comparability of these job classifications, as the differences seem too large, especially in retailing, finance, and insurance.

As mentioned above, the Japanese investment in capital goods has out-stripped that of the US quite dramatically as is illustrated by Table 5.

Table 5: Capital Equipment Investment per Employee
(in ¥1000, 1977, 1 US $=268.5)

	US	Japan
Steel	8,900	20,102
General Industrial		
Machinery	2,135	5,231
Electrical Machinery	2,555	2,427
Automobiles	2,272	6,377
Chemicals	7,861	26,269
Auto parts	1,550	3,427

Source: Economic Survey of Japan 1979/80, p. 133.
Note: The capital equipment ratio is calculated as follows:

$$\frac{\text{Average book value of tangible fixed assets at the beginning and end of a business term}}{\text{Average workforce at the beginning and end of a business term}} \ (\text{¥}1000/\text{worker})$$

This investment level is partially a function of savings and the relatively large gross fixed capital formation experienced in Japan compared to that of the US (see Table 6).

Table 6: Gross Fixed Capital Formation
(in $ Billion)

| | US | Japan | % of GNP | | Ratio US:Japan |
			US	Japan	
1961	90.45	17.64	17.0%	33.1%	.513
1965	128.91	27.01	18.8%	30.4%	.618
1970	170.21	72.71	17.4%	35.3%	.493
1975	249.45	161.63	16.3%	32.2%	.506
1979	426.41	319.88	18.0%	31.7%	.568

Source: National Accounts of OECD countries 1950–1979, Volume, Paris, 1981.

Productivity is also a function of favorable labor relations which in turn is linked to the management culture aluded to above. Table 7 shows the number of working days lost due to labor disputes in the two countries.

Table 7: US and Japanese Labor Disputes

| | 1000 man days lost | | Days lost/capita | | Ratio US:Japan |
	Japan	US	Japan	US	
1960	4,932	19,110	.0522	.106	2.03
1965	4,850	25,378	.0495	.131	2.65
1970	4,041	66,416	.0391	.324	8.29
1975	8,185	31,237	.0734	.146	1.99
1979	901	33,399	.0078	.151	19.4

The overall trade relationship between the US and Japan is perhaps the area of most concern to us at this time, and if the trends of the past 15 years are to continue, there is clearly reason for concern. Table 8 shows some of these developments.

Table 8: Japan–US Trade Development (in $ billion)*

	1965	1970	1975	1979
Japan's exports to the US	2.414	5.875	11.425	26.235
US exports to Japan	2.080	4.652	9.563	17.579
US deficit (100=balance)	86.2	79.2	83.7	67.0
Japan's exports to the US as a % of US GNP	.35%	.60%	.74%	1.11%
US exports to Japan as a % of Japan's GNP	1.59%	1.63%	1.89%	1.71%
US GNP	688.000	985.800	1,537.000	2,369.000
Japan's GNP	130.700	285.900	507.200	1,030.200
Japan's GNP as a % of US GNP	19%	29%	33%	43.5%
Japan's GNP/capita as a % of US GNP/capita	19.9%	41.5%	62.9%	81.1%
Japan's population as a % of US population	50.4%	50.5%	52.2%	52.5%
Yen exchange rate 1 US $=	361Y	358Y	296Y	219Y
% dollar devaluation compared to 1965 yen	0	.8%	18%	39.3%

*All values in current dollars and exchange rates (SAUS, 1980).

A. FALKENBERG

It is in the automobile industry that the US has felt the impact most strongly. The Japanese automobile industry is fiercely competitive and now has almost one-third of the market in the US; British, French and Italian cars have virtually been driven out of the US market and only the European luxury cars are left in the US. Even Volkswagen has been dealt a severe blow by the Japanese, not to mention the US auto-makers. Table 9 gives an overview of the world's automobile industry.

Table 9: US and Japanese Car Production
World Car Production 1979

Company	Country of Production		Total Units
General Motors	USA	6.445.087	
	West Germany	968.446	
	Canada	847.193	
	Brazil	208.131	
	UK	146.415	
	Australia	136.927	8.752.219
Ford	USA	3.075.131	
	UK	565.942	
	West Germany	546.957	
	Canada	500.839	
	Australia	111.336	
	Spain	232.432	
	Brazil	169.631	
	Belgium	316.618	5.518.886
Chrysler	USA	1.231.612	
	Canada	194.958	1.426.570
	Worldwide		
VW			2.148.555
Toyota			2.996.225
Nissan (Datsun)			2.337.821
Toyo Kogyo (Mazda)			971.421
Mitsubishi			938.517
Honda			801.869
Isuzu			424.788
Daihatsu			336.345
Suzuki			344.935
Fuji (Subaru)			334.290
AMC			343.194
USA			11.475.107
Japan			9.635.546
West Germany			4.249.725
France			3.613.458
USSR			2.080.000
Italy			1.632.289
Canada			1.631.661
UK			1.478.512

Source: Compiled from Wards Automotive Yearbook, 1980.

RESEARCH ON CROSS-CULTURAL MANAGEMENT

The automobile success has been due in part to the perceived quality difference between the US and the Japanese cars. Figs. 3 and 4 depict weighted aggregated quality scores for the two countries of cars sold in the US market based on the annual quality survey conducted by Consumer Reports. (5=much better than average, 1=much worse than average.)

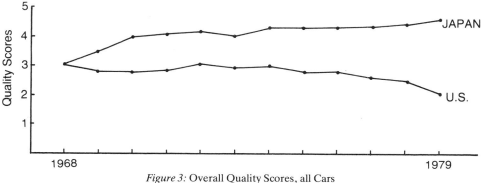

Figure 3: Overall Quality Scores, all Cars

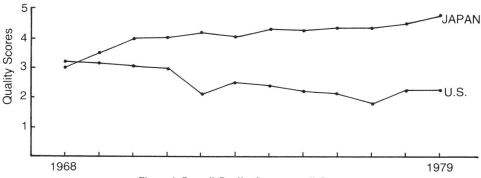

Figure 4: Overall Quality Scores, small Cars

(Falkenberg, Andreas W.: 'Modeling Market Share; A Study of the Japanese and US Performance in the US Auto Market', Forthcoming in the *Journal of the Academy of Marketing Sciences,* Winter 1985.)

This has resulted in a gradual increase of the Japanese market-share in the US market. The small car market is defined as including the Chevrolet Nova, Ford Falcon, and Dodge Aspen and smaller US and all Japanese cars. (For market-shares, see Figs. 5 and 6.)

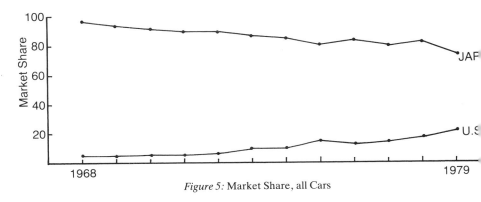

Figure 5: Market Share, all Cars

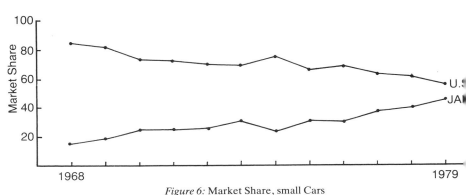

Figure 6: Market Share, small Cars

CONCLUSION

It has been argued in this chapter that the economic results achieved in Japan in the last century have in part been facilitated by unique motivational forces, a collectively oriented cultural heritage, a well-suited democratic institutional arrangement as well as by an active public policy facilitating economic and technological change. Several other nations share several similar traits, but few if any have matched the rapid development experienced in Japan. The lessons from Japan are hard to adapt to other cultures, especially those which put a higher priority on individual freedom and performance—or those which are suspicious of government's ability to fulfil the responsibility of planning for change. What might be adapted to other countries could be the emphasis on decentralized sovereignty which followed World War II. This trait is found both in the public institutions and in individual organizations in several advanced countries, and is rarely (never?) found in the less developed countries. Fig. 7 is offered as a summary of the arguments presented.

Figure 7

Results=F (Motivation,	Cultural Heritage,	Institutional Arrangements,	Technology, Economics and Industrial Policy)
Avoid —Humiliation —Foreign dominance	Long term cooperation —Physical heritage —Resources —Philosophy	Decentralized sovereignty —Women —Labor unions —Land reform	The government as a change agent —MITI and MOF —Industrial policy —Barriers
Gain —Recognition —Resources —Markets (survival)	Organizational characteristics —Employee relations —Decision making —Vertical groups —Group performance —Group credit —Harmony and face loss —Generalists —Mutual dependencies	—Economic decentralization —Educational emphasis Cooperating public institutions —Business —Regulators —Lawmakers	—Support programs —Financing —Public world wide marketing

REFERENCES

Business Week, July 06, pp. 60–75, 1981.

Business Week, July 20, pp. 115–118, 1981.

Drucker, Peter F., 'What is Business Ethics?' *The Public Interest*, No. 63, Spring 1981, pp. 18–36.

'*Economic Survey of Japan*', Economic Planning Agency, Japanese Government, Tokyo, 1980.

Falkenberg, Andreas W., '*Economic Effects of Cultural Differences; A Study of Japanese Success in the US Auto Market*' (Doctoral Dissertation), University of Oregon, Eugene, Oregon, 1982.

Falkenberg, Andreas W., 'Modeling Market Share; A Study of the Japanese and US Performance in the US Auto Market' (Forthcoming in the *Journal of the Academy of Marketing Sciences*, Winter 1985).

JETRO, 'White Paper on International Trade Japan 1980', published by JETRO, Tokyo, pp. 39/40.

OECD, '*National Accounts of OECD Countries 1950–1979*', vol. 1, Paris 1981.

Reich, Robert B., 'Made and Litigated in the USA', *Business Week*, October 27, 1980, pp. 28, 32.

Scott, Bruce R., John W. Rosenblum, and Audry T. Sproat, '*Case Studies in Political Economy: Japan 1854–1977*', Division of Research, Cambridge, Massachusetts, Harvard Business School, 1980.

'*Statistical Abstracts of the United States 1980*', US Department of Commerce, Bureau of the Census 101st Edition.

'*Statistical Survey of Japan's Economy 1980*', Economic and Foreign Affairs Research Association, Tokyo, December 1980.

'Wards Automotive Yearbook', Detroit, Michigan 1980.

CHAPTER 8

An empirical study of innovative behaviour in Poland

Krzysztof Obtój and Pat Joynt

INTRODUCTION

This chapter explores the innovation process in the context of successful innovations in Poland. Evidence from the integrated results of ten case studies suggests that several organization concepts need to be redefined or expanded. Among these are the concepts of an organization as a goal-seeking unity with a certain formal hierarchy and a defined domain, and the concept of society innovation rather than organization innovation.

Essential to the above is the concept and the associated process(es) of innovation. Innovation as a theoretical area of interest is rather new to the behavioral sciences and administrative and organization theory. Burns and Stalker (1961) and Lawrence and Lorsch (1967) are often considered to be the first empiric studies on the concept of innovation. With the introduction of the innovation concept, the traditional logic of testing hypotheses based on past behavior soon became very limited, because innovation by its very definition cannot always be considered as a summary of past behavior.

New logics and expanded thinking are required to cope with the concept of innovation and this is a central theme here. After a brief review of the theories of innovation in the next section, we will present a new method of researching this complex concept and the associated processes. The framework (grounded theory) and the associated technique (clinical case studies) will be presented in the methods section. Following this, a summary of the results of the ten Polish case studies will be made in an analysis section. Finally, the authors will draw conclusions and review some of the implications for the research presented here.

A REVIEW OF PAST INNOVATION THEORIES

The work of Burns and Stalker (1961) is essential to this study for two reasons: first, the concept of innovation is introduced in a contingency framework which will fit the context of this work; second, contingency theory is both implicitly and explicitly developed in their work. The study involved twenty Scottish and English firms, with an emphasis on the electronics organizational activity in each. The dependent variable was the system of management, and the independent variable was the environment. Both of these concepts were expanded; the management system to include organic and mechanistic, and the environment to be defined in terms of technology and market conditions.

The data for their research was gathered by observations, interviews, meetings and casual remarks with the managers involved. The empirical analysis was essentially descriptive and of a sociological nature, which allowed the writers a great deal of freedom in analysis of their data. This type of research model is virtually impossible to duplicate, and, while one can fault the research methodology, one must give credit to the work, for it has become one of the classics. It also fits into the methodological perspectives used in this study.

In analyzing the concept of structure or organization, Lawrence and Lorsch (1967) expanded the previous thinking of Burns and Stalker (1961). Two new concepts were introduced to describe structure, differentiation and integration. Differentiation means not only differences of segmentation and knowledge, but also includes attitudes and behavior. Essentially four subjective differences were considered on an individual as well as on a departmental basis. A functional orientation was used in analyzing organization departmentation, with the main emphasis on the marketing, production and research departments.

The first difference analyzed was the difference among managers in a variety of functional jobs as to their orientation towards goals. The next difference analyzed was that of time. Essentially, this was a measure of the time to solve typical problems that confronted the manager. Third, an interpersonal orientation analysis was used. The last dimension was formality of structure, which includes the degree of formality as well as the use of formal rules in guiding organizational activity. Lawrence and Lorsch (1967, p. 11) defined these notions of differentiation as 'the differences in cognitive and emotional orientation among managers in different functional departments'. The second concept used in defining structure was integration or coordination. This concept involves the state of interdepartmental relations, and includes not only an analysis of the relationship between departments, but also the devices used to achieve effective coordination. These devices range from simple rules, to individual integrators, to group integrators or committees. Galbraith (1977) and Davis and Lawrence (1978) extended the group integrators or committees to include temporary and permanent groups as well as matrix management.

Joynt (1979) in a study of 100 Norwegian organizations attempted to expand upon these earlier works by using a larger sample as well as a larger number of variables in this analysis. Part of this work is reported in Chapter 4; however, for our purposes here the findings on organization innovation are interesting. Using regression techniques, the following variables were found to explain organization innovation success: the use of groups under the supervision of a task or process oriented leadership; compromise was not used to solve differences of opinion between departments, however, coordination was essential. The organization tended to have an intensive 'core' technology (Thompson 1967) and existed in a complex internal and external environment.

Crozier and Thoenig (1976) studied the complex yet stable system of groups and institutions at the local government level in France. They found interdependence to be particularly visible each time an institution made a decision. Compromise was also necessary and the behavior was described as 'a game of defense, protection and non-communication. If there is steady resistance to coordination and formal adjustments, it is not because the players do not know one another, nor because they are far from one another, but because they belong to a complex and stable system which has other forms of regulation' (Crozier and Thoenig 1976, p. 550). The authors concluded that a new strategy involving a much less formalized approach is necessary to study this type of behavior.

Molitor (1974) studied the dialetical interplay among people, structures and procedures of Belgian bureaucracy in public administration. Molitor found a unique, permanent technique for negotiating compromise for key problems. Molitor called this group the 'pragmatic élite' and their behavior often resulted in a suppression of innovation. Downs and Mohr (1976) suggest that a set of new prescriptions are needed for research on innovation. They suggest a methodology of using interactive models which would be a significant departure from current research practices on the concept and associated processes of innovation.

Colignon and Cray (1980) expanding on the finding that 'pragmatic élites' or 'critical' organizations should be the focus of organizational research, especially with respect to organization change and innovation. Colignon and Cray (1980, p. 351) define a critical organization as 'one which has significant, transformative effects on the class relations of a society'. The concept of organization inherent in this definition differs considerably from the traditional ones. Rather than an entity moving towards a set of universally accepted goals, one may visualize the organization as 'a collection of individuals brought together in structured relationships of domination and subordination who form alliances that influence the direction of the organization' (Colignon and Cray 1980, pp. 351–352). The writers also go on to imply that time is also a factor and use the notion of 'critical moments'. Both the notion of critical organizations and critical or successful innovation moments are expanded in the study reported here.

Cherns (1980) suggests a circular relationship between the organization and the social environment. Many of the earlier studies on innovation, which have been reviewed in this section, used environment as an independent variable in the innovation process (Burns and Stalker 1966, Lawrence and Lorsch 1967, Galbraith 1971, 1977, and Joynt 1979), yet Cherns's argument and the results from the research reported here raise serious questions about the role of society. In this study we were unable to make the separation and found that in reality the concept of organization innovation in Poland should be relabeled 'society' innovation because of the many actors and societal influences involved.

METHODOLOGY

The theory of innovation has been dominated by two methodological approaches: the use of systems categories, and the empirical approach. The empirical approach concentrates on the testing of hypotheses using statistical operations such as regression or correlations analysis. Lawrence and Lorsch (1967), Khandwalla (1974) and Joynt (1979) point out that many variables and relations which cannot be precisely measured lie beyond the techniques available using the empirical approach. Despite its shortcomings the empirical approach has dominated the innovation literature in recent years. For our purposes, the implicit assumptions about rationality, causality and omnipotence of innovation processes, members, pathology or human conservatism—to cite some of the most popular cause *a priori* characteristics of the research—play an important role in the methodology used here. Further, it seems obvious that the inquiry of such a complex phenomenon as innovation requires a contingency methodology.

Flanagan (1954) proposed the clinical case study as an appropriate methodology for the study of innovation. This methodology has two important advantages in the innovation context. First, one does not have to accept *a priori* explanations, e.g. in the form of hypotheses and/or predictions. Second, the case study methodology provides the important postulate of total clinical analysis and understanding. Glaser and Strauss (1974) point out that the main aim in the study of complex organization behavior should be to understand how events relate to each other, and the main process consists of information collection and processing, but *not* in the form of hypotheses testing. Using this method, new information and facts gathered in research open new possible areas for inquiry, and research questions are constantly being reformulated. New categories or questions are constructed on the basis of new information and the criteria used for information collecting are changeable. Such a phenomenological perspective makes possible the adoption of basic variables or criteria for information selection more arbitrary. The goals of the research shift based on the relevance of the problem and the strategy of constantly reformulating the questions and categories allows one a better understanding of the complex process of innovation.

One of the major problems with the above 'open' approach is that of transformation gathering and integration. We used the following guidelines in the methodology adopted here:

1. The list of the main questions should be constructed, yet remain open and adaptive.
2. All persons connected, even in a remote way, with the innovation process should be interviewed. The interviews should be informal without notes being taken during the interview. Each of the main questions should be asked two to four times during the interview.
3. After an interview, the first description of the innovation process should be formulated. This becomes the main source for re-formulating the main questions.
4. All documentation should be analyzed from many points of view. The complex network of organizations and/or persons engaged in the innovation process should be constructed.
5. The past history of cooperation and conflicts between important persons and organizations should be taken into account.
6. The future perspectives for cooperation and the chances for success should be taken into consideration.
7. After these steps, the interviews should be repeated using other members of the research team if possible. This will help to avoid the problems of errors made during the interview by both the interviewers and those being interviewed.
8. Every conflict should receive maximum consideration by the research team, for conflict is often the best source of knowledge on how the system is functioning as a whole.
9. The monograph of the innovation process should be presented to every important member involved in the process with questions about its objectivity, validity, etc. The monograph should be provocative at this stage in order to get more information.

It is important to stress some of the aspects of the integration technique. Raw information and data are integrated into a complex monograph on a qualitative basis, and the research team's intuition and experience play important roles during this process. Subjective interpretations are used to create an objective description and explanation. The scientist, in a sense, moulds an objective reality from the many subjective interpretations obtained during the interviews. Thus, the goal of the research is a model of reality, and the process of model building starts with the first case and, for practical purposes, has no precise end. The first intuitions are enriched with the information flow and each new case aids in building the model. The model helps in systematizing and putting the facts in order and in such a way integrates the case studies. The feedback between the model and the case studies can be sketched in three different ways:

1. Categories of the model that match the facts.
2. Available facts that do not match any model category.
3. Categories of the model that do not match the facts.

The first point above is trivial. In the second point, one is rich in knowledge that should be used to enrich and modify the model. In the third point, the model categories are probably artifacts, and they should be displaced if one is sure that they do not represent the reality at hand.

The continual process of the above-described confrontation is qualitative, and one is often dealing with vague categories rather than precise indicators. The research goal strategy is to 'understand' and then to 'explain', and one is constantly generating questions, problems and hypotheses. The feedback between the model and reality guarantees a constant improvement and a dynamic type of model building.

The 'open' methodology we have presented can be graphically presented as in Figure 1. When one considers the complex, qualitative and dynamic phenomena often associated with the innovation process, it seems useful to use grounded theory (Glaser and Strauss 1974) modified by the clinical case strategy (Flanagan 1954, Obtój 1980).

RESULTS OF RESEARCH

The clinical study method, reviewed in the previous section, was used during the period 1977–1980 to analyze the innovation processes in the Polish economy. The cases concentrated on successful innovations, since the goal of the research was to study the entire innovation process and the mechanisms were enterprises and R & D units use of cooperation, and not innovation failure. The initial result from each of the cases was a 25 to 50 page summary that has been substantially reduced and integrated in the summary that follows.

The chemical and machine industries were the prime focus of this study, because they appear to have the best conditions available for innovation in a Polish context. The enterprises and research and development units from these industries are grouped into several unions, and all the unions in one branch form a ministry. The prime work of the ministry is concerned with day-to-day activities. All important decisions about investments are concentrated at the government level, and the government, in turn, relies on the Ministries and Governmental Planning Office opinions, and they can be considered as consultants in the process. In short, the organizations (enterprises and R&D institutions) are subordinated to the Ministry of Education and Technique if the innovation process is part of the so-

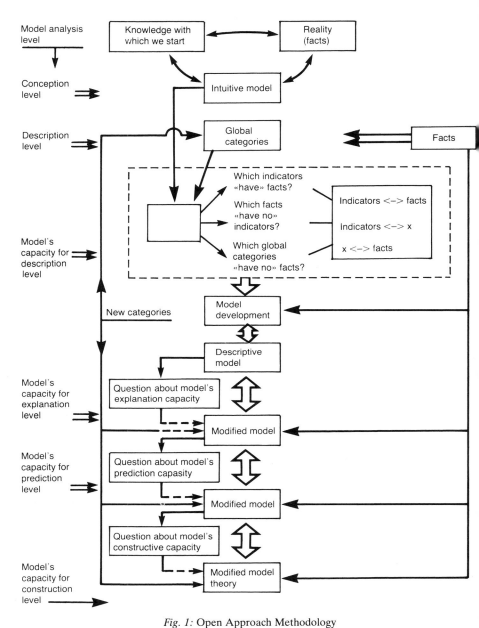

Fig. 1: Open Approach Methodology
Source: A. K. Kozninski, K. Obtój: 'Innovation process—the morphology of success', papers for Polish Conference on innovation, Warsaw, 1980.

---

called 'great projects', which are coordinated by that very ministry. In such cases a sort of matrix structure occurs. The formal structure of the industries is relatively simple as is shown in Figure 2.

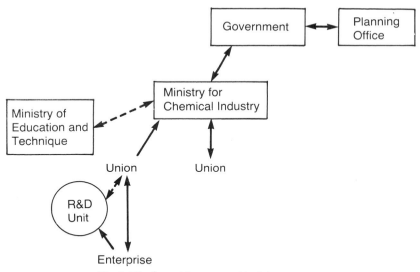

Fig. 2: The formal Structure of Polish Industries

Our research showed that the main members of the innovation process were motivated to attain two contradictory goals. The enterprises often attempted to become autonomous because cooperation created too many problems and conflicts. This usually resulted in the enterprise doing everything in order to achieve a planned level of production at any cost. This situation arises because the managers of enterprise are mainly judged on the production level basis, thus the income to cost ratio is not as important. On the other hand, the research and development institutions suffer from the same situation. The main uncertainty is created by poor cooperation links, and the obvious strategy is to use as few cooperation links as possible. The second premise is the system of rewards for managers and members of the R&D units, where the number of patents, articles and scientific works count most, and the industrial implementations are not as important. Of course total independence is unrealistic and impossible to achieve, but the weakness of the cooperation links and the system of rewards strongly support the tendency toward autarchy and autonomy. However, these tendencies are limited mainly by formal structure and technical constraints. The entire system is based on interdependence and the informal strategies result in an atomization of the organizational network. Peer relations are very friendly, but interrelations in an organizational context are weak or non-existent. The formal conditions are thus satisfied with a minimum of effort and cost within the self-sufficiency strategies.

We have attempted to sketch the complex behavior associated with the innovation process and, in summary, organizational behavior can be defined as the tendency toward autarchy and autonomy which involves a minimum degree of cooperation. At the same time, however, managers attempt to preserve an image of good cooperation and relations with each other. This idea is very important for political reasons, and one can assume that managerial self-images are also of equal importance in most cases.

Sometimes close cooperation among the organizations actually takes place. Departures from the mutual strategies described above can be observed in the successful innovation cases. These innovations are created by the special situations of a great chance or by threats of absolute coercion for the organizations involved. Both the enterprises and R&D institutions cooperate in such cases to get special benefits (e.g. investments, export possibilities, interesting international contacts and positive attitudes from political institutions) or to avoid threats or coercions (e.g. import restrictions, personnel reductions, etc.). In looking at the cases involving successful innovation we found three basic rules governing the behavior of the actors involved in the process. We define these rules as:

1. The rule of compromise.
2. The rule of exceptions.
3. The rule of fuzzy decision procedures.

1. The rule of compromise

Since the system is based on interdependence, the main threats are conflicts, yet conflicts are an essential ingredient in the innovation process, as was pointed out in the second section. Conflict, in the Polish context, often emerges between the enterprises implementing the innovation and the R&D unit. These conflicts usually have to be solved by indirect negotiations, using a third party. The actors often find this third party in the Union because of the Union's central position in the organizational network. Sometimes the actors agree on another type of mediator such as a political institution, the Ministry, or one of the well-known directors of a research and development unit. The mediator's role is very informal, and after many indirect information exchanges the solution must be a compromise. This compromise often creates absurd technical or organizational consequences, but these consequences are not important from many managers' points of view. The solution need not solve the problem, but it has to preserve harmony and equilibrium in the organizational network. The arbitrator or mediator knows this very well, and must play the role of the uninvolved third party. He cannot show even the slightest instance of being partial, and he cannot risk losing his prestige with the harmony of the system. The bargaining occurs between concrete persons or groups, and if the arbitrator denies this right to any party it will mean the decline of his influence, prestige and power. Also, the non-compromise position only creates new problems, so all parties are very much interested in a compromise—at any price.

There are special cases where the compromise is better for one person than another, and in such situations another rationality is used. Political interest, economic coercion, legal constraints and technical or organizational imperatives are then used, and with such arguments, the blame is laid on the system and not on any of the actors.

There are two premises which force this method of compromise. Open negotiations usually polarize the interests, conditions and goals resulting in the escalation of conflict and presumably a deadlock or a situation where one actor would have to retreat. Even the most powerful actors avoid domination because they are never sure about the future. There is therefore no problem in getting all parties to agree to indirect negotiations and compromises.

Second, conflicts are deeply hidden and camouflaged as they wait for the intervention of a chosen external actor—the mediator. In a completely atomized system such a strategy of conflict solving creates the possibility for compromise, and for yet another element in the innovation process.

2. The rule of exceptions

During the 1970s the Polish system lacked guidelines for resource allocations, and this forced the managers in the organizations involved to adapt to such a situation. Each investment or innovation was treated as something new or unique and the managers were able to increase their organizations' allocations, using the strategy of 'exceptions to the rule'.

Three tactics were used by the managers in order to increase the probability for allocations. First, the innovation was given the status of being very important socially, politically and economically. Second, the atmosphere of taking a great chance was created around the innovation in question, and third, a maximum number of organizations and managers were engaged in the innovation process.

The promoters of the innovation often used the plurality of their roles and the mass media to create emotions and attitudes positive to the innovation. Often the rationality associated with the innovation was forgotten or played a very secondary role. The important thing was to have a good coalition having access to the central government bodies. While all managers feel that their innovation is the exceptional one, not all of them try to promote the innovation in this coalition fashion.

The reason for not building a coalition for some of the innovations is the fear of failure. If the innovation was a failure, the external members of the coalition would feel cheated. The consequences become obvious—powerful members of a coalition would begin many inventions which might be very profitable but, being risky, would never see daylight. In conclusion, the innovation that is promoted has a very high probability of final success.

3. The rule of fuzzy decision procedures

The decision scheme in the Polish innovation process is quite different from the traditional March and Simon (1958) scheme of problem solving: search for alternatives, choice of solution, etc. or the processes reported by Lawrence and Lorsch (1967) and Joynt (1979). The greatest problem encountered in our studies was to find out by whom, when and why a decision was made or part of the innovation process occurred. The decision-making process is neither hierarchic nor lateral, neither democratic nor autocratic.

The many actors engaged in the innovation process create a system of complex temporary networks with the focal point being the promoter's success, where it is imperative to interact with the organizations and individuals that form the external coalition. We found that many members of the external coalition did not know who the other members were. Only the promoter knows all the members and thus serves as the go-between. Most of the contacts are of a bilateral nature with the promoter as the focal point with whom every member of the coalition is able to make contact without any problem.

The members of the coalition have varying degrees of influence, some having access to the decision centers at the governmental level. These members are very important, and a coalition without such members has a relatively low probability of final success. Members of the coalition use as many information channels as possible and, interestingly enough, we found that the channels were usually used in a way different to what was normally expected. As an example, a political channel was used to send economic and technical information and an organizational channel was used to send political information. The promoter and the external coalition members must find the correct channel or channels to relay the necessary information to the center, and redundancy is necessary for a successful innovation. The reasons for this are relatively simple, because the decision-makers in the center are usually reluctant to make decisions. They are perfectly aware that most of their information has an emotional and subjective rather than knowledge and objective, orientation. They experience the enormous flows of information, from many channels, and being aware of the poor reliability of the information system, they are unable to choose the proper innovation. Thus, the decision-makers try to do as little as possible to minimize the probability of errors.

The actors in the system are familiar with the above situation as well, because they helped to create it. In order to achieve their objectives (e.g. getting approval and resources for the innovation process) they constantly use the plurality of their roles to activate even more information channels and as many decision-makers as possible. The process of redundancy (both in the dimension of information flows and activated decision-makers from the Center) is necessary to increase the probability that someone, somewhere in the Center will act positively even by accident. Figure 3 illustrates the processes described above.

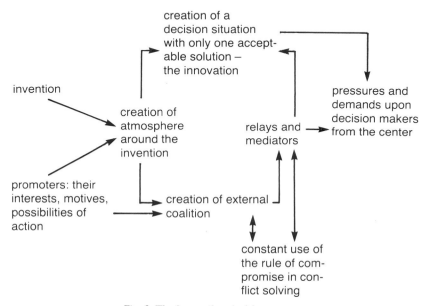

Fig. 3: The innovation decision process

Conclusions

The conclusions we draw from the research reported here tend to expand the horizons and domain of the existing theory rather than replace it. The review in the second section illustrated the development of the theory from individuals to groups to organizations to political systems. This study adds a new dimension where the political, economic, organizational, sociological and cultural factors interact in a complex way inside the organizational network. Using a network as the unit of analysis has presented us with some contradictions to the existing body of theory.

Burns and Stalker (1966) and March and Olsen (1978) found that informal roles played an important part in the innovation processes.

This was also found to be true in our study. However, the key promoter's role is much more complex, and it can hardly be called informal. Promoters use the plurality of their roles and the plurality of information channels in formal and informal ways. We want to stress that the 'informality' is constructed by the new, the inventive, and the unexpected. In other words, informality means that the formal elements of the system are constantly used in new and unexpected configurations (Lindblom 1959). The final effect is, of course, informal, but the way it is achieved can hardly be called informal. The formal–informal perspective requires a redefinition in this case.

Lawrence and Lorsch (1967) and Joynt (1979) found that successful innovative organizations often changed from individual integrators to group integrators or committees. This study enriches this conclusion. The coalitions developed during the process are very loosely integrated groups. As we have stressed, the individual promoters, in order to preserve their key position, do not allow high level integration to evolve. They prefer to act as relays and go-betweens in the complex network of engaged organizations. The main contacts are of a bilateral nature with promoters as one party and another organization as the second party. As the coalition is built around one mutual objective, and as connections and contacts are seldom and accidental (the promoters' case is an exceptional one), it vanishes quickly after the objective is achieved, because promoters stop playing their relay role. To conclude, the innovation coalition involves a very temporary and special communication patterned group. Another important and interesting aspect of the innovation process was the rules of the game in the Polish context. We want to stress once more the general characteristics of the game:

1. The rules of the game are the result of a complex and long-lasting process of collective learning by the system's members (Crozier and Thoenig, 1976). Implicitly, research stresses that a network is a system, yet few researchers attempt to prove it. We showed that the organizational network is more than just the sum of its parts, organizations and their relations. The collective game (and especially its rules) is evidence of this because it operates on the system's level only. Every member of the system can play his or her own game, but within the framework of the mutual rules of the system. Everyone is a prisoner of the rules, and this means nobody can escape from the rules without being punished by the rest of the organizational network members.

2. The game and its rules contradict the traditional view of the role of a formal hierarchy in the organization (Colignon and Cray 1980, Keeley 1980). It strongly contradicts traditional top-down perspective. We were able to show that the collective game sometimes becomes a substitute for the formal structure and even regulates the formal structure relations. It takes place tempo-

rarily, but nevertheless such phenomena deserve special attention. The traditional and still popular view of the organizational hierarchy, with its importance and power for the regulation of the organizational members' actions seems to be exaggerated, and newer theories involving 'loose coupling' analysis need to be encouraged. By creating a game, organizational members are able to escape from formal structure rules and influence. The formal structure still exists, but it is a camouflage rather than a regulator.

3. The latest research of Obtój (1984) shows that newly created organizations very quickly learn the game, its rules, and how to use them. It is a trial and error process but nevertheless a quick and efficient one. A two-year longitudinal study of one such organization (it has been the Coordination Office of one of the great projects) strongly supports the hypothesis that the game and its rules are not a specific and temporary phenomenon. Rather it is a means for the members of the system to constantly question the power and influence of the very upper levels of the organizational hierarchy. It is a simple and efficient way to influence the decision processes, and the actors involved gain the decision-making power that they formally do not process by using the rules described earlier.

It is interesting to note that in such situations everyone strongly and loudly criticizes the formal hierarchy, autocracy and the centralization of decision power, but nobody tries to change it. On the contrary, every possibility for change and decentralization is stopped and blocked by the 'powerless' members of the system. The system is an oppressive one, but the collective game gives the .possibility of possessing power and influence to everyone. Even the actors on the low levels of the hierarchy are able to stop or block the actions of coalitions made up of powerless actors. Most of the ideas concerning decentralization of the system come from the highest levels of the hierarchy, and each time they are stopped by other actors in the system who find centralization is the best cover for their actions (Kozminski, Obtój et al. 1980).

4. Our last conclusion is of a methodological nature. We are convinced that in order to understand individual behavior one must understand the nature and the rules of the system as a whole. Every system is based on individual interdependent relations. Maybe this remark is a trivial one, but too often research tends to emphasize the study of one-direction relations (relations of dependence). In order to understand the behavior and the rules of action of all members of the system, one must analyze interdepedence first. The picture of the system must be constructed first, and the image of the organization's course of

action follows. As this study shows, the understanding of system characteristics and the collective game that takes place allows us to explain the, at first, apparently irrational behavior.

March (1981) in a recent review of over 150 sources suggested the following five footnotes to change in organizations. It is beyond the scope of this study to redesign March's findings into our methodology, but one reaction constantly emerges as we read his footnotes. It is almost as if he wrote them with this study in mind. We have duplicated them below, underlining the most appropriate items:

1. Organizations are continually changing, routinely, easily, and responsively, but change within them cannot ordinarily be arbitrarily controlled. *Organizations rarely do exactly what they are told to do.*
2. Changes in organizations depend on a few stable processes. Theories of change emphasize either the stability of the processes or the changes they produce, but a serious understanding of organizations requires attention to both.
3. Theories of change in organizations *are primarily different ways of describing theories of action in organizations*, not different theories. Most changes in organizations reflect simple responses to *demographic, economic, social and political forces.*
4. Although organizational response to environmental events is broadly adaptive and mostly routine, *the response takes place in a confusing world.* As a result, prosaic processes sometimes have surprising outcomes.
5. Adaptation to a changing environment involves an *interplay of rationality and foolishness.* Organizational foolishness is not maintained as a conscious strategy, but is embedded in such familiar organizational *anomalies as slack, managerial incentives, symbolic action, ambiguity and loose coupling.*

SELECTED REFERENCES

Burns, Tom and Stalker, Gordon, *The Management of Innovation,* London: Tavistock Publications, 1961, 1966.

Cherns, Albert, 'Organizations as instruments of social change in postindustrial societies', *Organization Studies,* Vol. 1–2, 1980.

Colignon, Richard and Cray, David, 'Critical Organizations', *Organization Studies,* Vol. 1–4, 1980.

Crozier, Michel and Thoenig, Jean-Claude, 'The regulation of complex organized systems', *Administrative Science Quarterly,* December, 1976.

Cyert, Richard and March, James, *A Behavioral Theory of the Firm,* Englewood Cliffs: Prentice Hall, 1963.

Davis, Stanley and Lawrence, Paul, 'Problems of matrix organizations', *Harvard Business Review,* May–June 1978.

Downs, G. and Mohr, Lawrence, 'Conceptual issues in the study of innovation', *Administrative Science Quarterly,* December 1976.

Flanagan, James, 'The critical incidents technique', *Psychological Bulletin,* 4, 1954.

Galbraith, Jay, 'Matrix organization design', *Business Horizons,* February 1971.

Galbraith, Jay, *Organization design.* Reading, Mass.: Addison-Wesley, 1977.

Glaser, B. and Strauss, A. *The Discovery of Grounded Theory,* Chicago: Aldine, 1974.

Joynt, Pat, 'Contingency analysis for effective administration', *Omega,* 5, 4, 1977.

Joynt, Pat, *Contingency Models for Administrative Behavior,* Brunel University, 1979.

Knight, Kenneth, 'A descriptive model of the intra-firm innovation process', *Journal of Business,* October 1967.

Kozminski, A. and Obtój, Krzyztof, 'Innovations and new techniques and their implementation'. Research report for the Ministry of Machine Industry, Warsaw, 1980.

Lawrence, Paul and Lorsch, Jay, *Organization and Environment,* Boston: Harvard University (1967).

Lindblom, Charles, 'The science of muddling through', *Public Administration Review,* 19, 1959.

Mansfield, Eugene, *Industrial Research and Technological Innovations,* London: Longmans, Green and Co., 1968.

March, James, 'Footnotes to organization change', *Administrative Science Quarterly,* Decmber 1981.

March, James G. and Olsen, Johan P., 'Ambiguity and choice in organizations', *American Political Science Review,* 72, 1978.

March, James and Simon, Herbert, *Organizations,* New York: Wiley, 1958.

Mohr, Lawrence, 'Determinants of innovation in organizations', *American Political Science Review,* March 1969.

Molitor, A., *L'administration de la Belgique: essai.* Centre de Recherche et d'Information Socio-Politiques and Institut Belge de Science Politique, 1974.

Obtój, Krzyztof, *The cooperation between R&D organizations and enterprises: the rules of the game.* Ph.D. thesis, University of Warsaw, 1980.

Obtój, Krzyztof, Book to be published in 1984.

Keeley, Michael, 'Organizational analogy: a comparison of organismic and social contract models', *Administrative Science Quarterly,* June 1980.

Thompson, James, *Organizations in action,* New York: McGraw Hill, 1967.

Wilson, James, 'Innovation in organization' from *Approaches to Organizational Design,* edited by J. Thompson, Pittsburgh, University of Pittsburgh Press, 1966.

Woodward, Joan, *Industrial Organization: Theory and Practice,* London: Oxford University Press, 1965.

PART III

Values, Culture and Education

Education as an aspect of management success has been a central theme in much of the behavioral science approach to the study of management and organization. Despite this fact, little has been done in the area of cross-cultural or comparative studies to study the management education aspect in more depth. Granick's work of more than a decade ago should have served warning that management education is perhaps the key variable behind a country's degree of success on the international scene. We felt this issue to be so important that we have devoted a special section of the book to this theme, however we have restricted ourselves to two cultures—Germany and England and two works which in reality show us only the tip of the 'iceberg' involved. We hope the work of Nicholas and Locke will serve to open the way for much needed attention in this area.

CHAPTER 9

Cross-cultural research, technological change and vocational training: Methodological background and practical implications

Ian Nicholas

INTRODUCTION

Much of recent organizational research is 'contingency-oriented' and directed towards explaining organizational characteristics according to variations in the size, technology and the task environment of the organizations concerned.[1] The theory propounds that contextual factors partially determine organizational structure and thus influence behavioural consequences.[2] Similarly, there is acceptance that those in positions of power and authority, the 'dominant coalitions' of the firms, can exercise a series of 'strategic choices' and 'procedural options' that influence behaviour.[3] This in turn has led to an 'expansion' of the number and variety of moderating or intervening variables examined, ranging from person-job congruence, through organization communications, organizational climate, socio-technical conditions and so on, to ethno-cultural and socio-political dimensions.[4]

Findings from research of this nature have yielded a mass of valuable inter-connecting concepts and explanatory insights into the way organizations work but they appear to resist any form of reconciliation into a cohesive whole.

It is clear, however, that organizations develop differently; similarly, there is evidence that some combinations of context and structure produce organizational behaviours that can be both more effective and/or more beneficial to the individuals concerned.[5] Whether these result, however, from an organizational response to a series of environmental constraints, or arise from a judicious choice between a range of different organizational alternatives, would appear to be of little analytical significance. And yet, just as there are differences in the capacities of organizations to adapt to external factors, it is equally well documented that no single organizational design has positive effects in all types of environmental and technological contexts.

DEFINING THE ENVIRONMENT

It might well be that our current conceptualization of the term 'environment' is at too artificial a level. Without, however, denying the value of research into the interaction between the organization and its environment, perhaps our understanding of the way in which enterprises 'really' function can be enhanced if the analytical distinction between the two concepts is discarded.[6] This is not to deny the effect of some sort of environmental dimension; rather it has the intention of elevating the concept to a more national or 'macro' level where the factors in question are more of a social, cultural or institutional character. Any such notion of cross-national research into organizations, however, brings with it in its wake a series of new dilemmas and questions.

Not least of these—and we will come back to it later—is the question of what constitutes, say, a cultural dimension. Firstly, some consideration needs to be given to the purpose of any such cross-national research effort and what it might help to achieve. To some extent in the past, there has been a tendency for cultural variations to be submerged and regarded more as an unwanted cause of variance which detracted from the universal application of organizational theory. In spite of the tacit acceptance of cultural differences between countries, it was an over-sensitivity to the threat of a theoretical 'particularism' which restricted a more robust approach to the question of national differences. Indeed, there still lingers the convergency view that industrial societies will produce similar institutional patterns if for no other reasons than the dictates of technological determinism.[7,8]

And yet, at the same time, and in spite of evidence to the contrary, the suspicion still remains that there is some sort of 'universalism' that determines the way organizations go about their respective business— that there are some 'supra' dimensions that influence the 'actors' and the inter-relationships that they exhibit. These 'societal traits' are sufficiently pervasive to mould the social fabric of the overall environment under consideration and have a qualitative impact on the contingencies and structural variables that form part of any organization.

This 'societal effect approach' to organizational research has been propounded by Brossard and Maurice (1977)[9] and views such factors as training, education, task characteristics, working relationships and so on as constituent parts of the social culture. Their combination, and the manner in which they interact, influence the form that action towards a given organizational goal will take. It stresses the 'principle of functional equivalence', that is, it emphasizes the nature of different solutions to similar organizational demands, whether these are expressed in terms of the manufacture of motor cars, or in the desire to provide a rational base for meaningful and effective work.

The approach focusses on the way in which the actors construct organizations but, rather than simply looking for similarities and differences against a traditional organizational model, it concentrates on the 'socio-technical logics' of development. The similarities and differences, nevertheless, both *within* and *between* different cultures or countries are important—but their significance is dependent upon those societal factors that create and modify them.

TRAINING—AS A CULTURAL DIMENSION

A Historical Perspective—Comparison between the United Kingdom & West Germany

Training between say West Germany and the UK represents a good example of a cultural dimension that influences the way in which organizations might pursue different means towards a similar end. It is a particularly interesting comparison because it reveals a situation in which, historically, both systems started roughly from the same base, that of the mediaeval and craft guilds.[10] In addition, for much of their respective developments the influencing factors were economic and political in character, rather than strictly cultural. In the UK, the industrial revolution, although incorporating a range of technological advances of the time, depended more on the availability of raw materials and capital than on skills in the workforce. Moreover, the very success of the process of industrialization discouraged, or, perhaps more correctly, did not encourage, anything other than nominal developments in the training and recruitment of managers or skilled employees. This wave of industrial progress took place against a background of free enterprise and a liberalization of trade. These factors had the effect of stimulating the protective role of, on the one hand, the trade unions, specifically in terms of craft demarcations and the content of particular skilled occupations, and on the other, professional associations, with an interest in regulating entry and qualification standards at the higher levels. With successive governments adopting a laissez-faire position and rejecting any centralist view of vocational training, an increasingly individualistic approach gradually became more firmly entrenched: a thorough apprenticeship training could fit a person with the necessary qualification for a lifetime of work within a particular organization. Education, as such, certainly for people entering industry, was relegated to the school system whose task was to teach elementary subjects like the three R's. This philosophy still persists and is reflected in the commonly-held view that the job of schools and universities is to provide a general academic education with vocational preparation and training fundamentally remaining the responsibility of the factory or the office. This historical perspective may be seen to explain much of the predilection for science as opposed to technology and arguments revolving around the place of engineering in the arts-science-applied science hierarchy.[11] But it also accounts for the reluctance, until even comparatively recently, to introduce technology subjects at university level and indirectly explains the relative dominance of the professional associations in the UK.

This minimal degree of state interference in technological and vocational training did not apply to anywhere near the same extent in Germany. At the beginning of the nineteenth century, the separate German States played an active role in stimulating economic development by nurturing the residual vocational functions of the guilds. This, however, was aligned initially more in accordance with specific industrial groups and vocational interests in mind and, as these informal training arrangements gradually emerged as technical schools, they retained comparatively strong associations with industry. As in Britain, these schools were removed from the traditional university system and equally, there was a marked reluctance by them to accept vocationally-oriented educational facilities within their domain. The States, however, constantly aware of the need for industrial development, adopted a more resolute approach to this dilemma: they incorporated the technical schools into the universities and thus, by forming a series of technical universities, bridged the gap between traditional education and vocational training. At the same time, the new institutions maintained their links with industry and continued to provide engineering and other technically-oriented graduates to industry in increasing numbers.

The individualistic mould, as represented, on the one hand, by the 'purist' classical education of the 'gymnasium' versus vocational training on the other, continued unaffected by the changes in higher education until the beginning of the twentieth century. At that time, a dramatic reorientation in vocational training occurred. It was partly political in inspiration and directed towards maintaining the autonomy of small handicraft industries—only master-craftsmen, examined under State regulation were able to train apprentices and attendance at part-time vocational education during the period of training was henceforth to be compulsory.[12] But, perhaps more it was the result of a radical reassessment of the purpose of training under the guiding influence of the educationalist Kerschensteiner—he took the view that vocational education was as much education for life as training for a trade, and that only through 'practical work' could 'true character' of 'the useful human being' properly be developed, or the youth of the country 'fulfil their responsibilities towards the community'.[13] This change in philosophical direction was reinforced in the 1920s by Spranger's theory of 'Berufsbildung', which proposed that 'the way to higher general education is through the trade and only through the trade'.[14] Thus was it that the conceptual foundations of vocational training were established in Germany.

During this process of development other political initiatives took place which strengthened its impact. One crucial element was the reform of the chambers of commerce and industry into bodies, under common law, with enhanced powers to administer and control both the form and content of vocational training and the standards to be achieved. In addition, there had been established a series of special schools and institutions for particular trades and industries where foremen and middle management personnel could receive more advanced training.

Within Germany therefore, a tri-partite and hierarchically graduated system of technical education and training has evolved. Below the universities and technical universities are a range of institutions, each catering for the work needs, at different levels within the enterprise, for middle management, for prospective foremen and technicians and, below that again, a very comprehensive range of apprenticeships and other vocational trade courses. But equally of relevance is the ability to graduate from one level to the next higher and for this to be reflected in possible avenues of promotion within the firm.

These two perspectives of training have been presented in some detail to give some substance to that which might otherwise be seen as assertion. It is clear that, despite similar historical beginnings, vocational training in Britain, under laissez-faire liberalism, has evolved individualistically with only nominal state intervention being apparent, indeed, with only little public concern being expressed about its effectiveness, until comparatively recent times. Germany, on the other hand, saw the revival and retention of the association view and developed 'mechanisms' ensuring 'coverage', not only of the areas of skills and the necessary levels of proficiency to be achieved, but also in the breadth of application and the number of people potentially involved in the training. Furthermore, German training appears to be located more within a particular 'engineering speciality', that is, it tends to be more 'integrated' in character in that it is consistent with, and reinforces, the underlying connotations of 'Technik' by stressing the relationships that exist between production and the other associated 'disciplines' of design and development. Whilst a similar approach is also apparent in the UK, and from the 'engineering theory' standpoint the levels of attainment are probably equivalent, the emphasis on the 'production function' as an entity appears to be regarded as a matter of lesser significance. This is almost certainly related to the prevailing organizational patterns and to the ways in which newly-qualified engineers are traditionally 'accepted' and 'used' in Britain, but, paradoxically, this is tending to result in the development in parallel of training in Britain cast more in the 'engineering generalist' mould, that is, it is being directed more towards production management and embracing, to varying degrees, the different branches of engineering in the one course. This is rather different from current German practice but represents, under different cultural circumstances, a corresponding attempt to enhance the vocational relevance and practical orientation of the graduates concerned.

ORGANIZATIONAL DIFFERENCES

If the single theme of vocational training is pursued into the realm of the study of the organizations in Britain and Germany, it is not surprising to find evidence of the effects of these differing approaches on such questions as organizational structure, functional differentiation, degree of decentralization and so on. But, at the more superficial level, striking differences are also apparent: there is, for example, a lesser utilization of formally-qualified engineering personnel in Britain.[15] Similarly, whilst in Germany there is a tendency to regard Facharbeiter qualifications as a minimum requirements for engineering production work there is, in Britain, rather more doubt about the correspondence between tradesmen status and actual skills. This question of skills versus qualifications is brought more sharply into focus when computer numerical control (CNC) equipment based production is examined. There is a reasonably consistently held, albeit changing, view in Britain that CNC tends to result in operator deskilling and that CNC operation is more routine and involves less physical responsibility than comparable conventional work. This perception is less evident in Germany where CNC is seen as requiring further skills to cope with a continuously evolving spectrum of new tooling, more complex components, and improved programming techniques.[16] Furthermore, the use of CNC highlights other organizational characteristics. In Germany, CNC organization is fashioned so that it links foremen, chargehands, worker and planners around a common concern. The general principle adopted is that of attempting to develop a 'nucleus' of machining knowledge around which training, manning and other organizational policies are structured. This is particularly relevant in the case of foremen, who, in Germany, are deeply involved, not only in CNC operations, but in equipment selection, utilization of control system variants and so on. By contrast, their counterparts in Britain, have been largely bypassed by the introduction of CNC with the consequent lessening of control over jig and tool requirements, production demands and schedules, presetting arrangements, process and materials flow, and so on.[17]

The technical orientation of training, and the resultant emphasis on knowledge and skills, are associated with other organizational characteristics. Whereas in Britain, CNC has been adopted in such a way as to maintain planning department control and/or autonomy, or to segregate it from other sections of the production group, in Germany, operator and shop-floor planning/programming is much more frequently observed. This organizational pattern extends beyond the shop-floor: the line hierarchy, from foreman up through the management structure, is both more technical in orientation and more integrated with production engineering and other production functions. By comparison with the British type of organization, which tends to feature a greater amount of lateral segmentation between departments, with a numerically-strong technical staff on top of the works personnel, German organization is distinctive for small technical staff superstructures, usually more associated with supervision and management tasks, and linked more closely with the production workforce.[18]

This centrality of engineering and production in German plants is evidenced in a variety of other ways. Managerial control, for example, over different divisions or production sites is more intensive in technical respects, that is, in terms of product and process development and the achievement of production targets, deadlines and delivery dates. In Britain, by contrast, control occurs primarily through financial performance targets and indicators where the emphasis is on financial return. This comparison also extends to questions of the economic justification of new equipment: it has often been observed that British companies expect new plant and machinery to pay for itself more quickly than similar firms in Germany. This reinforces the view that British companies tend to emphasize profits as a company goal whereas German firms stress the technical and production preconditions necessary to achieve returns.[19]

These comparisons, highlighting similarities and differences, could be extended if other national and cultural dimensions, such as the framework of industrial relations, economic conditions, employment patterns and so on, were to be included. The question remains, however, about the 'use' to which the findings of such studies can be put.

APPLICATION OF CROSS-CULTURAL RESEARCH FINDINGS

Socio-Economic Conditions

In the study mentioned above concerning the introduction and use of CNC, it was evident that certain changes in the socio-economic structure, notably associated with competitive and marketing strategies, were taking place and these were having a marked effect upon production and other corporate policies. Enterprises, both in Britain and in Germany, stated that they were, indeed being forced, increasingly to cater to small market 'niches' rather than for homogeneous mass markets. More individualized, customized products, with a greater number of product variants, were seen as being required. Product innovation, as part of this development, was also tending to lead towards increased component complexity with the inherent consequence of increased financial costs associated with work-in-progress and finished stock.

Financial Considerations

Thus market-oriented and financial considerations are pointing in the direction of more complicated machining processes and both smaller batch sizes and correspondingly more frequent conversion. A modern CNC machine is ideally-suited technically to handle such product requirements. This increased variability of batches, however, has implications for organizational processes; it is not one, for example, that can be handled bureaucratically through a conventional increase in the division of labour—rather, it requires a greater degree of flexibility and adaptability, at the level of the operator and the machine. Each CNC operator is likely to have to deal with a greater and more frequently-changing range of jobs.

Whilst the machines are becoming more sophisticated they are also easier to program. It is no longer necessary to be an EDP specialist to 'instruct' the machine even in the manufacture of highly complex components. The need for separate and specialist information workers is reduced; rather, programming becomes an integral part of the job and a vehicle by which the vocational expertise of its users is increased. It is indeed of significance to observe that the crucial 'bottlenecks' in production are not information-processing and calculating difficulties—experience indicates that these are still associated with tooling, materials, feeds and speeds, and faults and breakdowns, but, if anything, their significance has been enhanced. But of equal importance is the fact that skills in handling these 'metal removal' problems are only developed on the machine. It follows that whilst 'new' skills may be required, increasing emphasis needs to be placed on the maintenance and evolution of 'traditional' craft skills for, only in this way, is the necessary level of flexibility and adaptability capable of being developed.

Socio-Technical 'Logics'

We would, however, also go one step further; we would suggest that German companies, by the nature of their general organizational arrangements and their emphasis on technical training, have an 'in-built' advantage over their British counterparts. In Germany, there is an increasing recognition of the merits of an approach which relies strongly on craft worker skills, and further, one which purposefully sets out to integrate any 'new' skills requirements with those more traditionally attained. In the German context this transition would appear to be a 'natural' development; in the British context this is by no means so evident. But, this depolarization of skills and qualification structure is quite within the present 'logic' of CNC development and application, not because it is a necessary consequence, but because it appears to be consistent with economic success.

THE POTENTIAL TRANSFER OF CULTURAL CHARACTERISTICS

It is, of course, impossible to import a set of cultural dimensions and incorporate them within another national environment. If however, it is possible to identify one or a number of crucial 'elements' of 'good practice' exhibited within one setting, it should not be impossible to 'borrow' such a concept and attempt to 'insert' it into the realm of institutional 'reality' within another setting.

From the research findings described above there appears to be some evidence that there are substantial differences between Germany and Britain in the extent and orientation of technical training, the way in which this skill and knowledge is integrated into the production function, and the extent to which lateral segmentation between departments occurs. These factors in themselves would seem to represent sufficient justification for pursuing this general form of investigation. But a case can be made for following up the process and attempting to devise strategies for incorporating views and philosophies found useful elsewhere within the 'home' culture.

This can be conceptualized at a number of levels, for example, the national level, and include considerations associated with changes in the education system, of privilege, class and elitism, attitudes towards status and sectional 'solidarity', of professionalism, the resolution, or at least the regulation, of conflict and so on.[20] But if we restrict ourselves to that of the level of the individual organization, a number of additional issues appear to be relevant and, without attempting to be exhaustive nor to list them in any particular order of priority, to include such questions as:

—the degree of trust, discretionary power and responsibility that management is prepared to confer upon employees, that is, in more general terms, the nature of managerial control and supervision, where and how it is to be exercised and the extent to be the formalization of procedures and the centralization/decentralization of authority is desirable/feasible;

—the nature of the appropriate 'operating nucleus'/'technical core' around which the manufacturing processes should be organized, that is, the degree of flexibility, adaptability and co-operation necessary, and the relevant craft/technical skills, such as machining, programming, setting, etc., expertise needed within the nucleus, but including also the manner in which 'ancilliary' services such as scheduling, tooling, materials, quality and performance reporting and so on are to be provided;

—the quality of the 'formal' organizational relations by which 'other' services such as design and development, production engineering, industrial engineering, etc., facilities are integrated with the operating nucleus. These include questions associated with the nature of existing communication procedures, organizational structure, considerations such as the 'accepted' degree of delegation, the role of multi-disciplinary teams, specialized departments, advisory groups, etc., the extent of any managerial 'overload' and so on;

—the nature of any 'informal' element of organizational dominance, precedence or established priorities that exists between, for example, production and tehnical services, production and maintenance, production and planning and/or scheduling and so on, and the 'barriers' to effective overall operations that these relationships may confer;

—the degree to which modified career and progression paths (including changes in the remuneration structure and packages) can influence both the 'learning' patterns of the individuals concerned, and result in changes in the character of existing 'boundary' conditions both within the organization, and between it and its external environment;

—the nature, form and content of training programs, both for operators and for supervisory and management personnel, and the effect that these can have not only on the more specific 'management' items cited above, but also, and equally if not more importantly, on the prevailing organizational 'culture'.

CONCLUSION

This form of organizational thinking is not easy. First and foremost it requires a good understanding of the national characteristics, both of the countries concerned and of the organizational 'themes' that result. Secondly, however, there is the important element of judgement: these general issues are delineated by both opportunities and restrictions—by what might be desirable but, on the other hand, by what might appear to be feasible. This, of course, is dependent upon the specific situation and the circumstances that may warrant some form of intervention. But the very nature of this dilemma emphasizes the rationale for well-constructed research initiatives into the cross-cultural complexities of organizational action, especially if it includes the additional aim of attempting to modify the practices within one country which appear to impede performance.

NOTES

1. See, e.g., Pugh, D. S., D. J. Hickson, C. J. Hinings and C. Turner (1968) 'Dimensions of Organizational Structure', *Administrative Science Quarterly,* Vol. 13, pp. 65–91.

Idem (1969) 'The Context of Organization Structure', *Administrative Science Quarterly,* Vol. 14, pp. 91–113.

2. See, e.g., Blau, P. M. and R. A. Schoenherr (1971) *The Structure of Organizations,* Basic Books, London & New York.
   Child, John (1973) 'Predicting & Understanding Organization Structures', *Administrative Science Quarterly,* Vol. 16, pp. 168–85.
3. Thompson, J. D. (1967) *Organizations in Action,* McGraw-hill, New York.
4. See, e.g., Morse, J. J. (1975) 'Person-Job Congruence & Individual Adjustment & Development', *Human Relations,* Vol. 28, No. 9, pp. 841–61.
   Muchinsky, P. M. 'Organizational Communication: Relationships to Organizational Climate and Job Satisfaction', *Academy of Management Journal,* Vol. 20, No. 4, pp. 592–607.
   Hellriegel, D. and J. W. Slocum (1974) 'Organizational Climate: Measures, Research and Contingencies', *Academy of Management Journal,* Vol. 17, pp. 255–80.
   Silverman, D. (1970) *The Theory of Organizations: A Sociological Framework,* Heinmann, London.
5. Porter, L. W., E. E. Lawler and J. R. Hackman (1975) *Behaviour in Organizations,* McGraw-Hill, New York.
6. Maurice, Marc, Arndt Sorge and Malcolm Warner (1978) 'Societal Differences in Organizing Manufacturing Units. A Comparison of France, West Germany and Great Britain', Ninth Congress of Sociology, Uppsala.
7. Kerr, Clark, J. T. Dunlop, F. H. Harbinson and C. A. Myers (1973) *Industrialism and Industrial Man,* Penguin, London.
8. Hickson, D. J. (1974) 'The Grounds for Comparative Organization Theory: Shifting Sands or Hard Core?' British Sociological Association Conference, Leeds.
9. Brossard, Michel and Marc Maurice (1976) 'Is there a Universal Model of Organization Structure?' *International Studies of Management & Organization,* Vol. 16, pp. 11–45.
10. Sorge, Arndt (1978) 'Management, Technical Education and Training as a Public Concern in Britain, France and Germany', International Institute of Management, Report IIM/DP33, Mimeo.
11. Lawrence, Peter (1980) *Managers and Management in West Germany,* Croom Helm, London.
12. Taylor, M. E. (1981) *Education and Work in the Federal Republic of Germany,* Anglo-German Foundation, London.
13. *Op. cit.,* p. 17.
14. *Op. cit.,* p. 25.
15. Sorge, Arndt, Gert Hartmann, Malcolm Warner and Ian Nicholas (1981) 'Micro-electronics & Manpower in Manufacturing: Applications of Computer Numerical Control in Great Britain and West Germany', International Institute of Management, IIM/LMP 81–86, Mimeo, Chapter 7.
16. See Sorge, Arndt, *et al., op. cit.,* Chapter 5.
17. *Op. cit.,* Chapter 5.
18. *Op. cit.,* Chapter 6.
19. *Op. cit.,* Chapter 2.
20. Dahrendorf, Ralf (1982) *On Britain,* BBC Publications, London.

CHAPTER 10

The relationship between educational and managerial cultures in Britain and West Germany
A comparative analysis of higher education, from an historical perspective

Robert Locke

The current flap in many countries over education is only the most recent in a long line of similar preoccupations which stretch back at least into the second half of the nineteenth century. In Europe, two countries, Britain and Germany, whose economic performances and educational systems varied and vary significantly, have often experienced the same sort of investigatory passions. Since education is a vast topic, this investigation process has been equally vast but recently attention has focused specifically on higher education and business-industrial management. This chapter pursues that theme. Therefore, it ignores the many aspects of management and higher education which do not clarify the relationship between them in order to concentrate on the points of contact. In both countries, the structure, content and purpose of business education not only are and have been influenced by the nature of the relationship existing between the educational and business-industrial worlds, but, it is argued here, so has managerial performance. Accordingly the subject will be treated under the following rubrics:

1. The contacts established in Germany and England between higher education, business and industry.

   a) The German yardstick
   b) Comparative English experience

2. The effect which the historical interrelation between higher education and management had, has, and perhaps will have on managerial performance in each country.

   a) The corporate level
   b) The operational level

THE CONTACTS ESTABLISHED IN ENGLAND AND GERMANY BETWEEN HIGHER EDUCATION AND MANAGEMENT AND HOW THEY DIFFERED IN EACH COUNTRY

The German yardstick

Since it is to be argued here that managerial cultures in Germany and England have been greatly affected by deeply rooted educational traditions, it is best, at the outset, to make the salient features of these traditions quite clear. Moreover, since the German experience is to be used as a yardstick with which to measure the British, the higher education of German business and industrial 'managers', will be handled first. It is, of course, impossible to describe traditional higher education in Germany in much detail here. For our purpose, it suffices to say that the German university was, by the mid-nineteenth century, unique in one crucial way: it stressed scientific research. We owe to the German university the infernal injunction that exists everywhere today to do research and publish or perish. Already in the nineteenth century, the first question asked about a German professor was, what has he published? This research imperative entails a specific conception about the nature of knowledge: in every field there is an accepted body of truth, but this body of truth is only a stage in our knowledge about the world. Science is an investigative process through which our knowledge is tested, deepened and perfected, which means that the process, scientific research, is itself integral to the transfer of knowledge through the teaching function. These ideas about the nature of knowledge were not peculiarly German. What made the Germans different was that they had managed by the nineteenth century to institutionalize them in their forms of higher education. In the Germanic world of Middle Europe the PhD was a research degree as was the *Habilitation*.[1] Few who aspired to a professorship in a German university attained their goal unless they had proven their research capacities by the completion of a doctoral thesis and a *Habilitationsschrift*. Indeed research projects were undertaken on the undergraduate level.

This meant that the Germans did not neglect the sciences in the nineteenth century. Indeed the term science *(Wissenschaft)* applied there to all fields of knowledge because knowledge in every field was subject to systematic, disciplined research and development. The Germans not only pursued natural science *(Naturwissenschaften)* but turned history, art, languages, i.e., the humanities, into *Geisteswissenschaften*. Moreover, German universities were engaged in a professional education which taught medicine, law and theology as *Wissenschaften*. The footnote, the article, the thesis, the book took over as the humanities ceased to be a medium primarily for the inculcation of *culture générale* (although there were still pretentions in that direction) and professional knowledge the exclusive, jealously guarded possession of private groups (the doctors, the lawyers), to become objects of scientific inquiry. German universities were centers for serious scholarship and research.

Since this was the university tradition, no self-respecting discipline or institution of higher education could hope to find acceptance in German academia unless it conformed to the research model. And people, when they set about establishing schools for technicians and businessmen, wanted, because of the great prestige of German university *Wissenschaft*, to obtain acceptance. Consequently, when the engineers, merchants, businessmen and educators founded technical institutes and business schools in Germany, they sought to make much more of them than glorified trade and commercial schools.[2] The professors and their students had, however, to counter effectively the oft repeated accusation, emanating from the universities, that engineering and business studies were somehow not scientifically respectable. They did so by making engineering and business studies part of applied natural and economic science, science which demanded research based on the most exacting methodology.

In their educational forms, therefore, the new technical institutes and business schools sought to copy the universities. Since the university research tradition was objectified in academic degrees, gaining the right to grant them became an avid preoccupation of the newcomers. In engineering, where economically related higher education developed first, it was a long climb, but by 1900 students in the technical institutes were officially authorized, in the best traditions of *Wissenschaft*, to acquire doctorates *(Dr.-Ing.)*, the first engineering doctorates in the world. Indeed, in that year, in Prussia, the King-Emperor, William II, an admirer of scientific technology, granted the engineering schools the right to issue the two degrees (*Dipl.-Ing.* and *Dr.-Ing.*) that placed them, formally, on the same level as the universities.[3] Research facilities, moreover, were expanded impressively, particularly during the two decades before the First World War. The Royal Institute of Physics, which was created at Charlottenburg, aroused the admiration of the international scientific community. It was the most spectacular example of the numerous electrical, chemical, mechanical and metallurgical laboratories established in German technical institutes for students as well as professors. Detailed descriptive articles with accompanying photographs, that the German engineering journals frequently published, testify to the elaborate and thoughtful care with which these teaching-research laboratories were installed.[4]

Thus the German engineering schools, the technical institutes, had, by the turn of the century, managed to integrate themselves into the *Wissenschaft* tradition. At the same time that they improved their scientific stature, moreover, they also multiplied in number and increased in size. By 1900 schools existed throughout the Empire: in Charlottenburg (Berlin), Brunswick, Danzig, Hannover, Munich,

Dresden, Stuttgart, Aachen, Darmstadt, Karlsruhe and Breslau. These eleven technical institutes and the three mining schools (Berlin, Freiburg and Claustal) formed the already renowned German system of higher education in engineering. Two sets of statistics illustrate their growth. The first shows the phenomenal increase in their student population during the last decades of the nineteenth century.[5] Whereas the German population increased in this period by ten percent, the number of students increased by 171 percent, from 5,361 to 14,734. The second statistics show the rapid increase in the membership of the German engineering fraternity *(VDI)*.[6] The similarity between the two rates of growth was not accidental. The *VDI* was more than a powerful supporter of the technical institutes. Its leadership was recruited largely from their graduates. Indeed the director of the *VDI* during these critical growth years (1856–1890) was Franz Grasshof, professor in the Technical Institute of Karlsruhe.

Over the past eighty years, moreover, these German technical institutes have carried on this *Wissenschaft* tradition, unabated. Between the war the schools almost doubled their enrollment.[7] More students, furthermore, were not just crowded into the same facilities for, even during the difficult Weimar years, German technical institutes managed to expand and modernize their research laboratories and workshops.[8] These expansions, moreover, continued, after a short respite, across the chasm of the 1945 collapse.[9] German technical institutes (e.g. Aachen, Munich, Karlsruhe), many of which are now called universities, are not only good engineering schools but also excellent institutions for scientific research—institutions which continue to offer the same degrees and possess the same first rate research facilities that they had under the Empire.

The technical institutes were joined, if somewhat later, by new forms of higher business education, the *Handelshochschulen*. The first German business school was founded at Leipzig in 1898. Cologne got a school in 1901 as did Frankfort on the Main. Thereafter a number of new schools were organized in quick succession (Aachen, 1903; Berlin, 1906; Mannheim, 1907; Munich, 1910; Königsberg, 1915, and Nuremberg, 1929). Before the proper research study programs could be established in the schools, one needed to have the professors to run them, and these professors had themselves to have passed the required tests. To find such men in 1900 was impossible for the simple reason that business economics as a systematic recognized study did not exist. The first professors of business economics, therefore, were academically speaking, i.e. from the university's perspective, not properly qualified. They were either secondary commercial school teachers, men drawn from business or industry, or, if academics, men trained in other fields (economics, political sciences, law, etc.). Nonetheless, this first generation of professors, enticed by the rigors of *Wissenschaft*, rapidly repaired these 'deficiencies'. By 1920 it was possible to acquire the full range of undergraduate and graduate degrees in business economics, and the possession of such research degrees became increasingly important for appointment to professorships in business schools. Indeed it became exceedingly difficult for people without them to get a chair. In just one generation the German professoriat in business economics, therefore, became a self-recruiting, orthodox elite, comparable in training and outlook to the elite holding down faculty positions in older university disciplines.

It also became a serious group of researchers who provisioned themselves with all the scholarly appurtenances deemed necessary for this essential professorial task. The oldest periodicals in business economics, Schmalenbach's *Zeitschrift für handelswissenschaftliche Forschung*, known today as *Schmalenbachs Zeitschrift für betriebswirtschaftliche Forschung*, and Heinrich Nicklisch's *Zeitschrift für Handelswissenschaft und Handelspraxis* were founded, respectively, in 1906 and 1908. They were research organs from the first which not only published articles on numerous topics but reviewed, critically, current books and articles, foreign and domestic. To this periodical literature, which expanded significantly after World War I, must be added publications in book form.[10] By 1938 the ninety-nine business economists listed on the membership rolls of the Association of German Teachers of Economic and Social Sciences, had authored 465 and co-authored or edited 565 works, amounting to 10.40 per person.[11] Among these volumes were the elaborate bibliographical and research references characteristic of every scientific discipline. Professor Erich Schaefer's *Das Schriftum über betriebswirtschaftliche Marktforschung* and Kurt Schmalt's *Betriebswirtschaftlicher Literaturführer* were books of this kind. But the really impressive achievement came with the five volume *Handwörterbuch der Betriebswirtschaftslehre* (concise Dictionary of Business Economics) published under the general editorship of Heinrich Nicklisch. First printed in 1926 and kept up-to-date in subsequent editions, this 1,520 page reference work was a monument to business economics in Germany. It placed before professors and students a complete bibliography of both foreign and domestic works on most aspects of the subject.

As a corpus, the writings show, therefore, that business economics had become the discipline of the research-oriented faculties of the new business schools. The professors were fully conscious of what they were doing and what it signified in German education. As early as 1910, one observer at the Vienna Congress on Commercial Education could report:

One could clearly see how the business schools in German speaking regions had begun to develop into teaching and research institutions in economics and how the Latin countries, with their very different academic *(Hochschule)* goals, strived more and more to copy and to hold fast, tenaciously, to routine business practice.[12]

VALUES, CULTURE AND EDUCATION

All the scholarly accoutrements of academic business economics served to create a sophisticated science in the best traditions of German *Wissenschaft*. The professors, in their research seminars and in their research projects, and the graduate students, engaged in thesis work under the guidance of these professors, who replenished their ranks from the academically most successful research students, developed the discipline. The knowledge generated was taught to students primarily on the undergraduate level. Since a thorough theoretical education was necessary to complete the scientific instruction considered to be essential for any qualified degree holder *(Diplom-Kaufmann)*, the teaching function was no mean task. It made demands that increased as the science was developed, on students and teachers alike.

In 1900 students could complete the comprehensive undergraduate education in two years. In 1926, the length of the study period was increased to three years. At the same time the numbers enrolled, despite the First World War and the financial crisis of the Weimar Republic, increased impressively. By 1928, total enrolment reached 3,119 students, 516 auditors *(Hospitanten)*, and 1,330 attendants at public lectures.[13] In that year over 16,000 received degrees from a business school *(Dipl.-Kaufman* or *Dipl.-Handelslehrer)*. After World War II the study period for the undergraduate degree was increased to four years. Currently students in German universities spend on the average ten semesters (five years) to complete their undergraduate studies *(Diplom-Kaufman)*, two years to complete a doctorate and three to finish a *Habilitationsschrift*. At the same time that the scientific study periods increased, the attendance at the business schools grew enormously. In 1958, 24,200 people graduated in economics in West Germany, most of whom were in business economics; 6,200 received doctorates. Since then there has been a veritable explosion in business economics as it has become the fastest growing discipline in German universities and colleges.[14]

So much then for the forms of higher education in engineering and business economics, their historical development, and how they reflect the *Wissenschaft* tradition. The content of these new German disciplines has, of course, changed considerably over time. This is true in engineering studies because, although the German technical institutes were the first schools in the world to introduce engineering specialties (mechanical, civil, chemical, electrical, hydraulic engineering, etc.), subsequent scientific progress has not only significantly altered the content of these studies but added new ones. It is important, too, not to forget that the content of business studies has changed over the years. Indeed, from the viewpoint of the manager (and hence of this study) the changes in business education have been more significant than those in engineering and science, for transformations in content have affected forms of education as well.

'Management' per se was not in fact studied before the Second World War in Europe and scarcely in America. People studied institutional (banking, insurance, industrial administration, etc.) and functional (marketing, accounting, personnel, etc) subjects. We still study institutional and functional subjects in business and management but the focus on management as a special profession, as a specifically academically learnable generalist skill (science) embodied in such studies as decision theory, strategic planning and operations research, is a recent phenomenon. Consequently, the content of business studies in the pre and post World War II business school differed enormously.

Since German business schools had grown to maturity before 1940, their prewar curricula consisted of institutional and functional courses. If one looks briefly at the subjects listed in a German business school catalogue of the time, however, this does not appear to have been entirely the case. Although functional and institutional courses are listed, they formed part of a coordinated study called business economics *(Betriebswirtschaftslehre)*. This did not happen in America, where little attempt was made to integrate institutional and functional disciplines into one science. That difference Professor Kurt Schmaltz had to explain to the Americans when, in 1930, he published an article in *The Accounting Review* on 'The Business Periodicals of Germany'. He pointed out that 'periodicals like *The Accounting Review* and *The Journal of Accountancy* simply do not exist in Germany, at least not as scientific periodicals. The German periodicals cover the whole field of business economics. They can best be compared with the *Harvard Business Review*, although even there the fields of finance and marketing are especially emphasized.'[15] The Germans seemed, therefore, to be studying the structure and operations of the firm as an integrated, multifaceted discipline in which the functional and institutional subjects were submerged. This, however, was not completely true.

The illusion of an integrated study arose because in *Betriebswirtschaftslehre* instead of the functional and institutional parts being integrated into a whole, the whole was swallowed up by one of the functional parts. Whereas in America functional studies in accounting, marketing and finance flourished alongside each other and constituted the mainstay of business school curricula, in Germany accounting completely overshadowed all others. Thus the German business schools concentrated, aside from institutional studies, on accounting or accounting-oriented business technologies. The statement, however, should not mislead, for the German achievements in this respect were most impressive. For centuries, first skilled mechanics and merchants and then engineers and businessmen had lived apart professionally, separated by a belief, rooted in practice, that they had different if not incompatible functions. Even the scientific management movement, which emerged in all advanced countries, including Germany, after 1900 did not heal this rift. It was the achievement of engineers—e.g. F. W. Taylor in America, Henri Le Chatellier in France, George Schlesinger in Germany, to name a few—not accountants. When accounting was treated in the scientific management movement, it was handled primarily by production engineers from the engineering point of view.

The effort, as far as accounting is concerned, to amalgamate the production and the merchant function came in Germany from the professors of accounting in the new business schools. Initially, few people realized that this was to be their purpose. The schools were called *Handelshochschulen* (Commercial High Schools) and the study *Handelswissenschaft* (Commercial Science), clearly disclosing commercial origins. Merchant guilds and chambers of commerce set up and financed the schools in their, the merchants', image, and professors dealt with balance-sheets, profit-and-loss, i.e. financial accounting. But early there was dissatisfaction with this emphasis. Eugen Schmalenbach, the greatest figure in the pioneering generation of German business school accountants, criticized one of the leading Berlin professors, Johann Schaer, a man who contributed mightily to the conversion of commerce from a practical craft into a learned science, for clinging too tightly to the commercial world.[16] Schmalenbach did everything in Cologne to extend the study of accounting into industry and he, with the support of men like Nicklisch in Berlin, imposed his views. 'Schmalenbach's contribution,' one of his students, Professor Alfred Isaac, could write as early as 1922, 'is to have helped the factory take its rightful place in business studies. Schmalenbach led the way towards the amalgamation of commercial and industrial accounting into one science.'[17]

The result was a flexible instrument of managerial control. German academic accountants worked out an accounting science that could be applied to any kind of firm. Armed with economy theory, they developed new forms of balance-sheet accounting, explored cost accounting for both manufacturing and commercial businesses, investigated inflation accounting, integrated financial and cost accounting, devised excellent uniform accounting procedures for comparative business purposes.[18] The work was so impressive that the translators, in a preface to the 1959 English edition of Schmalenbach's *Dynamic Accounting*, noted:

In preparing this book for publication . . . (they, the translators) felt they were providing teacher, students, and all who are interested in accountancy, with something which has not previously been available to them (in England). This book does not set out to be a technical handbook of bookkeeping and accounts, but it is an attempt to present the subject in its proper perspective, as a branch of economics. Few men have been better qualified to bridge the gap between economics and accountancy than was Professor Schmalenbach . . . Surrounded by a group of brilliant technicians he demonstrated how accountancy could embrace costing, statistics and planning, which, together with financial accounting, represent the four cardinal points of economic control, and the true reflection of the operations of a business.[19]

Considering that the book was published nearly forty years after its ideas were printed in German, this is high praise. But it should not obscure the fact that the science which the German professors developed and called business economics *(Betriebswirtschaftslehre)* was essentially management accounting.

It is important, moreover, to explain the effect which the German pre World War II achievement in business economics had on the development of their discipline after the war. Past business education cannot affect present unless its influence is projected through people and institutions into present business education, and this projection only becomes comparatively significant when the relative capacity of the past to affect the present differs significantly from country to country. Even before the Second World War, the Americans had developed studies in marketing and finance to a far greater extent than the Germans. During and especially after the war, the evolution of functional studies proceeded apace principally in North America, in the fields of organizational behavior and personnel, for example. In addition, these and the traditional fields of business knowledge (i.e. marketing, accounting, finance) were basically affected by auxiliary sciences (applied mathematics, statistics, electronic data processing, psychology, sociology and economics).

More importantly, there was, as noted, the reorientation of business schools in America from functional fields of knowledge to management per se. Decision-making, leadership, group dynamics, and related topics became the focus of attention in an effort to educate 'managers'. It became *de rigueur* among American management specialists to talk about the necessity, because of the rapidly changing needs of management, for life-time continuing education. Better to give students a minimum education on the undergraduate level and then in MBA and post-experience education to allow the active manager to keep in tune with his career needs as he perceives them— career needs that, as he moves into higher management, require more and more the skills of the 'generalist'. Thus the content of American business education changed, and so did its structure; for, although pre-experience undergraduate education flourished, too, a rapidly developing MBA and post-experience education became the 'generalist' form of management education par excellence. By the 1960s American business schools were more numerous and quite different from their prewar version.

In West Germany, the past was literally physically projected into the postwar business school. In 1965, an investigation showed that, of the 78 full professors *(Ordinarien)* teaching business economics in West German universities, 26 had been born between 1895 and 1904, 10 between 1905 and 1914, 19 between 1915 and 1924, and 23 between 1925 and 1934.[20] At least 36 of the 78 (47%), then, had been completely educated before the Second World War and hence exposed

VALUES, CULTURE AND EDUCATION

almost exclusively to the accounting business economics taught before 1929. Most of the others, moreover, had been educated either partially before the war or in the immediate postwar period by a professoriat rooted in the prewar *BWL* tradition. Of course, numerous retirements since 1965 have brought more people into the business economics professoriat from the postwar generation. But, considering that it was virtually impossible to get an appointment as a professor in business economics in a German university without having come through the established system *(Promotion, Habilitation)* and that it did not profit the Germans academically to get degrees in America, even the postwar German generation was heavily subjected to the indigenous traditions in business economics, and consequently, unlike the West Europeans, less susceptible to and more critical of the Americans.

This can be seen most readily from the functional content of postwar German business studies. Brinkmann, for instance, in a survey of students in the Northrhine–Westphalia region (conducted in 1967), concluded that studies of the new business technologies [operations research, electronic data processing, and personnel management—*(Menschenführung-Sozialpsychologie)*—] 'were only cursorily taught or were not taught' by German business faculties.[21] On the other hand, his questionnaire shows that all students in *Betriebswirtschaftslehre* took bookkeeping as a preliminary requirement *(Propädeuticum)* and had as an obligatory subject in their final examinations *allgemeine Betriebswirtschaftslehre*, which remained heavily accounting oriented.[22] All business students were also examined on two functional subjects selected from a list of options. But this exercise of choice had not led to major changes. Peter Matthias' study (1973) of business economics majors at Göttingen and Hamburg shows, for example, that only 16% (113 out of 713) chose operations research as an examination elective, and it was the only new (post World War II) subject among the top six most frequently selected examination options (unless organizational theory, which despite its prewar origins made its greatest advances after the war, is included among them).[23] The other choices were quite traditional: commerce 47% of the students (335 out of 713); auditing and taxation, 41% (295 out of 713); industrial administration, 39% (258 out of 713); banking, 31% (218 out of 713).[24] Thus the students either had no opportunity to select many of the new subjects (e.g. personnel management, electronic data processing, operations research) or generally ignored them. The fact that so many students chose auditing-taxation (which are accounting subjects), industrial administration (in which cost accounting traditionally is very important), banking and commerce (in which financial accounting is stressed), indicates the extent to which the content of prewar business administration was projected into the postwar period.

Yet this evidence should not be misinterpreted. Since traditional

German business economics was accounting dominated, since most of the newer functional disciplines were American developed, and since there is always a time lag in the transfer of knowledge, the predominance of the older technique persisted for a long time. But there was and is nothing about the *Wissenschaft* tradition that set(s) it against scientific innovation. On the contrary that is its very essence. In this context it is instructive to note that operations research, which the 1967 study shows was hardly taught in German universities, had already, by 1973, been selected by 16% of the students in Hamburg and Göttingen as an optional examination subject. Students and young professors, especially, were eager for change.

University reforms in the late 1960s, moreover, produced structural changes in German university governance which facilitated transformations in university curricula. No longer were full professors *(Ordinarien)* considered uniquely to be members of the various faculties and charged accordingly with the responsibility for the organization of curricula and the surveillance of examinations. This responsibility was transferred from the full professors to the university faculties, where all academic teaching staff had voting rights. Consequently the examination regulations could be more easily altered. To the traditional examination subjects in business economics were added new ones and the professors to teach them.[25]

In the 1970s, therefore, business school curricula developed rapidly in Germany. OR has become a standard examination subject; personnel or human resource management has made similar strides to become another standard, if optional, examination topic.[26] Elements of other disciplines (law, sociology, social psychology, statistics, mathematics, etc.) have profoundly influenced the content of the older disciplines, too, so that they are very different from what they had been just 15 years ago. The transformation became especially marked when electronic data processing finally invaded German business economics. The adoption of new business techniques and perspectives (EDP, decision theory, systems analysis, etc.) greatly altered the content of traditional studies in accounting and organizational structure.

German academics, moreover, have shown strong interest in *Praxis*. The Curricula Reform Committee *(Studienreformkommissionen)* that have been operating in each German state since the student unrest of 1968 have stressed the relationship between university and society. The law even states that among the educational goals of the university (and this is a distinct departure from the old *Wissenschaft* tradition which was concerned with cultivating rigorous thinking) is the preparation of the students '. . . for their occupation and social roles'.[27] Business economists have, to further this end, increasingly paid more attention to case studies and project teaching techniques and students have been encouraged, either before or during their university studies, to do work periods in a firm.[28]

If the German *Wissenschaft* tradition has easily accommodated the new sciences generated at home or abroad, it has, nonetheless, resisted new educational forms, and therewith, much of the form-dependent content, exhibited in the American example, of business education. Business studies remain, in Germany, under the influence of the *Wissenschaft* tradition, according to which professors perceive of their activities as scientists. Mention could be made of the comprehensive examination systems and the long periods of study devoted to theoretical subjects at undergraduate and graduate levels which have characterized German business economics for decades. But the most significant difference in German business education, from the American point of view, has been its resistance to the 'generalists' approach to management education. German students take up general management problems in their specialties—a decision theory approach is integral nowadays to accounting, personnel, marketing and other specialties. But German academic business economists have been true to their prewar traditions. There are no MBA programs, no taught courses for post-experience or doctoral students.

The pull of *Wissenschaft*, moreover, has been felt at lower level technical and commercial educational institutions as well as in the technical institutes and business schools. Traditionally these technical and commercial schools (*höhere Handelsschulen* and *Ingenieur-schulen*), which pre-dated the technical institutes and *Handelschoch-schulen* and whose expansion happened at as least as fast a pace, escaped the *Wissenschaft* tradition. They taught practical skills in commerce and engineering to their students. After the creation of the technical institutes and business schools, it became customary for these lower schools to recruit their faculty from the ranks of the *Diplom-Ingenieure* and the *Diplom-Kaufleute*. *Wissenschaft* entered the sub-university schools in their person and with them came the striving to emulate superiors, that is, to acquire the status of *Hochschulen* themselves. These strivings bore fruit in the 1970s when *SPD* governments in many states of the German Federal Republic elevated these higher level technical and commercial schools to the rank of technical colleges *(Fachhochschulen)*. The '. . . promotion to a *Hochschule* and therewith incorporation into the university system', was possible only because people in these lower schools, recognizing the validity of *Wissenschaft*, wished to adopt the 'research outlook'.[29] Their attitude illustrates how this university-inspired *Wissenschaft* tradition has, since most technical institutes and business schools had themselves previously been lower grade technical and commercial schools, acted like a magnet, drawing lower echelon schools almost inexorably into the research science orbit.

Yet, if *Wissenschaft* has been important to the development of the form and content of higher education in engineering and business economics in Germany, it has not acted alone. Any practising manager or engineer reading these pages could readily understand why. Engineering and business management are as much skill as science. Peter Lawrence, in his book on *Managers and Management in West Germany*, has made this point, as far as engineering is concerned, quite forcefully. 'The "applied science" label', he noted,

implies some misconception of engineering work . . . The output of science is knowledge; the output of engineering is three dimensional artifacts. Much scientific work takes place in laboratory conditions where the influence of undesirable variables has been controlled: most engineering work is conducted 'on site', and is subject to environmental influences. Scientists who study things, seek ideal solutions and universally valid laws (knowledge). Engineers who make things, seek workable solutions which do not cost too much.[30]

Ian Glover, moreover, has made much the same point about the manager's job. 'The classic "scientific management" view of the manager as a "decision-maker" . . . concerned with the flow and use of "hard" information, with relationships amongst job-holders, with organization and position in the hierarchy is a fiction.'[31] The working manager concentrates on tasks, on functions; his first duty is to get the job done and that job is the same as the engineer's, the making and selling of a three-dimensional object not the creation of knowledge. Indeed the knowledge required by the manager is fragmentary and comes from more than one field. The production manager needs to know some psychology as well as some physics, the personnel manager some physics as well as some psychology. Most of the information manager's use is, moreover, not scientific at all. It is based on hunches and private information gained in short talks. 'Executive work is best conceived of as being skill-specific, rather than knowledge-specific; knowledge, skills, experience, are all necessary, none exclusively or even predominately.'[32]

Nothing, therefore, is wrong with science or skill; both are needed for the good manager or engineer to succeed and a good system of higher education in engineering or business economics promotes both. Eugen Schmalenbach underscored the non-scientific component in his new discipline when he compared it to economics in 1919. 'Economics and business economics', he noted,

handle, to a large extent, the same material *(Stoffe)* but they do not have the same spirit *(Geist)*. Economics is a philosophical science with philosophical characteristics. Business economics . . . (is not). Chemistry and mechanical technology are closer in spirit to business economics than is economics. Business economics is purposeful. It must think purposefully.[33]

Schmalenbach did not disparage economics. It, like other university disciplines, contributed a great deal to 'knowledge'. For business economics, however, economic theory was not true or false, in a philosophical sense, but useful or worthless, in a technological-skill sense. On the other hand, Schmalenbach did not conceive of business economics, chemistry, mechanical engineering, etc., as mere vocations. Knowledge *(Wissenschaft)* and skill *(Kunst)* were required in them to achieve their ends. As an educator, he conceived of his mission to impart both.

All men were not as clever as Schmalenbach. The allure of *Wissenschaft* was so strong in Germany that many lost sight of the fact that academic business economists and engineers were not just scientists, i.e., knowledge seekers, but technologists, i.e., purveyors of purposefulness. Besides, combining the two was not easy since practicality and scientific speculation make difficult bedfellows. Moreover, since education in engineering and in business had traditionally been training in skills *(Kunstlehre)*, the emphasis on science, especially in the beginning, was needed as a counterbalance in order to add an essential element to these studies. Nonetheless, the Germans have managed rather successfully to maintain a homeostasis between *Wissenschaft* and practical purposefulness in their system of engineering and business education.

Although there have been grumblings about the *Fachhochschulen* becoming too theory oriented since the reforms, the real problem, from the standpoint of retaining a balance between *Wissenschaft* and practicality, has been with technical institutes and business schools, for they have been most smitten, and for a longer time, with *Wissenschaft*.[34] In the technical institutes, this ability to keep their feet on the ground has been obtained by a continual close cooperation with industry. Men in *Praxis* paid close attention to them when they were being developed in the nineteenth century. As one engineer wrote in 1913:

> While the state scarcely uses the technical institute, except for the education of its construction engineers, German industry fully understands how to make the technical institute serve its purpose by extracting practical profit from its scientific activity. Industry not only gets its technical personnel from the graduates of the technical institutes but also top people for industrial administration. Consequently, industry follows the development of the technical institutes very carefully. It tries, and quite successfully because of industry's representation on the German Commission for Technical Education, to influence the form and content of instruction in technical institutes, and makes sure that institute laboratories undertake research of practical interest by providing the industrial machines and equipment and the wherewithal for the school laboratories to carry out these industrially desirable tasks.[35]

This cooperation, moreover, was expressed quite early by the recruitment, especially from high technology industries, of engineering professors from *Praxis*. This policy of recruitment has been maintained to the present. To do so, the technical institutes have had to deviate from normal university practice. Although a university professor is required to have a *Habilitation* to qualify scientifically for his chair, in engineering this proviso has been constantly ignored. Professors of engineering frequently only have doctorates *(Dr.-Ing.)* and sometimes have no doctorates at all, for what is legally stipulated is a *Habilitation* or its 'equivalent', which has come to mean, for engineering, proof that, while working in industry, the professor has made a contribution through publications and/or the acquisition of patents to the advancement of engineering knowledge.

Members of a common culture, engineering professors and engineers in industry cooperate closely with each other. Working engineers frequently come to professors with their problems, which are often given to students as doctoral projects. Undergraduates, who are required to do industry-related work projects and to spend some months working in industry (the *Praktikum*) during their studies, are also given a practically oriented scientific instruction. The cooperation between industry and technical institutes is as much a part of engineering education as *Wissenschaft*, and it has a long history.

In business economics this cooperation with business and industry has been less successful, especially since World War II. A prolonged effort to create a scientific discipline has led to the business economists in universities and *Hochschulen* to distance themselves from the practical purposiveness that Schmalenbach had set for them after the First World War. The tendency is expressed most straightforwardly in professorial recruitment. Whereas engineering has avoided the *Habilitationsschrift*, business economics, conforming to general university practice, has become a 'discipline of the book', i.e., its professors must do a *Habilitationsschrift* and cannot, routinely, rely on an equivalency to qualify for their posts. Since this qualification requires years of full-time academic study, and business economics has (since 1969) dropped the mandatory *Praktikum* at the undergraduate level, German professors of business economics frequently either do not have any management experience or very little. Inevitably, therefore, they have come to stress the scientific nature of their work in terms of the accumulation of knowledge, knowledge that may or may not be immediately applicable in practice. Just as inevitably perhaps, although individual professors maintain close teaching, consulting, and research contacts with *Praxis* and their students are particularly anxious about *Praxisbezug* (relationship of their studies to business), the relevance of academic German business economics to the workplace has been questioned.

Still it is wise not to exaggerate the estrangement of academic business education in Germany, compared to engineering, from business and industry. This is true in one sense because of the effect that German business economics has had on engineering education. Even before the First World War professors, practising engineers, and government bureaucrats perceived a need to introduce economic subjects into engineering curricula. The concern led to the creation of a special major, that of the *Wirtschafts-Ingenieur* (Economics-*Ingenieur*), established in the technical *Hochschule* (Charlottenburg) in 1921 and to similar programs in other engineering schools subsequently.

VALUES, CULTURE AND EDUCATION

The *Wirtschafts-Ingenieur* study program (which consists of half engineering and half business economics subjects) explicitly recognized the fact that the economic dimension is just as important to the manufacturing business as the purely technical one. The business economics content of the *Wirtschafts-Ingenieur* programs has, to a large extent, been the product of German business schools. It was Willy Prion, a business economist (no engineering degrees), who organized the *Wirtschafts-Ingenieur* program and ran it between the wars, and business economists have continued since that time to hold down chairs in German technical institutes (particularly those teaching *Wirtschafts-Ingenieure*).[36] Moreover the discipline taught has been developed in the business schools where these professors, before they moved to technical schools, got their degrees. Professors of business economics in technical institutes have kept close contacts with their colleagues in business schools. They are members of the same professional associations.

The *Wirtschafts-Ingenieur* is not universally popular. Some feel that the study program is a half-way house between two genuine subjects, that it would be, consequently, better to have students train in engineering or in business economics and not half learn both. Still, the *Wirtschafts-Ingenieur* have been successful in industry. They seem, in fact, since they are trained in engineering schools, to have developed the same close relationship with industry (especially with *Wirtschafts-Ingenieur* working there) that is typical of the engineers in technical *Hochschulen*.

Yet the *Wirtschafts-Ingenieur* program is rather small. It is, moreover, only a shared responsibility of the university-based business economists. To say, therefore, that a good relationship has been established between business economists (working in *Wirtschafts-Ingenieur* programs in engineering schools) does not gainsay the general criticism of German business schools as being *praxisfremd* (divorced from *Praxis*). And it cannot, compared to the engineering schools be gainsaid. But that has not, from the point of view of the practical education of German managers, had a particularly deleterious effect. In order to understand why it is necessary to recall the traditional form and content of business studies in Germany. This education is scientific (in the sense that doctoral theses and *Habilitationsschriften* are research projects for the expansion of knowledge) and specific pre-experience (in the sense that students for first degrees have no managerial experience and are taught functional and/or institutional subjects, e.g., accounting, banking, etc.). Consequently German business schools have never gotten directly involved in the teaching of management to active managers. There are, it was noted, no MBA courses in Germany, no university sponsored post-experience education. From the perspective of *Praxis* this might be seen as a good reason for thinking that German business education has become divorced from the problems and purposes of active managers and that this separation has harmed their education. Such a conclusion, however, depends on how much one thinks the skills as opposed to the knowledge component in management education can or should be learned in a university.

In effect, a homeostasis between *Wissenschaft* and practical purposiveness in German business education is achieved through a division of educational labor. Both academics and active managers recognize the skill dimension of the management function. As Ihno Schneevoigt, Chief of Personnel, IBM Germany, observed, '. . . the young manager needs to know how decisions in a firm are made, how firm operations, . . . how specific planning processes run'.[37] But he added that teaching this is the province of the firm. Post-experience education of managers, management education per se, in Germany, therefore, has been conducted through in-house training or extra-mural non-academic training schools where the programs, like those in-house, are directly responsive to the requirements of their clientele—the business and industrial firms that pay for them. This education permits the firm to teach—to the extent that it is teachable—the management know-how which has nothing to do with science (although scientific knowledge can be of use there), while at the same time leaving to the university business school, in the form of its pre-experience first degree programs, the functional and theoretical background education which the complexity of modern business and industrial management increasingly requires of its new employees.

All students in German business schools specialize and most major in traditional subjects (accounting, marketing, finance, banking, insurance, etc.). All students, moreover, get a good theoretical knowledge of statistics, EDP, micro-economics and macro-economics. The significance of the technical factor for business management, moreover, is not ignored. Although business schools make a valuable contribution in this respect to the technical institutes, they also include technical and engineering subjects in their own programs. Indeed sometimes they are mandatorily required of business students. At Stuttgart University, for example, 20 percent of the courses taken by every student in business economics (regardless of whether he intends to go into marketing, finance or other non-engineering related fields) must be in technical engineering subjects. Peter Lawrence has observed that the concept of 'management' as a separate subject and 'management' as a separate profession has never taken hold in German industry. 'Germans are much less prone than the Americans . . . to think in terms of "management", in the sense of some phenomenon which can be extrapolated, analyzed and talked about in general terms . . . German managers think about the functionally specific rather than the managerially general.'[38] German education in business economics, because of its functional emphasis, contributes to this practical purposefulness.

Comparative English experience

These, then, are the achievements of the Germans in higher technical and business education and the yardstick against which English experiences can be measured. The key to German education and the chief point upon which to concentrate in an English comparison is the relative balance attained between *Wissenschaft* and practical purposiveness. At the outset it can be stated that English traditions in education did not create this balance. On the contrary, in England, the first industrial country, the university and the business-industrial community always treated each other with indifference if not distrust or hostility. People who needed skilled qualifications to work in business or industry acquired them on-the-job; and people who were admitted into state-recognized professional associations—accountants, engineers, etc.—were trained in the same way. They were apprenticed in factory, workshop, or office for a period of time deemed necessary to learn profession or trade. Not until the late nineteenth century (aɪ ¹ thereafter) did these professional or trade associations even recogniz the importance of any formal written entry examinations. The examinations adopted were, moreover, when they came, quite practical in nature in that they were drafted by working professionals to ascertain the candidate's knowledge of current practice. There was never any suggestion that the body of knowledge examined represent the fruits of scientific discipline or inquiry.

Nor was there any suggestion that people attend a college or university in order to qualify for managerial jobs. In engineering the scientific content of the subject was recognized when the engineering associations, accepting an engineering degree as a partial fulfilment of their entry requirements, waived one of their qualification examinations and shortened the apprenticeship period for degree holders. Nonetheless, the engineering associations overlooked the university educated for decades. As late as 1950 90 percent of those who became mechanical engineers in England were non-university educated, that is, they had studied part-time on-the-job and gained admittance through examination.[39]

Moreover, when the engineering associations eventually accepted the usefulness of a university education, they did so in a purely engineering sense only. As late as 1930, an engineer, Professor Burstall, proposed that business and management courses be added to the engineering curricula at universities. But *The Engineer*, which published Burstall's suggestion, opposed it. 'We have always held,' the editor stated, that apprenticeship or pupilage is an absolutely essential element in the education of an engineer. Indeed, if we had to choose between an extension of the college course and workshop training, we should unhesitatingly select the latter . . . Possibly technical schools and universities might be made more useful to young engineers by the introduction of the subjects Professor Burstall . . . suggests but we do not believe that any amount of college education in them can ever take place of the day-to-day touch which is given by a few years as an apprentice or pupil.[40]

A few months before, the editor of *Mechanical World and Engineering Record*, another spokesman for the engineering associations, had written in a similar vein:

In these days of organised college courses it is well to remember that in the last analysis the leaders in our industry are produced from one source—they are the products of workshops or factories . . . It may be said that they are scientific without being scientists. A list of past presidents of our senior engineering institutions would include many names of distinguished leaders whose unique merit consisted in a highly developed mechanical instinct which was sufficient to guide them to the right point of view on any problem connected with their work. Without anything more than this valuable intuition many of our great engineers of the past would continue to be eminent to these days. A perusal of the correspondence and inquiry columns of engineering journals and the proceedings of institution meetings makes manifest the fact that the real difficulties of engineers are principally those of a practical character.[41]

These professional engineers had not understood that the knowledge essential to engineering could not be acquired on-the-job anymore than, as they correctly observed, the skills necessary to the engineer could be learned in class.

This reticence towards higher education was shared by that other large professional group whose prominence within business management had, since the nineteenth century, been increasing—the accountants. By 1900 students could take accounting courses in some British universities and the availability of such courses augmented as the century progressed. But the accounting societies resented and resisted any incursions into their territory. They had a monopoly that permitted them to decide who could become a recognized accountant and they did not take kindly to those who suggested that accountancy should be learned in universities. A Mr. Paterson expressed this general prejudice before an assembly of Incorporated Accountants in 1911:

I find, and I think it is the experience of all who have carefully examined the cases that came under their notice, that a student who has been in a good office, and who has the natural ability to assimilate what he sees and reads, makes a better accountant than the man who starts off with the halo of a university education (Applause). I think that our method of examination, subject to certain qualifications, is a far better test than even a degree in economics in the Berlin University (Hear, hear!). We get far better results from a practical examination than from one in mere theory.[42]

This sort of resistance continued right up through the Second World War. In 1950, 'the vast majority of accounting students in the British Isles prepared with the aid of correspondence schools' for their

VALUES, CULTURE AND EDUCATION

examinations while working as 'articled' clerks in an accountant's office.[43] And English accountants continued to utter the old clichés about the superiority of apprenticeship and to honor it in practice.[44]

If the men in practice ignored the universities, the men in the universities returned the disdain. English universities were, to use C. P. Snow's famous phrase, beset by two cultures. The first, the older, in the arts and humanities, was cultivated in the English public schools and in Oxbridge. It was not really an education at all, in the academic sense, because knowledge was incidental to its purpose. Rather it was designed to develop the 'leadership qualities' of an elite by bringing teacher and taught together in 'leisure and confidence'. It sought to impart 'effortless grace, casual assurance', and the 'light touch in command', qualities of an essentially esthetic nature which were necessary for the preservation of a primarily landholding leisure class elite's cultured way of life.[45] Although the arts and humanities provided the educational content of the system, its goal was the 'Gentleman-Ideal'.[46] Whereas in Germany universities became centers 'for scholarship and knowledge', at Oxbridge they functioned 'as a nursery for gentlemen, statesmen and administrators'.[47] History, art and languages were not, therefore, subjected in England to the constraints of *Wissenschaft*.

Neither, moreover, were the liberal professions. Universities did not have professional schools; the liberal professions in England were strictly speaking no more part of the system of higher education than the incorporated engineering and accounting associations just mentioned. Like them, the liberal professional groups, with the exception of medicine, evidenced no great interest in scholarship and science, in 'knowledge' as a systematic search for the truth. Their 'knowledge' was a rather esoteric systematized body of received customs and practices which were acquired by the newcomer on-the-job and through independent study for professional qualifying examinations. If they had this in common with all English trading, engineering and merchant associations, the professions, and among them especially the lawyers, had very little else. As Ian Glover explained:

> Britain's economy turned industrial too early and too slowly to get rid of essentially aristocratic attitudes towards occupations and the rise of knowledge for practical ends. Knowledge was to be conspicuously consumed, not used as an input to the development of skill. Hard work was for the lesser breeds. None were keener to make such attitudes their own than the middle-class arrivistes, among whom the new professional occupations must be counted.[48]

Glover's point is that the London-based merchants and overseas traders, who were close to the court and government, sought to adopt aristocratic values and that they did so, educationally, through their attendance at public schools, by embracing the 'Gentleman Ideal'. Professional education, therefore, had just as little to do with science, industry and commerce as Oxbridge education. Both were based on the humanities, the study of which was supposed to form the heart and mind of young men destined to higher, i.e., non-industrial service. Consequently, professional education like university education was blamed for the deplorable state of science during the nineteenth century and the resulting unbridgeable gulf, because of the indifference if not outright hostility of those educated in the humanities toward science and industry, between the two cultures.

However, that second culture, science, if a much more recent addition to English universities, exists. British science is distinguished to a very high degree. And English universities are not only recognized today as scientifically among the more fruitful in Europe but as having been so for some time. The number of British Nobel Prizes won before as well as after World War II is alone sufficient testimony of this achievement.

But science has manifested itself quite differently in English higher education than has *Wissenschaft* in German. To begin with, although economics has long been inside the pale, 'science' has traditionally been restricted in English studies to natural science. More importantly, even though within the English educational system a sharp distinction arose between the arts and sciences, an even greater one emerged between science and vocationalism. This distinction existed in the nineteenth century in German education, too. No group of people had a greater disdain for vocationalism than German university professors. They were engaged in a higher calling, in the non-practical *(zweckfrei)* search for truth, in a value-free environment.[49] Useful knowledge, knowledge that served special interest had no place in *Wissenschaft*. That is why German universities, refusing to accept engineering and business economics as proper scientific subjects, left them originally to fend for themselves and why these subjects were developed originally in special schools *(technische Hochschulen* and *Handelshochschulen)*. This separation from the university but retention within the *Hochschule* system permitted engineering and business economics to develop into a third science, the technologies that Schmalenbach talked about, which combined *Wissenschaft* with practical purposiveness. The English system of higher education tended to ignore this third science. English universities accepted one of its components as 'applied science'. It was classified under the science part of the *arts* and *sciences* knowledge division, and accorded, as Peter Lawrence wrote of engineering, '. . . a junior, dependent and subordinate status under the aegis of science'.[50] The other, the practical purposiveness part of the 'third science', was ignored and hence left to shift for itself outside the university.

There is no doubt that engineering, compared to the 'pure sciences', has accordingly been poorly treated in English higher education. And there is no doubt that business economics has suffered at the hands of economics an even worse fate. In 1902 the newly appointed economist

VALUES, CULTURE AND EDUCATION

in London, Edwin Cannan, '. . . argued that the practical usefulness of economic theory was not in private business but in politics'.[51] At Cambridge, where mathematics had become an entrenched discipline, analysis and the search for the fundamental economic tenets, rather than the interpretation of facts, fascinated economists. In Germany academic business economists before World War II had borrowed heavily from economic theory to develop a management accounting useful to the firm. In Britain marginal analysis was cultivated in economics but the will to apply it to business problems was missing. English economists considered these problems, as one scholar wrote in 1937, '. . . to be the domain of second rate minds, incapable of aspiring to the scholarly economist's highest level of activity: the development and perfection of the classic theory and the theory of distribution'.[52] Such sentiments left very little place in universities for business and management sciences, even less than that afforded engineering.

Consequently, engineering and business (commercial) studies experienced a very different fate from the German. Although Cambridge and Oxford established chairs in engineering (but at Oxford not until 1907), the numbers involved were ludicrously small. Indeed at Oxbridge even the natural sciences were neglected. Between 1880 and 1900 only 56 students at both universities received a Bachelor of Science (B.Sc.) honors degree. Numbers, moreover, speak rather eloquently for the position of engineering studies even in the famous Redbricks, the civic universities. There were only 1,129 students of engineering in all the universities of England and Wales in 1913—at a time when there were ten times that many in the German technical institutes.[53] Between the wars the total output of graduate engineers in Britain was comparatively small (9,997). German technical institutes alone had twice as many students in 1923 as British universities had graduates in engineering between 1925 and 1939.[54] And this leaves out the large number of students in German universities, particularly in chemistry, who, between the wars, were studying technological subjects.

The form and content of English engineering studies were also quite modestly developed compared to the German. The failure of engineers to take much interest in business economics has been noted. No *Wirtschafts-Ingenieure* programs were started in Britain before the Second World War (indeed none was started until five years ago, i.e., 50 years after the program started in Berlin). The English engineering student studied for a much shorter period of time as an undergraudate than did the German. As for graduate studies, they were almost non-existent in England. The last point is important because a graduate degree program is essential to an academic discipline's deep involvement research. No one suggests that the professors and students in English universities were incompetent, but the form and content of

English studies before the Second World War were certainly, by German standards, insufficiently research directed.

The state of business or commercial education was even worse. At Oxford and Cambridge, because of the 'vocational' bias, no commercial subjects were taught, including accounting. Accounting courses were provided in civic universities where, in a few, undergraduate degrees in commerce could also be obtained. But the numbers involved were small and graduate research degrees were non-existent. The content of the commerce degree programs, moreover, was not on a par with the German. To develop, business economics needed to be wedded to theoretical economics. But the historical school of economics, from which business studies could profit least methodologically, flourished at the civic universities. The London School of Economics did move in the right direction in the 1930s. During a reorganization of the school in 1932, a graduate section on commercial education was added. This department's research goal was, in part, '. . . to find and perfect the methods of economic analysis that were susceptible of being used' on practical business problems and 'to let theoretical analysis guide and at the same time be guided by practical studies'.[55]

The results were encouraging, but they came too late and in too limited an institutional scope to alter significantly the nature of commercial studies in England before the war.

The failure to develop higher education in engineering and business economics left England almost as a beginner as the country faced the difficult problems of reconstruction and development after World War II. It is not necessary to catalogue fully the great strides that higher education has made in both fields since the war. In engineering a growing sense of technological inferiority has prompted great expenditures on higher education.

The organization of the great centers of science and technology at Manchester and Strathclyde and the expansion of Imperial College London, the development of Churchill College, Cambridge, and the creation of some, if less renowned, nonetheless, excellent universities of technology elsewhere testify to this preoccupation.

In business studies the changes have been even more radical. When the British set out after the war to establish a system of management education, they were not, because of an absence of tradition, burdened like the Germans by the past. Since they did not have a qualified corps of professors or well-defined programs, and inasmuch as their rich ally was eager to help, they sent scores of students (partially with financial aid from affluent American foundations) and experts to study in and to study American business schools. These students and experts brought management sciences, imbibed in America, back to the newly created or renovated business schools where they (the students and experts) ensconced themselves in professors' chairs. The British also invited American academics and management education experts into their schools. English business study programs, in their actual content, greatly resemble the American.

The limits to American influence, therefore, have come primarily from the continuing influence of those English business and academic traditions that had stymied the development of business education in the first place. In effect, immediately after the war, despite the urgency of reconstruction, the English university community resisted change. The consequence, for the period up to 1960, was as follows: little undergraduate education in business took place in universities. Business helped organize post-experience education for its own managers, either in-house, or by sending them to non-university institutions (like the Henley Staff College). Pre-experience education in management sciences was done in public sector institutions. These institutions (colleges of technology, colleges of commerce, etc.) had a long educational tradition—in the education of working and lower middle class children, primarily in technical and commercial subjects, at the sub-university level. These public sector institutions created, then, the Diplomas in Management Studies (DMS) and the ordinary and higher national certificates and diplomas (ONC, OND, HNC, HND) which so many English managers possess today.

Since 1960, higher education in business and management has expanded rapidly in Britain. Nonetheless during the expansion the anti-vocational prejudices of the university and the anti-intellectualism of the business community affected the emerging system. Both have, in effect, been expressed in the way the system has expanded. English universities, even after 1960, have continued to question the intellectual validity of business studies. A comparatively small number of students, until quite recently, graduated in management and business (as late as 1975 they numbered for all universities in the hundreds).[56] The recent enrolment increases, moreover, do not necessarily prove that this intellectual snobbery about business studies has been abandoned, for the least academically qualified secondary school leavers have opted for university business study programs.[57]

Although its institutions had been in sub-university education for a long time, the public sector's entry into higher education occurred in the 1960s, when the newly established Council for National Academic Awards (CNAA), a uniquely degree granting but not a teaching agency, began to award degrees to people who studied in the public sector. Public sector institutions, therefore, unlike the universities, were not empowered to grant degrees, but only to provide the courses, subject to approval by the CNAA, which led to the CNAA degrees. The fact that so much of the post-1960 degree work has been in public sector CNAA-sanctioned courses (especially in the newly organized polytechnics) has probably reinforced the university's anti-business penchant. Questions were raised about the value of the CNAA as opposed to a university degree. They were supposed to be equivalent. Since, however, the first degree students in the public sector were frequently people who failed to gain entry into university, and those who taught them lacked the academic qualifications of university instructors, equivalency was much in doubt.[58]

University skepticism, moreover, has been enhanced by the fact that the public sector education has been subjected to the influence of the particularly virulent deep-seated anti-intellectualism of English business and industry. By their origin as trade schools, public sector institutions were and are vocational in spirit, tuned to the mundane needs of business and industry. Public sector funding, moreover, is provided by local and regional governmental authorities, which represent business and industrial interests to a great extent, and whose generosity is conditioned by the 'usefulness' of the education. Practicality has, therefore, been the hallmark of public sector education. Professors are often drawn from practice and are not, from the university's viewpoint, particularly well qualified. Teaching, not research, is their business. This teaching, moreover, is done to a large extent on-the-job. All CNAA first degree business study programs are organized on a sandwich principal, i.e., with periods of study alternating with periods of work in a business or industrial firm.[59] The entire educational procedure in the public sector reflects that deep conviction in English business education that experience is the best teacher.

The emphasis on practicality and experience, moreover, has influenced English graduate education. Much, if not most, graduate education in business and management studies takes place in the business schools. English business schools, at least many of them, including the most prestigious (London, Manchester, Cranfield, Henley, etc.) are not, although technically classified as such, 'normal' university institutions. Much of their funding must, unlike that of other university departments, be earned from outside sources, i.e., from services rendered to and paid for by governmental and business organizations. The English business schools, therefore, are not, like the German, isolated from the outside world. The financial independence, which permits the German professors to develop their disciplines according to the canons of *Wissenschaft*, does not exist in the English business school, and there is a dark suspicion that this is the case because the rest of the English university scientific community does not think business studies are indeed respectable *Wissenschaft*.

English business schools, therefore, have not developed into traditional academic institutions. Their professors do not have the 'scientific' qualification, many not possessing PhDs. Their publications are skimpy (both in bulk and content). Often, for certain fields like accounting, professors have the professional qualification (which

VALUES, CULTURE AND EDUCATION

satisfies the demands of a powerful professional association, e.g., Chartered Accountants) rather than the PhD (which satisfies those of science). The English business school has followed the educational precepts of the American business school, with its stress on short term post-experience and MBA courses.

This practical emphasis, moreover, seems to have been the unavoidable consequence of the influence that business and industry have had on the business schools. It is poignant to observe how business school professors downplay their academic interests and qualifications when approaching *Praxis*. What a contrast to German professors of business economics who insist that their discipline, as *Wissenschaft*, has much to offer business and industry. It is even more poignant to see, despite these efforts in England, how unsuccessful the schools have been. Their relative failure is expressed in the difficulties English business schools have had with enrolments. Although approximately 75,000 new managers join British business and industry yearly, the business schools have not managed to educate many of them. At a time when 40,000 MBAs graduate yearly in America, only 800 emerge from British business schools, and a large percentage of them (40) find employment in American or other non-British owned firms (in Britain).[60] English business schools might have tried to find a home in the halfway house between the practical world and academia, but they have not, because of the traditional antagonism between them, been particularly successful.

THE EFFECT WHICH THE HISTORICAL INTERRELATION
BETWEEN HIGHER EDUCATION AND MANAGEMENT HAD, HAS,
AND PERHAPS WILL HAVE ON MANAGERIAL PERFORMANCE IN
EACH COUNTRY

We are ready to confront the difficult problem of the relationship between higher education and managerial performance, past, present, and future (?) in Germany and Britain. Before looking at this relationship, however, something has to be said about the other variable, managerial performance. It is not a question here of measuring, according to some general scheme, how individual managers or groups of managers perform. Managers work in organizations. It is organizational efficiency, specifically managerial effectiveness expressed through organizational efficiency, an efficiency obtained within an historically evolving international organizational context which is to be clarified.

Organizational evolution has been quite complex. This has been less true perhaps at the factory level. Although factory unit size has increased, and, consequently, factory organization size, too, the greatest managerial changes have occurred at the corporate level. Alfred D. Chandler, Jr., in his influential *Strategy and Structures*, first drew attention to how the corporation model emerged, in America, beginning shortly after the First World War, from the dominant product, functionally organized corporation which had, itself, emerged, c. 1900, from the simpler business and industrial organizations of the nineteenth century.[61] Chandler argues that American capitalists in a changing technical world, with new marketing strategies to match new technologies and products, set out to create and created the corporate structure necessary to their strategy. Their corporate success, therefore, had resulted not from conquest of monopoly power but from the creation of more efficient enterprises by more efficient managerial structures and methods. Professor John Child explains:

> With diversification the number of co-ordinating and communication linkages . . . increases more than proportionally. The divisional structures 'uncouples' some of these linkages by building new subsystems (divisions) composed of units which have intense interaction around common product or geographical needs, and by reducing the number of other links needed to connect one subsystem to others. Broadly speaking, it has been found that . . . firms which match their organization structures to their strategies tend to perform somewhat better than those which do not make this match.[62]

In the late 1960s and early 1970s this corporate structural change was considered to be one key to managerial efficiency.

From a purely knowledge-skill capability viewpoint, management at the top had to differ from management at operational levels. Derek Channon, in his study of British enterprise pointed out that 'the widespread adoption of a strategy of diversification and a multi-divisional organization highlighted the need for a large number of general managers without which the potential advantages offered by strategic and structural change would be lost'.[63] There has, of course, been considerable difference of opinion over the years about the management skill appropriate to top corporate staffs. In 1980 two Harvard University professors, Hays and Abernathy, questioned, in particular, those which American top management had. 'Since the mid 1950s,' they observed,

> there has been a rather substantial increase in the percentage of new company presidents whose primary interests and expertise lie in financial and legal areas and not in production . . . High level American executives come and go . . . Top management posts are filled from the outside . . . The business community . . . has developed a preoccupation with a false and shallow concept of the professional manager, a 'pseudo-professional' really, an individual having no special expertise . . . [64]

This is an interesting indictment of American top corporate management. It is echoed, moreover, by recurrent attacks on the faddish, cookbook recipe nature of management policies—Return on Investment, Market Share, Portfolio Diversification—which at one time or another were used, almost exclusively, as yardsticks with which to measure performance and often did more harm than good. The current emphasis on product design and production, on engineering, on disinvestment, on in-house recruitment of top men, is an attempt to correct the superficiality of an MBA generalist approach to corporate management which Hays and Abernathy think has got American industry into some trouble. But the new emphasis does not deny the need for top corporate management to be engaged in general policy formulation, strategic planning, etc.—functions essentially different, and requiring different knowledge and skills, from those of managers concerned with daily operations. One factor to be considered, when evaluating the impact of the educational system on German and British entrepreneurial performance, is, therefore, its ability to provide the expertise necessary to the tasks of the headquarters' staffs.

A second factor, however, is operational level middle and lower management skills. Although they are more customary, i.e., traditional, functional specific skills (accounting, marketing, etc.) which are needed for the planning and control of everyday operations, they are nonetheless essential to successful management. The individual expression of these skills—indeed the ability to express them most fruitfully—depends on the organizational structure and culture at operational as much as it does at corporate levels, and that organizational structure and culture itself depends on the educational culture's ability to affect the operational organization milieu as well as to teach specific skills to individuals. This discussion of the relative impact of higher education on entrepreneurial performance in Britain and Germany, will, therefore, focus on both corporate and operational management.

(a) CORPORATE LEVEL

Stacks of books have been written about the anti-business, anti-industrial character of the English educational system. The Oxbridge predominance in the corporate boardroom, the public school man in the City, the imbalance between classical and science education, the 'Gentleman-Ideal'—all and more have been cited as examples of an educational tradition inimical to British business and industry. But, as noted in the first part of this paper, British higher education has conformed, just like British business and industry, more thoroughly than German to new corporate structures emanating from America. The presence of post-experience and MBA programs in British business schools and their absence in German testify sufficiently to this fact.

Moreover, these parallel developments in business, industry, and education seem to interrelate and reinforce each other. German management appears to be weak in the particular skills—strategic financial and corporate planning, marketing, portfolio analysis—needed by headquarters' staffs in the large multinational, multidivisional corporations. At least this was the conclusion reached by an American consultancy firm—Booz, Allen, and Hamilton—a decade ago in its report to a German government agency on the state of

German management.[65] Whereas the German emphasis on pre-experience, functional engineering and business sciences was considered to be responsible in the 1960s, at least in part, for the failure of German corporate managers to adopt 'superior' (i.e., American) management methods, German managers were praised for being production oriented, for their failure to succumb to the 'generalist' approach to management, for their thorough knowledge of the functions within the firms (that they had learned during years spent in various departments before being promoted up the hierarchy to command). British corporations, by contrast, are notorious for the paucity of production and design engineers among their directors and headquarters' staff. German engineering education, with its high standard knowledge-skill combination seems to be responsible for the large percentage of engineers in German corporate management; British engineering education, by contrast, with its neglect of formal in favor of practical education, particularly in production engineering, has not helped the cause of engineering in the boardrooms.

Nonetheless, judgments about the effectiveness of German and British business education are, from the corporate headquarters' perspective, quite different. A member of the board of a major German corporation complained recently about the failure of German academic business economics to be of much assistance in strategic planning.[66] This firm, when it turned outside for advice, relied on American-based management consultancy agencies (McKinsey and BCG) and Harvard, IMEDE, and INSEAD professors. Professors in top British business schools, compared to German, would be similarly useful. No doubt the *Wissenschaft* tradition is responsible to a large extent for this estrangement between German BWL and *Praxis*, for it has deprived German professors of the contacts which are essential for them to understand realistically and deal effectively with the problems of German corporation executives.

The relative reluctancy, compared to the British, of German firms to adopt multi-national, multi-divisional corporate forms might also confirm this judgment about the relationship between corporation management and education. Of the two countries, the one that has converged on the postwar American corporate model most completely is Britain. The 1973 study by Sauvant and Mennis proves this most graphically. The authors note that:

relatively recent and accurate data are available on the distribution of MNC (multinational corporation) headquarters. In 1968–69, 7,276 corporations in the United States and 14 West European countries had affiliates in one or more foreign countries. The United States alone is the home country of 2,468 or 34 percent of all MNCs; Britain, West Germany, France and Switzerland account for 3,631 or 50 percent.[67]

If the United States outdistanced the European countries, within Europe, as the following tables show, Britain outdistanced West

Germany even more; and when the comparative size of the British and West German economies is considered this disparity is even greater.[68] Moreover, not only does German business invest directly abroad to nowhere near the extent of the British, but the same evidence also indicates that this German investment is not taking place in a divisionalized structure. It is obvious, since the amount of German direct foreign investment (production of foreign affiliates, third column in the table in footnote 68) is not going into production but '. . . into the expansion of foreign distribution networks. For instance, the three major West German chemical companies maintain about 80–90 percent of their affiliates abroad solely for the purpose of distribution'.[69] This amounts to an expansion of a functional department not true divisionalization.

Distribution of Parent Corporations and Their Affiliates by Home Countries (1968–69)

Home Countries	Number of Parent Corporations	Percentage
United States	2,468	33.9
United Kingdom	1,692	23.3
Federal Republic of Germany	954	13.1

Size of Parent Corporations by Home Country and Affiliate Network

Home Country	1 Country	Number of Parent Companies with Affiliates In			Total
		2–9 Countries	10–19 Countries	More than 20	
United States	1,228	949	216	75	2,468
United Kingdom	725	805	108	50	1,692
Fed. Republic of Germany	448	452	43	11	954

Of course, different German and British corporate structural evolution might be accounted for by factors that have little to do with education (e.g., different markets, different product lines, in each country's economies). Moreover, even if the importance of the educational factor is admitted, it might be an effect, more than a cause of corporate structural change, i.e., the educational systems respond differently to the different managerial requirements of the British and German corporate structure. Usually, however, there is a reciprocal effect between educational and corporate institutions in the sense that the corporate leaders get the education they want, but the education they want has a lot to do with the education they got. Accordingly, the fact that German corporate managers 'think', as Peter Lawrence has noted, 'about the functionally specific rather than the managerially general', much more than the American or British probably has much to do with the fact that German business education has been, more than the American or British, devoted to the education of functional specialists rather than to the development of generalist management skills. To the extent, therefore, that English traditions in higher education—in this case the absence of one in business education—have enabled the British to establish the educational forms necessary to promote the management required to develop in the multi-national, multi-divisional corporate structure, and the German traditions—because of their perpetuation of older business school forms quite different from American ones—have not, and to the extent that the development of the new management corporate structure has increased the efficiency of top management to deal with strategic and long range planning, the British achievement in higher education has been more pertinent to top management needs than the German.

(b) THE OPERATIONAL LEVEL

Studies of German and British management reveal considerable differences at the operational level. These differences need to be explored before the educational traditions can be evaluated in terms of operations management. One very perceptive piece of research, done some years ago by Maurice, Sorge, and Warner, will be used for this purpose.[70] This study compared British, French, and German firms, paired and matched according to size and production type, that faced nearly identical problems. The researchers drew up a scheme of the operational managerial hierarchy as follows:

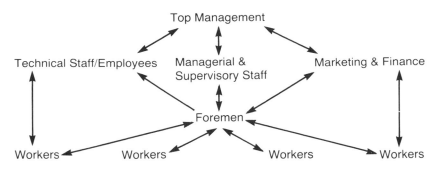

Fig. 1. The operational managerial hierarchy.

And they evaluated the management hierarchy in the firms in terms of three blocks of variables:
1. *The configuration of the organization;* breakdown of the labour force into categories as shown in the hierarchy (above), and numerical ratios between the sizes of components, as well as sizes relative to the total workforce.
2. The joining of individual tasks into work positions, and the coordination of work activities; this could be called *work structuring and coordination.*

VALUES, CULTURE AND EDUCATION

3. The acquisition of qualifications and competence, and the progression of individuals within typical careers; these constitute the *qualification and career systems*.

Comparisons under the first category showed that, although in every branch of technology (unit production, large batch/mass production, continuous process production) the German work units were substantially larger than the British (and hence should be more bureaucratic); staff size was larger in the British than the German units (see following chart).

		Germany	Britain
=Percentage of foremen in works	Unit production	4.0	5.7
	Large batch/mass production	3.5	3.8
	Continuous process production	15.8	16.5
=Percentage of managerial & supervisory staff in works	Unit production	28.8	21.6
	Large batch/mass production	(no data available)	
	Continuous process production	37.4	25.5
=Percentage of technical staff employees/works	Unit production	25.0	39.9
	Large batch/mass production	2.3	6.5
	Continuous process production	11.3	16.7

Maurice, Sorge, and Warner, p. 69, 1980.

Although these statistics show that the German staff was smaller than the British in relationship to the line, this was not always the case. German managerial and supervisory staff was larger than British but British technical staff larger than German. These differences indicate that German managerial hierarchies in the firms were not as tall as British but German managers' span of control was much greater. If we think of technical staff as an advisory function, moreover, the line dominated the staff in German factories even more.

Work structuring and coordination, the second variable, also differed. The *flexibility* and *cooperation* between different production jobs were greater in Germany than in Britain; the differentiation between the function of production and maintenance was sharpest in Britain. Both sets of activities were clearly separated in the latter country and workers rarely crossed over from one area into another. Indeed, on the British shop floor, supervisory activities were dominated by the technical services. German foremen, on the other hand, were freer to detail workers to other jobs during a shift. German production workers often did easy repair and maintenance jobs themselves (thereby eliminating the necessity to call in technical services). In other words, the style of work and management differed in German from British factories.

The third variable was the qualification and career systems. The flatter an organizational structure, the greater the spans of control, and the more, as John Childs noted, 'the competence of manager and subordinates' needs to rise.[71] Hence the style of work, i.e., the nature of individual tasks, was not only different in the British and German factories but the skills were, too, i.e., the German managers being much broader in scope and of a higher technical quality than the British. Greater skill permitted production workers in German factories to cross over to maintenance and production managers to become part of technical staff at some point in their careers and vice versa. Style and skill, therefore, had considerable influence on the structures of these firms. German firms were not as tall as British and were less formal. The border between line and technical expert in Germany tended to disappear; in Britain it was quite pronounced.

The Maurice, Sorge and Warner study ignored marketing and finance managers. Fortunately, a study by Turnbull et al. gives us some insight into how British and German managers worked in marketing at operational levels. The study is based on interviews of 800 marketing and purchasing agents in six countries. Each interviewee was asked about the marketing and purchasing experience he had had with firms in the other five countries. British firms were rated poor in meeting delivery deadlines (which requires close cooperation between production and marketing), and in offering new technology to their customers (which requires close cooperation between research and marketing), etc. The British were, in fact, at or near the bottom and the Germans almost at or near the top (second only to the Swedes) in every category judged. The investigators explained:

> The market staff in German companies have an exceptionally high reputation, not only for their technical competence but also for their commerce ability. In technical matters, the German suppliers are found to be innovative and at the forefront of development. They stress technical excellence and high quality, rather than emphasizing price . . . They keep buyers informed of developments and follow up on product application in customer firms. Their export experience has given them a very sound knowledge of how foreign firms operate . . . They are outstanding in speed and punctuality of deliveries.[72]

This statement reinforces that of Maurice, Sorge and Warner about the high technical competence of Germans.

These investigations show, therefore, that the German and British organizational structures and systems differed, when they did, because of a contrast in shared values. Peter Lawrence asserts that

> Germans do not counterpose thought and action, intellectual ability and practical prowess, engineering knowledge and commercial aptitude, inventiveness and profit, professions and non-professions, detailed knowledge and 'the overall view', line and staff, production and maintenance, or work and style.[73]

Lawrence makes this statement because he obviously feels that the English do counterpose 'thought and action, intellectual ability and practical prowess . . .' and because he believes that their view of reality had a lot to do, compared to the German, with the poorer performance of the British operational unit.

Two points can be stressed here. First, although more comparative studies are needed, there is no reason to believe that those just examined are incorrect. They indicate that the German managers are not only better qualified but that they operate within a more flexible and effective organizational structure which is itself a reflection of the nature of their qualification. Secondly, these distinctions between German and British operational management cultures seem to be nourished by the very different educational cultures described in the initial section of this chapter.

The connection can be perceived by looking at the educational backgrounds of German and British managers. In a 1976 survey of its members (4,525 questionnaires answered out of 10,000 mailed), the British Institute of Management (BIM) discovered that 42 percent of the membership did not even have two 'O' level secondary school certificates. One German survey in 1973, which looked at management from the foreman level to board level, shows that 19 percent of the managers did not have the *mittlere Reife* (the German 'O' level equivalent).[74] The BIM study, moreover, revealed that 55 percent of British managers did not have two 'A' levels. More German managers had the *Abitur* (secondary school advanced level certificate). Since the German *Abitur* (until very recently) required four 'A' level examination subjects, more German managers had passed more 'A' level subjects than British.

The secondary education of German managers, therefore, seems to be much better than the British. This has probably resulted in the better communication and information gathering skills that were noted in the Turnbull et al. study of marketing and purchasing agents. British managers are notorious for their poor language knowledge. A German canvass of 6,490 managers in 45 German corporations, employees having the rank at least of 'Meister' (foreman) or 'Gruppenleiter' (supervisor), showed that 72 percent of them had 'language competence' at least in English, and 26 percent at least in French.[75] Inasmuch as foreign language study is an integral part of the German system, a good secondary school education certainly provided the German managers with a basic foreign language skill that British managers are notorious because of a deficient education, for being without.

A comparison of the post-secondary but sub-first-degree educational level of German and British managers leads to similar conclusions. The BIM survey of its members shows that 27 percent of British managers had Higher National Certificates (HNC) or Higher National Diplomas (HND) and that 36 percent had acquired the Diploma in Management Studies (DMS) or its equivalent. German management surveys do not look very closely at the subdegree education of German managers, but when they do they show that those with diplomas from Higher technical or business schools (now *Fachhochschulen* but formerly *hoherere technische- und Handels-schulen*) were certainly no greater in relative numbers than the certificate and diploma holders from British colleges and polytechnics. But this numerical equality does not mean that these managers had equivalent subdegree level educations. As noted, the people studying for the HNC, HND, or DMS do not and did not need to have secondary school qualifications on a par with those required by *Fachhochschulen*. The *Fachhochschule* entry '. . . in British terms would be somewhere between GCE "O" and "A" levels, probably closer to "A" levels'.[76] Of course, this requirement has been set higher recently; nonetheless, in the past a *mitteler Reife* ('O' level) requirement (plus a completed apprenticeship) was still the standard. In Britain entry into HNC, HND, and DMS courses is open to 'practical' men (people not just without degrees but without 'A' level secondary school qualifications). Moreover, people in *Fachhochschulen* study full-time for three years (a minimum); those in Britain study two years part-time for the HNC, two years full-time for the HND, and six months to one year full-time for the DMS. This signifies less that the British managers have received a greater 'practical' education than the German (since the German *Fachhochschule* education is quite practical and requires a student work period) than that the balance between science and practical purposiveness, which has always been the hallmark of the German educational system, has been achieved to a greater extent by the Germans in their subdegree education of managers.

The story at the degree level is again much the same. Many more educational profiles have been made of German than British managers. They show a marked presence of university graduates in German management, anywhere between 50 and 78 percent.[77] These results compare favourably with the British. One comparative survey of corporation executives, for example, registers 40 percent British with university degrees compared to 78 German.[78] Since the number of university degree holders is significantly less in the management of smaller family-owned enterprises and in the lower and middle management levels of larger ones, these figures exaggerate the presence of university graduates among German managers. Profiles of German managers which include a broader spectrum of management and companies reduce the share of university graduates to, according to the survey, between 30 and 35 percent. The BIM survey recorded the number of first degree holders in its membership at 28 percent. Although this survey probably exaggerates the number of graduates in British management, and their appearance in strength, in any event, is much more recent in Britain than in Germany (Hartmann's 1954 survey shows, for example, that 31 percent of German managers had university degrees) this 28 percent compares favourably with the German.[79]

Still these degrees are not really comparable. First degree studies in England are of a much shorter duration (three years compared to at least four and usually five or six) in Germany. The difference in duration alone has prompted Germans to consider their first degrees (*Diplom-Ingenieure, Diplom-Kaufmann*, etc.) to be the equivalent of the British master's degree. Since the systems are different, it is hard to measure degree equivalencies. But there is no doubt that German managers with first degrees, even if the number with such degrees is not much larger at lower and middle management levels than the British, have a greater academic training than their British colleagues.

At the postgraduate degree level, British managers lose out academically to the Germans in qualitative as well as quantitative terms. The BIM survey shows that only eight percent of British managers have higher degrees (MA, MBA, MSc and PhD). Because the statistics presented in the BIM study do not distinguish between postgraduate degrees, they do not indicate how many British managers hold doctorates. Obviously the numbers could not be very large, inasmuch as the combined total, including master's degrees, is only eight percent. When one considers that a survey of top managers in a major industrial region (Rhineland-Westphalia) shows that 61 percent of the members of corporation boards, and other surveys show that half of the degree holders in their manager sample hold doctorates, clearly the extent to which German managers possess doctorates greatly surpasses that to which the British do. If the Germans claim that their first degree is the equivalent of the British master's is allowed, moreover, then the general postgraduate level of education among German managers would be even higher. Since master's programs in Britain are usually not research directed, only the PhD is comparable to the German postgraduate doctorate. The number of German managers with a research-oriented graduate education, therefore, clearly predominates at this level.

These surveys of educational qualifications show the long-term impact of the different academic traditions on the British and German manager. They also show the different type of academic training that these traditions have brought about in the operational management community within each nation. German managers with university degrees have been educated almost exclusively in engineering (about 50 percent), law (about 25 percent), and business economics (about 25 percent). The number with pure science degrees or with arts degrees is insignificant. Among British managers there are more arts and humanities majors, more pure science degrees, fewer degrees in business economics and in law than in Germany. It could be argued, then, that British education has prepared its operational managers less carefully or usefully for technical and business functions because of the impact of the 'Gentleman Ideal' and the 'Pure Science' tradition on the educational structure and values of public schools and ancient universities.

More significantly, the evidence indicates that these educational traditions have directly shaped, for better or for worse, the operational management cultures outlined in the Maurice, Sorge, and Warner, and the Turnbull et al. studies. Because German systems of higher education combined *Wissenschaft* and practical purposiveness, they helped inculcate those shared values that observers, like Lawrence, perceive to be the strength of German operational management. Lawrence believes that the success can be attibuted principally to engineering, since well-educated engineers are to be found at every echelon and in almost every function in German manufacturing. Brinkmann has shown, moreover, that graduate engineers and *graduierter-Ingenieure* (from the *Fachhochschulen*) are employed in sales.[80] This utilization of highly educated engineers or applied scientists in commercial function is an old tradition. Higgins, reporting on the German chemical industry in 1906, observed, after a thorough inspection of German plants:

... We find in the technical departments, chemists engaged as analysts, as research chemists and as technical men. The first class treats the works materials and products, analyses the products of other firms, attempts to detect infringement of patents, etc. The research chemists are under the direction of the finest chemists in Germany, for example, Duisburg and Berthsen. A list of the chemists who have been employed from time to time by these firms shows that the best brains have been attracted. The technical men are concerned with the dyeing properties of the products. In this department, all the dyestuffs of their own and of their rivals are used under all conditions, and thus the properties determined ... The men who do the dye-testing ... are generally university graduates, who come there to be trained as travellers (salesmen) or as technical men. Some go out as representatives all over the world, while others stay at home as super-intendents of different departments ... No industry employs more graduates and no industry is more prosperous. The men gradually rise and occupy the highest positions, whereas a man without a High School (technical institute) or University training finds a difficulty in advancing. A 'good practical man', as the saying goes in England, might discharge his duties all right, but as a rule he cannot suggest improvements, keep in touch with progress through the journals, etc.[81]

The combination of *Wissenschaft* with practical purposiveness in German engineering education, moreover, obviously fosters the disappearance, at the operational level, of the contradiction between 'thought and action', and the ability of German engineering managers to move back and forth between technical staff services and production services, thus blurring the distinction between staff and line and contributing to the task-oriented atmosphere which is also seen to be the strength of German operational management. High technical knowledge at every management echelon, which corresponds to equally high educational preparation, contributes to the ability of

VALUES, CULTURE AND EDUCATION

German managers to exercise larger spans of control, and, hence, to more line than staff managers.

Moreover, the contributions of academic business economists to the shared values extant in operational management must not be overlooked. Much of the German engineers' awareness of commercial and administrative questions comes from this source, either indirectly, through the influence German business schools exercised on German technical schools, or directly through the education received in the business schools proper. The influence of business economics on engineers is expressed most clearly on-the-job in the person of the *Wirtschafts-Ingenieur* who is frequently employed in controller and production functions. And the fact that the technical and salespeople cooperate so well with each other has almost as much to do with the business economist's awareness, through his education, of the technical task, as the engineer's of the commercial. The ability, moreover, of the German managers to produce high quality products at reasonable prices and to deliver them on time has much to do with the adoption, and operation for decades, of efficient, largely business school developed and taught accounting based control systems. Brinkmann's 1967 survey of German firms in Rhineland-Westphalia shows that a higher percentage [from 33 to 56 percent (depending on management level) in factory accounting; from 38 to 46 percent (depending on management level) in auditing] had degrees in economics or business economics.

That a high percentage of German managers, especially at upper levels, posesses postgraduate research doctorates, moreover, certainly helps explain why German management sees no contradiction between inventiveness and profit, and why German firms have succeeded particularly well in high technology manufacturing. Active German managers willingly participate in the work of the technical and scientific community. Peter Lawrence observes that, among German engineers, those with the highest salaries (i.e., those higher in the employment hierarchy and hence those most probably higher in management) are engaged in 'technical-scholarly activities'. He records the following data on the German engineers queried in a survey:

	Entire sample	Highest paid	Engineers with good final examinations
—Percentage with technical publications (books and articles)	30	44	55
—Percentage who give technical talks or lectures 'outside' their firm	36	53	54
—Percentage with patented 'discoveries'	24	37	31

Source: p. 83, Peter A. Lawrence, *Technische Intelligenz und Soziale Theorie*, Munich: Minerva Publikation Saur GmbH, 1981.

It is interesting to observe that there is less difference between engineers with good final examination results and patented discoveries than other engineers who 'patent discoveries'. This indicates that 'good examinations' are not necessarily indicative of technical creativity (especially when the quality of the patented discovery has not been evaluated). Nonetheless, the Lawrence study does confirm the research orientation of engineers in German management. Lawrence has also noted that '. . . technical-scholarly activities are very much commoner among German engineers than among their British colleagues'. No doubt the relative degree of exposure to scientific culture in their systems of education has prompted different patterns of behavior in the managers' active professional careers.

The catalogue of educational-management interrelationships can be repeated for the British with inverse effects. The taller management structures, the shorter spans of management control, the higher proportion of staff to line employees, the dominance of the line by the technical service—all these attributes of the British operational unit, ascertained in comparative factory studies, reflect the contempt of the scientists for the technologist, and the man of knowledge for the man of action, which is ingrained in the English system of higher education. The fact that English top management is composed of accountants and arts graduates rather than engineers, and that it puts profit ahead of inventiveness, must certainly result, at least in part, from an educational system that looks on technologists as narrow-minded specialists incapable of appreciating 'the overall view'.[82] And the fact that British production engineers are not as well educated as German must have something to do with their relative incapacity to unify 'thought and action', 'intellectual ability and practical prowess' on-the-job. All these particular educational features combine with the generally lower educational level of British managers (especially at the middle and lower hierarchic levels) to create the less homogeneous, less flexible British operational organization.

CONCLUSIONS

Because the British provide an education more appropriate to the central staff managerial needs of the multi-national, multi-divisional firm, and the Germans have developed an education more suited to the management of operational units, the benefits and handicaps of the educational traditions are not one-sided. Of the two advantages, however, that of the Germans was and still is the more enviable. In order to understand why this is true, it is necessary to consider the question of adaptability.

Those in the 1960s who espoused the American corporate and top management model, seemed to think that it would not only bring about the desired efficiency in European industry but that its adoption would be relatively easy to accomplish. In effect they seemed to adhere to a culture-free convergence view about organizational and management change. 'The convergence thesis expresses a belief in the workings of the "invisible hand" applied to the diffusion of knowledge. Sooner or later knowledge gets codified, after which diffusion and, hence, convergence, becomes inevitable.'[83] The convergence theory, then, as far as management is concerned, is predicated on the idea that '. . . where problems and the technical means available for solving them are similar, social groups which may differ widely in cultural outlook will find similar ways of tackling them'.[84] The question is, can the transfer of the requisite knowledge, skills, and attitudes be accomplished as easily as the advocates of the culture-free convergence theory believe or is this transformation subject to serious culture specific constraints?

To answer this question, it is necessary, when assessing the culture-free convergence argument to know what is actually being discussed. To clarify the point it is useful to turn to the recent discussions about the excellence of Japanese management, presented, for instance, in the book by Pascale and Athos on *The Art of Japanese Management*.[85] In the book the authors talk about the seven S's of management, three of which are 'hard' and four 'soft'. The hard S's, Strategy, Structure, and Systems, are emphasized in Western business circles. And it is these which people mostly have in mind when they stress convergency. This is obviously true of those who apply the Chandler strategy and structure thesis in Europe. It is also true of most work in the Aston school in Britain. Their research concludes that large organizations adopt pretty much the same sort of bureaucracies everywhere and implement the same type of control systems to police them. But what about the four soft S's, Staff, Skills, Style and Superordinate Goals (Shared Values)?

Pascale and Athos tell us that they give structures and systems life and that 'the tremendous success of many Japanese companies comes through a meticulous attention to the soft S's'.[86] Hence the possibility that one firm could have the same strategies, structures, and systems as another but not do as well, because of the differences in effectiveness of the soft S management methods employed. Moreover, these soft S's are most susceptible to culture-specific influences. Childs and Kieser argue as much in the following passage:

> If it is allowed that both contingencies and cultural factors are likely to assist in the shaping of organization structure and roles, the question arises as to where these two streams of influence fit together. Our data suggest that the cultural factor has more bearing upon modes of individual conduct and interpersonal relationships, and it is precisely at this level that one would expect the products of socialization to be manifested most strongly.[87]

These internalized cultural values can create an entirely different atmosphere in similar structures and systems. Boisat points out, for

example, in his study of Hitachi and English Electric, that employees, sitting in similar organizational structures, look outward into society (e.g., at other job possibilities) in one firm (English Electric) and up the hierarchy in the other, i.e., remain psychologically inside the organization and loyal to it.[88] And David Granick noted, in an article on
'Managerial Incentive Systems', that his study

> points away from the convergency theory of national societies, for it suggests that, even if industrially developed countries should evolve toward some similar socio-economic system whose production units are large bureaucracies, this alone would not make their incentive systems similar and thus might leave quite distinct the activity outputs of the industrial bureaucracies in the different cultures.[89]

This outlook differs from the culture-free convergency theory, then, in that it attributes current business success and predictable future success to deep seated culture-specific consequences which are difficult, if not impossible, to transfer from one country to another. Peter Lawrence's study of *Managers and Management in West Germany* is a book from this camp; for Lawrence attributes German relative success to culture-specific phenomena that are largely alien to British life and hardly, perhaps not even desirably, because of different and cherished national cultural values, transferable to British firms.

The point is that these four soft S's are not only important to managerial efficiency in England and Germany, and that they are culturally rooted in the educational traditions of each country, but that the effect that they have on managerial and organizational adaptability differs at the corporate and the operational level. It is possible that the success of the German firm will depend more than it has in the past on its capacity to diversify into new product lines and penetrate foreign markets, and that success in these respects will require wider adoption of multi-national, multi-divisional corporate structures. Consequently, the German business schools, with their devotion to pre-experience education and *Wissenschaft*, might continue to shirk the task of providing the requisite managerial skill needed by top corporate management. If this happened, the effect on German corporations might not be particularly nefarious. Since the numbers of people in headquarters are relatively few, German firms can have the requisite people trained abroad, train them themselves, or, as they have already done, call upon foreign-trained professors and/or consultants, for advice in strategic planning. Reliance on culturally different foreigners, moreover, should not pose great problems because the expertise required—strategic planning, portfolio analysis, etc.—is of a cognitive nature, easy to learn by people of diverse cultural backgrounds, and, because of its relatively culture-free character, taught much the same way whether in Singapore, London, or Munich. Moreover, if the

VALUES, CULTURE AND EDUCATION

German corporation failed to acquire the marginal skills necessary at the strategic level and suffered, the results might not be too damaging for German industry. The excellence of the traditional functional management–education relationship in Germany promises to make business and industry attractive enterprises on the operational level, even if the operational units are divisions of more skilfully managed foreign headquartered multi-national, multi-divisional firms.

The British have much the greater problem. Although British industry, not German has conformed earliest and more thoroughly to the American multi-divisional, multi-national management model, the economic performance of British industry, compared to German, has been poor: corporate profits, poor labor productivity, declining share of world exports. Moreover, not only do British firms perform worse, but the divisions of American firms in Britain and of British firms overseas (located outside Britain) have greater productivity and profitability than divisions, located in Britain, of British-based firms.[90] There is, therefore, considerable difference between the British and their American and German rivals at the operational level. This indicates that the differences in operational management in Germany and Britain (described in the studies of Maurice, Sorge, and Warner, and in Turnbull et al.) are culture specific in nature and that the capacity of the most expert corporate management to improve the organization and managerial performance of its operating units is limited. It could be argued, therefore, that to the extent that British education has provided the expertise for the British multi-national, multi-divisional firm (i.e., its capacity to diversify more readily into more profitable operations be they overseas), and has not furnished the expertise needed at the operational level, it has prepared the way (and still prepares) for the prosperity of the British headquartered multi-national firm and for the rapid decline of national industry. It could also be argued that the ability of the British to eliminate these operational educational deficiencies is restricted, for the faults, like the virtues of the German system, are embedded in the value systems of the people.

NOTES

1. Although the German doctorate is a necessary step for those who subsequently do the *Habilitation*, the two degrees are of a different order. The *Habilitation* is essentially a degree for those who wish to be a professor in a *Hochschule*. Few people in business or industry, therefore, have the *Habilitation*. Many people in business and industry, on the other hand, have research doctorates.
2. See, Ch. II, 'The Graduate Engineer and Industrial Performance', in Robert R. Locke, *The End of the Practical Man: Entrepreneurship and Higher Education, Germany, France, Britain, 1880 to 1940* (Greenwich, Conn.: JAI Press, 1984).
3. For a reaction of contemporary engineers to reforms see, 'Reform der hoeheren Schulen', *Zeitschrift des Vereins deutscher Ingenieure* (afterwards *ZVDI*) XXXIV:50 (Dec. 15, 1900), p. 651. Also the enthusiastic response in the technical institute,

Charlottenburg, to the Emperor's decrees granting the right to give these degrees is well described in D. Blumenthal, 'Erinnerungen an Slaby', *ZDVI*, IV:9 (May 1, 1913), pp. 204–06.
4. See the *ZVDI* for the period in question.
5. *Table II.1.* Attendance at Technical Institutes

School	Number of students		
	1890	1900	1910
Charlottenburg	1,640	4,343	2,943
Munich	882	2,476	3,062
Darmstadt	318	1,674	1,768
Karlsruhe	571	1,538	1,343
Hannover	580	1,458	1,770
Dresden	403	1,161	1,447
Stuttgart	496	1,034	1,224
Aachen	198	567	916
Brunswick	273	483	663
Danzig	—	—	1,315
Breslau	—	—	117
Total	5,361	14,734	16,568

Source: Deutscher Ausschuss für technisches Schulwesen; *Berichte aus dem Gebiete des technischen Hochschulwesens*, IV (Berlin, 1912), Anlage 2:b.

6. *Table II.2:* VDI Membership

Year	Number of Members
1856	172
1866	1,215
1876	3,212
1886	5,630
1895	10,995
1905	19,581

Source: 'L'Association des Ingénieurs allemands', *Mémoires et comptes rendus des travaux de la société des ingénieurs civils de France* (1906), No. 1, December 22, p. 886.

7. Technical Institutes & Mining Academies in Germany (Number of full-time students)

Year	Number of Students
1914	12,297
1916	2,576
1918	3,036
1920	21.218
1922	27,019
1926	21,762
1928	20,811
1930	22,466

8. See the report of a visiting English team, during the 1920s, on German technical institutes, in which the excellent German facilities are described, in Donald Cardwell (ed.), *Artisan to Graduate. Essays to Commemorate the Foundation in 1824 of the Manchester Mechanics' Institute* (Manchester, 1974).

9. Students' enrollments in West Germany, studying uniquely three subjects—construction, mechanical and electrical engineering—grew as follows:

1949	6,423
1954	9,965
1960/61	20,664
1964/65	25,885

10. See, Ch. IV, 'German Business Economics: The Educational Achievement', in Locke, *The End of the Practical Man* . . .

11. Institut fuer angewandte Wirtschaftswissenschaft, *Die wirtschaftswissenschaftlichen Hochschullehrer an den reichsdeutschen Hochschulen und an der TH. Danzig, Werdegang und Veröffentlichungen* (Stuttgart, 1938).

12. Felix Werner, 'Die Betriebswirtschaftslehre und die Handelshochschulen', in *Zur Entwicklung der Betriebswirtschaftslehre, Festgabe zum siebzigsten Geburtstage von Hofrat Professor Robert Stern* (Berlin, 1925), p. 22.

13. Number derived from issues of the journal of the *Verband deutscher Diplom-Kaufleute*, 1920 to 1929.

14. Statistics on people studying economics in Germany after the war are as follows:

Year	Economics	Business Economics
1949	→ 8,319 ←	
1954	→ 18,229 ←	
1960/61	6,873	11,324
1964/65	11,521	16,240
1972	11,080	25,149
1977/78	14,152	33,570
1981/82	15,819	50,084

15. Kurt Schmaltz, 'The Business Periodicals of Germany', *The Accounting Review*, V (1930), pp. 231–34.

16. Reiew by Schmalenbach of Schär's Allgemeine Handelsbetriebslehre, I (Leipzig, 1911), in *ZfhF*, VI (1911/12), pp. 201–09.

17. Alfred Isaac, 'Neuere Entwicklung und Stand der Industriebetriebslehre', *ZfVDDK*, III:4 (July, 1922), p. 2.

18. Ch. IV, 'German Business Economics: The Theoretical Achievement', in Locke, *The End of the Practical Man* . . .

19. Eugen Schmalenbach, *Dynamic Accounting* (London, 1949). In translators' note, p. 6.

20. 'Betriebswirtschaftslehre, Theorie und Praxis im Streitgespraech', *Die Volkswirt-, Wirtschafts- und Finanz-Zeitung*, Vol. 19, No. 27, July 1965, pp. 1426–28, p. 1428.

21. G. Brinkmann, *Die Ausbildung von Führungskräften für die Wirtschaft* (Cologne, 1967), p. 119.

22. Peter Mertens, 'Der gegenwärtige Stand von Forschung und Lehre in der Betriebswirtschaft', in *Bildung und Wettbewerbsfähigkeit,* Sonderheft 12:81 ZfbF, pp. 40–54.

23. Peter Matthias, *Studien und Berichte: Determinanten des beruflichen Einsatzes hochqualifizierter Arbeitskräfte. Zur Berufssituation von Diplom-Kaufleuten* (Berlin, 1973).

24. They add up to more than 100% because the students could select two subjects for examination.

25. George Turner, 'Vergleich des deutschen Ausbildungssystems mit den Systemen anderer Länder', in *Bildung und Wettbewerbsfähigkeit . . .*, p. 84.

26. For a good description of changes in this field, see Karl-Friedrich Ackermann, 'Hauptströmungen und gegenwaertiger Entwicklungsstand der Personalwirtschaftslehre an den Hochschulen in der Bundesrepublik Deutschland', in Fritz Bisani and Hans Friedrichs, eds., *Das Personalwesen in Europa. Standard und Entwicklung des*

Personalwesens in den einzelnen europäischen Ländern. Part I, Reports from the International Colloquium 13–14 Oct. 1977, Essen, Germany.

27. Norbert Kluge, Ayla Neusel & Ulrich Teichler, *Beispiele praxisorientierten Studiums* (Bonn, 1981), p. 8.
28. Until the late 1960s an obligatory work period was required of all students. It was dropped during the expansion of the 1970s almost everywhere (except Nuremberg). Efforts are being made now to make some sort of *Praktikum* a part of *BWL* studies.
29. Kluge, Neusel & Teichler . . ., p. 11.
30. Peter Lawrence, *Managers and Management in West Germany* (London, 1979), p. 97.
31. Glover, Ian, 'Professionalism and Manufacturing Industry', in Fores and Glover, *Manufacturing and Management* (HMSO, London, 1978), pp. 115–31.
32. *Ibid.,* p. 121.
33. Eugen Schmalenbach, 'Selbstkostenberechnung', *ZfhF,* XIII (1919), pp. 257–99, 321–57, p. 259.
34. Before they became *Fachhochschulen* ten years ago, the higher lower-level technical and commercial schools had a skill rather than a scientific orientation. All their students, as a guarantee of familiarity with workshop and office routine, had been required to complete a formal apprenticeship in a technical or commercial trade before entry and to do a *Praktikum* in business and industry during their studies. Although students in *Fachhochschulen* are still required to do a six months' *Praktikum* in office and factory and their professors, to insure a close acquaintance with *Praxis*, are required, by law, to have at least five years' work experience (and many in fact have more), the apprenticeship proviso has been dropped for entry into both the technical and commercial *Fachhochschulen*. For those who want to keep the *Fachhochschulen* as sanctuaries of practical office and workshop oriented training, the recent changes have been disturbing. Some even claim that the acquisition of *Hochschule* status 'has produced an identity crisis' in the schools. 'On the one hand, the old specific value of the technical and commercial schools as a training center for craftsmen was lost; on the other, the adoption of a research outlook has been only conditionally possible, for it has harmed the schools' traditional relationship with *Praxis*.' It is too early to know if these fears are being justified. Kluge, Neusel & Teichler . . ., p. 11.
35. Quoted in Martin W. Neufeld, 'Die technischen Hochschulen Preussens bei der Beratung des Staatshaushaltsetats für das Etatsjahr 1913', *ZVDDI,* IV (July 1, 1913), p. 323.
36. The number of people studying to be *Wirtschafts-Ingenieure* has never been very large but it has grown steadily, especially since the war, from 689 in 1958, 800 in 1960, 1,515 in 1964, to 2,616 in 1970.
37. Schneevoigt, 'Die Ausbildung der Wirtschaftler aus der Sicht der IBM Deutschland GmbH', in *Bildung und Wettbewerbsfähigkeit*, p. 96.
38. *Managers and Management in West Germany*, . . ., p. 94.
39. Joel E. Gerstel and Stanley Hutton, *Engineers: The Anatomy of a Profession* (London, 1966).
40. *The Engineer,* CXLIX:3884 (June 20, 1930), pp. 689–90.
41. LXXXVI:2238 (Nov. 22, 1929).
42. C. Hewetson Nelson, 'Professional Education', *The Incorporated Accountants' Journal,* XXIII (Oct. 1911), p. 20. Paterson was speaking after a talk given by Nelson during a general discussion.
43. N. H. Stacey, *English Accountancy: A Study in Social and Economic History, 1800–1954* (London, 1954), p. 248.
44. See, Ch. 'The American Challenge', in Locke, *The End of the Practical Man. . .*
45. Gellert, Claudius, *Vergleich des Studiums an englischen und deutschen Universitäten* (Munich: Bayerisches Staatsinstitut für Hochschulforschung und Hochschulplanung, 1983), p. 4.
46. *Ibid.*

---

47. Eric Ashby, *Technology and the Academics* (London, 1948), p. 68.
48. Glover, 'Professionalism and Manufacturing Industry', . . ., p. 125.
49. Gellert, *Vergleich* . . ., p. 26.
50. *Managers and Management in West Germany* . . ., p. 97.
51. Edward Cannan, 'The Practical Usefulness of Economic Theory', presidential address to Section F of the British Association for the Advancement of Science, Belfast, September, 1902, reprinted in R. L. Smyth, ed., *Essays in Economic Method* (London, 1962), p. 188.
52. John Jewkes, 'L'Université de Manchester', in *Cinquantenaire de la Revue d'économie politique,* special number, 1937, pp. 112–13.
53. Donald S. L. Cardwell, *The Organization of Science in England* (London, 1957), p. 129.
54. Michel Sanderson, *The Universities and Industry* (London, 1972).
55. Arnold Plant and Lionel Robbins, 'La London School of Economics', in *Cinquantenaire de la Revue d'économie politique,* special number, 1937, pp. 66–78, p. 76.
56. First Degrees in Business and Management Studies and in Accounting at British Universities

Year	Men	Women	Total
1973–74	568	84	652
1974–75	642	104	746
1975–76	886	131	1,017
1976–77	1,110	173	1,283
1977–78	1,253	283	1,535
1978–79	1,360	329	1,689
1979–80	1,471	419	1,890
1980–81	1,552	544	2,096

University Grants' Committee: *Detail of First Destinations of University Graduates,* 1975–1981. These figures do not include graduates in economics, many of whom would have been in applied economics. Nor are students in combined majors (i.e., business and economics, or business and engineering, etc.) included. Even with them, however, British university graduates compared to German would be very limited in number. There were, for example, more than 50,000 students in BWL and over 15,000 in VWL in West German *Hochschulen* in 1980.

57. Herman Bayer and Peter Lawrence, using statistics published by the Universities Central Council on Admissions, have observed that the top British students in 'A' levels opt for the humanities or pure science. The following table shows, for example, 'The proportion of students admitted to British universities' with good 'A' levels, by field of study, in 1974:

Subject	Proportion of students with good 'A' levels admitted
Top three: (of 13 subjects)	
Medicine	45
Classics	38
Mathematics	36
Bottom three: (of 13 subjects)	
Civil Engineering	12
Mechanical Engineering	11
Business Management	5

Source: Herman Bayer and Peter Lawrence, 'Engineering Education and the Status of Industry', *European Journal of Engineering Education,* 2 (1977), pp. 223–27.

A survey of the career choice of British graduates (the class of 1960), moreover, shows that 50 percent of those that obtained First Class Honors Degrees and one third of those with Upper Seconds wished to ignore business and industry and remain within the university. '. . . There was no question', the investigators observed:

that in terms of preferences the professions and perhaps most seriously of all, management, appealed particularly to the academically less qualified man . . . Key posts in the industrial sectors are for one reason or another distinctly unattractive to those who have shown themselves most able to absorb an intellectual heritage.

Source: R. K. Kelsall, Anne Pool and Annette Kuhn, *Graduates: The Sociology of an Elite* (London: Methuen & Co. Ltd., 1972), p. 85.

58. A recent study of comparable institutions in the University and the Polytechnic sectors shows that research (measured in terms of publications) is much stronger among university academic staff:

Numbers of reported arts and sciences publications
1970–1979

Institution	Arts	Sciences	Institution	Arts	Sciences
Universities					
Bangor	2,161	2,575	Hatfield	209	650
Bath	1,638	2,584	Huddersfield	1,188	589
Belfast	2,445	6,105	Kingston	707	920
Durham	2,720	2,785	Central London	488	664
Kent	1,950	1,590	Oxford	803	672
Leicester	3,077	4,577	Paisley	213	686
Salford	834	4,668	Plymouth	407	1,090
Stirling	1,632	1,455	Sunderland	492	948
Warwick	2,457	2,461	Wales	364	751
York	2,919	1,956	Wolverhampton	406	274
Total	21,833	30,756		5,277	7,244
Percentage	41.5%	58.5%		42.2%	57.8%

Source: W. O. George and B. C. Thomas, 'When the Lines become Blurred', in *Times Higher Educational Supplement*, No. 593, March 16, 1984, p. 13.
Such studies do not, however, answer the question whether the research funding agencies are prejudiced against polytechnic staff as opposed to university and hence discriminate against them. If that were the case then the fewer publications might have little to do with research talents and more to do with institutional snobbism.

59. Witness the controversy in *The Times Higher Educational Supplement* over the failure of the universities to adopt the sandwich style of teaching, leaving it to the polytechnics. The implication in the feud is that the sandwich style is suited more to vocational than scientific instruction, i.e., to polytechnics than universities.

60. See, Ch. 'Management Education in Britain', in Richard Whitley, Alan Thomas and Jane Marveau, *Masters of Business? Business Schools and Business Graduates in Britain and France* (London: Tavistock Publications, 1981).

61. Alfred D. Chandler, Jr., *Strategy and Structure: Chapters in the History of Industrial Enterprise* (Cambridge: The MIT Press, 1962).

62. John Child, *Organization: A Guide to Problems and Practice* (London: Harper and Row, 1977), p. 148.

63. Derek Channon, *The Strategy and Structure of British Enterprise* (London: Macmillan, 1973), p. 227.

64. *Harvard Business Review,* July–August 1980, Vol. 58, No. 4, 67–77, p. 74.

65. Booz, Allen and Hamilton Report, English translation, in 'German Management',

International Studies of Management and Organization, Arts and Science Press Inc. (Spring/Summer 1973).

66. In an interview conducted March 17, 1984, with a man whose name, out of respect for confidentiality, cannot be given.
67. Karl P. Sauvant and Bernard Mennis, 'Corporate Internationalization and German Enterprise, A Social Profile of German Managers and Their Attitudes Regarding the European Community and Future Company Strategies', University of Pennsylvania, The Wharton School, Philadelphia, Penn., 1974, p. 21.
68. 'The available evidence', Sauvant and Mennis pointed out, '. . . suggests that West German business . . . has not reached the degrees of internationalization of other comparable countries.'

The table given below indicates for selected home countries the degree of their internationalization. The first ratio—annual direct investment outflows over GNP—suggests that West Germany, as measured in relation to its economic potential, had been investing abroad during 1965–1979 to the same degree as Britain and the United States. The second ratio—annual outflows over exports—indicates that for West Germany, as compared to other countries, exports are still considerably more important than foreign direct investment. This becomes even clearer if the last ratio—foreign production over exports—is examined. In the case of the United States, foreign production is three and a half times higher than exports, and in the case of Britain one and a half times. In the case of West Germany (and Japan), on the other hand, foreign production is only 15 percent of her exports—a truly significant difference.

The relative significance of foreign direct investment for selected home countries (averages 1965–1969)

Country	FDI[a]/× 100	FDI[a]/× 100	Foreign Production[b]/× 100
	GNP	Export	Exports
United States	0.4	10.3	350
United Kingdom	0.4	3.0	143
France	0.2	2.4	n.a.
Japan	—	—	15
Federal Republic of Germany	0.4	2.0	15

a=Foreign direct investment; annual outflows.
b=Production of foreign affiliates; based on estimates for 1967 only.

69. Sauvant and Mennis . . ., p. 3.
70. Marc Maurice, Arndt Sorge, Malcolm Warner, 'Societal Differences in Organizing Manufacturing Units: A Comparison of France, West Germany, and Great Britain', in *Organization Studies*, I:4 (1980), pp. 59–88.
71. John Child, *Organisation* . . .
72. Peter Turnbull and Malcolm Cunningham, *International Marketing and Purchasing: A Survey among Marketing and Purchasing Executives in Five European Countries* (London: The Macmillan Press Ltd., 1981).
73. *Managers and Management in West Germany* . . ., p. 181.
74. Quoted in Lawrence, *Managers and Management in West Germany* . . ., p. 65.
75. Sauvant and Mennis, p. 21.
76. Lawrence, *Managers and Management in West Germany* . . ., p. 65.
77. Lawrence discusses these many surveys in the chapter 'The Background of German Management', in *Managers and Management in West Germany*.
78. *Ibid.*
79. The BIM survey probably exaggerates the percentage of university graduates because more university graduates are probably in the BIM than are in the British management population in general. Moreover, probably a higher percentage of

university graduates was in the group that returned the BIM questionnaire (45% of those queried) than in the group that did not.

80. G. Brinkman, *Die Ausbildung von Führungskräften für die Wirtschaft* (Cologne, 1967). p. 119.
81. Sydney Higgins, *Dyeing in Germany and America, with a chapter on Colour Production, a Report* (Manchester: The University Press, 1907).
82. As Sword-Isherwood has pointed out, managers with arts and humanities degrees believe:

    that scientific or technical training is in some way narrow and does not fit a person to take general and far sighted decisions. It is less difficult (in their eyes) for the non-technically educated person to take sensible decisions in a technically sophisticated industry without technical knowledge. ['British Management Compared', in Pavitt, Keith, ed., *Technical Innovation and British Economic Performance* (London: The Macmillan Press Ltd., 1980), p. 89]

    The old two-cultures conflict, therefore, is projected into corporate management to its detriment.
83. M. Boisot, 'Convergence Revisited: The Codification and Diffusion of Knowledge in a British and Japanese Firm', *Journal of Management Studies*, XX:2 (April 1983), p. 188.
84. *Ibid.,* p. 159.
85. Richard T. Pascale and Anthony G. Athos, *The Art of Japanese Management* (New York: Warner Books, 1981).
86. *Ibid.,* p. 1.
87. John Child and Alfred Kieser, 'Organizational and Managerial Roles in British and West German Companies: an Examination of the Culture-Free Thesis', in Lammers, *Organizations Alike & Unlike* (London: Routledge and Kegan, 1979), pp. 251–71.
88. Boisot, 'Convergence Revisited . . .'
89. David Granick, 'Managerial Incentive Systems and Organizational Theory', in Lammers, *Organizations Alike & Unlike . . .*, pp. 76–96.
90. Michael Edwardes, 'British Industry and Industry in Britain', in Fores and Glover, *Manufacturing and Management . . .*, pp. 9–23.

PART IV

Cross-cultural management in the 1980s

An epilogue is necessary in a book with such diversity as this one. We feel, strongly, that this diversity will serve to stimulate further work in the area of managing in different cultures. All people start out as equal members of the human race; however, climate, traditions, and many other factors are often the background for different management behaviors. A well-placed hand shake, smile or word may make a critical difference in attempting to manage in the framework of another culture. It all depends on . . . And that's why we hope you found the book interesting!

CHAPTER 11

Epilogue

Malcolm Warner

INTRODUCTION

It is a testament to the term 'culture' that it continues to dominate the debate about managing in different national contexts. The literature in which 'culture' is used as an organizing concept is clearly now so extensive that its hegemony (at least of usage) is apparent, even though the weight of findings which claim to show its influence is exaggerated, grows constantly. Why is the former still true, and the latter also the case?

I shall *first* look at the contributions to the present volume, and *second* compare the diversity of the approaches with some now classic cross-national studies in the field.

THE DIVERSITY OF APPROACHES

This paradox may be explained by several factors. First, the term 'culture' trips from the tongue rather easily; it is linguistically facile. Next, the concept appears to have 'a common sense' justification. Third, it is a catch-all term, which has proved to be useful when other casual factors have not been offered as explanations.

The anecdotal basis of studies of comparative management ensured, at least in the early days, that differences could be ascribed to 'culture' in so far as they could not be put down to other common factors present.

This is not to say that the 'universalistic' approach has been wholly abandoned, but the role of 'contingency' has been increasingly emphasized. 'Convergence' may or may not be fashionably advocated these days; the real question remains *which* contingency, or contingencies, are germane to explaining differences between countries. If 'culture' is put forward as a candidate, the question is what precisely is meant by such a term, and whether what it purports to describe is the case.

When the vast literature that later accumulated of a more 'scientific' type was put to the test, as say by Roberts (1970), it was clear that more questions were left unanswered than were satisfied. Since then, further studies have summarized the studies at hand (Haire et al. 1966; Heller and Wilpert 1979; IDE Group 1981 etc.), and the degree of discontent remains perhaps even higher than previously. Nonetheless, it is difficult to approach the topic dispassionately, as the use of culturalist arguments has now become part of 'conventional wisdom' among many students of management.

As Heller has noted earlier:

> One should approach culture the way one would an aggressive patient—without prejudice but with a resolute intention not to be bowled over or hoodwinked into prescribing either a placebo or the patient's own pet medicine. Caution is needed because of the extraordinary multifarious use to which this term has been put in the past. Resolution is essential because the concept has attracted a large and possibly growing following among devotees who are more easily offended than put off by reasoned argument. (pp. 14–15, present volume.)

Yet, as he also points out, the term 'culture' is sometimes used so uncritically that in some contexts a sentence would make as much sense without using the word, as with doing so. It is rarely identified as 'a defined category' and is often employed as 'a residual category'.

Heller has concluded that we might more usefully look at 'the capacity of a given situational anchorage to attract cultural values'. If we could identify the relevant variable, we might then use a term to describe the factor concerned, such as 'centralization-control', if this were relevant. Heller argues that this would avoid the elitist use of the term 'culture'.

The degree of imprecision which is involved is considerable. Terms like 'cross-cultural', 'socio-cultural', and so on abound. There are now probably over a thousand empirical studies on management and 'culture'. Drent argues that culture may have a direct reference upon the organization, whereas the latter in time shapes individual behaviour. Cultural factors also influence attitudes and values, and hence make the organization go in one direction or another. Laurent, in his chapter, tested the hypothesis that the national origin of European managers determines their view of what proper management should consist of.

As Negandhi has observed in his chapter:

> During the last 20 years or so, much has been written on the impact of socio-cultural variables on management practices and effectiveness. In spite of the voluminous writings, there is as yet no clear-cut answer to the specific impact of the socio-cultural factors on management. Accordingly, the issues of applicability, transferability, and utility of advanced management know-how and practices have remained cloudy, if not controversial (p. 71, present volume).

It is difficult, and expensive, to do this over a wide range of countries. Only a few studies manage to attempt to derive very specific data in this area over more than two or three national contexts.

Negandhi, much earlier in his chapter, points out that the nations he is describing 'are more heterogeneous in their environments and socio-cultural heritage than many of the industrialized countries'. He uses the term 'socio-cultural variables', and seeks to tease out their impact on management. In his review of the literature he concludes that these studies suggest that there is 'no one-way of doing things', and he does not dissent from this view. But he does go on to argue against 'the cultural imperative hypothesis'.

Joynt, reporting in the present volume on studies done in four different countries (America, Germany, Denmark and Norway), argues that there are differences between cultures and that 'cultural maps' may help managers to better accommodate the differences between cultures. However he is ready to concede that 'the abstract words used to describe management and organization may vary enough between cultures to make comparisons very tentative in nature'.

In a similar vein, Hessling argues that the convergence-divergence debate is largely academic and that indigenous economic organization (public-private) needs an institutional rationality. This is not only management but especially occupational skills at operational and intermediate levels. Transfer of knowledge is not similar to the transfer of capital goods and needs a case research component.

Falkenberg examined Japanese management and argued that economic performance was helped by specific national/cultural factors, such as 'extraordinary motivation', favourable institutional arrangements and so on.

Obtój and Joynt in their study of innovation in large bureaucracies found that the type of methodology played a major role in obtaining information that might not exist in previous *empirical* studies. Perhaps one of the limitations one must contend with in cultural studies is that of a restricted domain with respect to the traditional concepts and models used as they tend to have a 'Western' bias.

Nicholas in his preceding chapter discusses environmental constraints, in terms of the 'societal effect approach' and looks at training and education as contingencies. In a historical comparison between the UK and West Germany, he looks at training 'as a cultural dimension'.

Locke in his contribution to the present volume is less concerned with theoretical issues in this debate and looks at the influence of past systems of management on current systems in the German and English cases, 'as a distinct historical development'. In his hands, the term 'culture' is not explicitly used, but terms like 'history' or 'tradition' are put forward. He then looks at the role of these factors on current forms of business education in these two countries.

I shall not go beyond the above summary of the approaches contained in the present volume. The detailed text is there to be re-examined by the reader. It would be useful to set the chapters against some now classic cross-national studies, and offer, *en passant*, some comments about the type of survey-approaches used.

RELEVANT PARALLEL STUDIES IN THE FIELD

In an important study, Haire et al. (1966) carried out research on managers in 14 countries and derived area-clusters (Nordic European, Latin European, Anglo-American and Developing Countries). On a rather more grandiose scale, Hofstede (1980) covered 40 countries within a single multinational corporation, and found clusters not dissimilar to the above research. Hofstede provides four basic benchmarks against which each country can be measured. First, the Power Distance Index (PDI); second, the Uncertainty Avoidance Index (UAI); third, the Individualism Index (IDV); and last, the Masculinity Index (MASC). These respectively purport to tell us how far managers in a given country accommodate to authority (or not), avoid uncertainty (or not), pursue an individualistic course (or not), or exemplify male chauvinstic values (or not).

The empirical basis for Hofstede's generalizations appears at first sight to be heavy-weight indeed. His data cover 116,000 responses from employees of a single (American-owned) business corporation, drawing on sub-samples in forty countries both developed and on-the-way to development. He argues that people carry 'mental programs' which are developed in the family in early childhood and reinforced in schools and organizations, and that the self-same programs contain a component on national culture. They are most clearly expressed in the different values that predominate among people from different countries.

Cross-cultural studies, if we may generalize, proliferate in all the social sciences, but they usually lack a theory of the key variable: culture itself. Names of countries are usually treated as residues of undefined variance in the phenomena found. 'Culture's Consequences' aims at being specific about the elements of which culture is composed.

The multinational firm, code-named 'HERMES', in which Hofstede (1980) carried out his research, is well-known, and no prizes are given for identifying it. But the author does not tell us enough about the special characteristics of this company (see pp. 55–57), especially its particular penchant for conformity by its employees and its lack of enthusiasm for unionization and unions given half a chance.

Moreover, the survey, large and impressive though it is, was originally designed for purposes other than those Hofstede aspires to in the book (and articles that have previously appeared). The scales used, for example to measure power-distance, are less than satisfactory and would surely have been more elaborate if a full-blown academic research project had been originally intended. On the other hand, it is a tribute to Hofstede's originality that a fascinating and substantial book has been developed out of the data and analyses.

As far as long-term equilibrium is concerned, Hofstede believes:

> . . . the stability of national cultures over long periods of history is achieved through a system of constant reinforcement, because societal norms lead to particular political, organizational, and intellectual structures and processes, and these in turn lead to self-fulfilling prophecies in people's perceptions of reality, which reinforce the societal norms. It is difficult to recognize this process in one's own culture. A deep and often painfully acquired empathy with other cultures is required before one becomes sensitive to the range of societal norms which our genus 'homo sapiens' has been able to invent and to the relativity of our society's norms. We find this eloquently expressed in the quote from Pascal at the beginning of this book: 'There are truths on this side of the Pyrenees which are falsehoods on the other' (p. 373).

The IDE International Research Group (1981) covered 134 organizations in two sections, over 12 countries, found a Nordic-Anglo-German cluster and a Latin one but only strongly for service sector employees vis-à-vis metal sector ones. The research was carried out in 12 countries (Belgium, Denmark, Finland, France, Germany, Great Britain, Italy, Israel, Netherlands, Norway, Sweden, Yugoslavia). Some 30 social scientists from 18 research institutions took part. The project development phase lasted from May 1973 through May 1975 and comprised pretesting and a pilot study in eight countries. Field research of the main data collection phase started in the beginning of 1976 and lasted through 1977. Data analyses first on a national and then on an international comparative basis, took place in 1977 and 1978. The publication of two volumes describing the project and its cross national results took place in 1981 (IDE Group 1981a, 1981b).

The basic assumption of the research is that formal rules and regulations on industrial democracy act to bring about mainly (though not exclusively) new processes of participative behaviour. It is assumed that this participation will lead to different patterns of power distribution, which can be demonstrated in the context of organizational decision making. The central theoretical issue was to establish whether existing patterns of decision-making and influence-sharing vary significantly as a consequence of different national arrangements for participative management, or to what degree they are due to other intervening factors.

The more democratic, legal participative systems, it appeared from the results, do make a difference, for example by modifying the impact of hierarchy. In addition, the effect of institutionalized norms on evaluation of and interest in participation is also noteworthy: there is convincing support that the national participative system (PS) does make a difference, although its effect is uneven over the wide range of variables and levels examined in the study.

Heller and Wilpert (1981) looking at managerial behaviour over 8 countries found no consistent cultural pattern. They included France,

Holland, Israel, Spain, Sweden, the United Kingdom, the United States and West Germany. The authors believed that:

> Consensus decision-making, which was so strongly advocated in the United States in the 1950s and 1960s, usually involves a group and our European managers had, as we saw, a number of important reservations about the appropriateness of committee procedures in many realistic business situations. It is not our intention to advocate the Japanese ringi system so much as to stress that there are alternative methods of influence and power-sharing which meet the stated objective. The objective is to use available skill and dormant motivation to improve the quality of decisions. Whether this is achieved in a group setting or not is beside the point. In line with the relativism of our model, we would predict that consensus methods based on time-consuming work in groups are appropriate in some circumstances but not in others (p. 49).

The judgement skills of those who are managed is of crucial importance as a predictor of managerial competence rather than just the skills themselves. American top managers score highly here: British managers much less so. Indeed the latter do not come out too well in the international comparisons. *Organization structure, technology (depending on the sector), national differences and environmental uncertainty, the authors claim, loom large as determinants of managers' behaviour: clearly important findings. Thus, there is a clearly articulated contingency theory, of managerial competence and power here and one which will have a major impact on future research in the field.*

The authors, however, do not accept any facile views concerning culture as a contingency.

> Our findings suggest that any proposition exclusively expounding the culture-free or the culture-bound theorizing of management behaviour should be viewed with great caution (. . .) This holds also for sweeping generalizations about 'cultural clusters; that appear to conform to readily available preconceived notions of cultural affinity between countries or those encompassing simplistic world views (p. 50).

This would seem to take issue with the approach offered by Hofstede. Their approach is more eclectic and complex. They argue that only:

> . . . by linking all three aspects, societal contexts, normative frameworks, and the microstructural facets of task and skill patterns can we hope to comprehend more thoroughly the dynamics and social consequences of one of the main organizational problems of our time—participation (p. 115).

These are only a few examples of research that has been carried out on a survey-basis. The first two studies reinforce the 'common-sense' view, taking given stereotypes. The second pair of studies is more cautious in its findings.

CONCLUDING REMARKS

A major drawback of all research based on very large samples is that there is so rich a pudding that an inordinate number of sixpences can be found in it, that is to say one can almost 'prove' any theory one wishes to test.

I would argue in favour of a catholicity of approaches. The wide range of chapters in the present volume testifies to the richness of ongoing research. *Taken together with* survey-findings, a more *critical* approach to 'culture' as a variable is possible.

The state of the art is such that we need to question and study our assumptions regarding the cross-cultural basis of managerial and organizational behaviour. There are no simple solutions or recipes. More research is needed and more sophisticated data-analyses must be made. Fashions in interpretations come and go regarding the source of this or that 'economic miracle'. The contribution of managerial style to variances in national prosperity cannot be easily teased out. A multi-disciplinary approach is needed, and greater attention, in my view at least, to performance of organizations and societies at both micro- and macro-levels.

REFERENCES

IDE Group, a) *Industrial Democracy in Europe.* Oxford University Press (1981);
b) *European Industrial Relations.* Oxford University Press (1981).
Haire, M. et al. *Managerial Thinking: An International Study.* Wiley, New York (1966).
Heller, F. A. and B. Wilpert, *Competence and Power in Management Decision Making.* Wiley, New York (1981).
Heller, F. A. and B. Wilpert. 'Managerial Decision Making. An International Comparison', in G. W. England et al.: *Functioning Organization in a Cross-Cultural Perspective.* Kent State University Press, Kent, Ohio (1979).
Hofstede, G. *Cultures Consequences*, Sage Publications, California (1980).
Roberts, K. H. 'On Looking at an Elephant', *Psychological Bulletin,* 84, pp. 327–350 (1970).

About the contributors

Frank Heller is Director for the Centre for Decision Making Studies at the Tavistock Institute of Human Relations in England. His work in the areas of decision-making, field research and comparative studies is well known internationally.

Pieter J. D. Drenth is Professor of Psychology at the Free University of Amsterdam in the Netherlands. He is presently Rector Magnificus of the University.

André Laurent is Professor of Organizational Behaviour at INSEAD, Fontainebleau, France. He was formerly Study Director at the Survey Research Center, Institute for Social Research, University of Michigan, USA.

Pat Joynt is Professor of Organizational Behaviour at the European Institute for Advanced Studies in Management in Brussels as well as at the Norwegian School of Management in Oslo.

Anant Negandhi is Professor of International Business at the University of Illinois, Urbana Champaign, USA. Born in India, his work stands central in the area of International Management.

Pjotr Hesseling is Professor of Business Economics at Erasmus University Rotterdam (formerly Netherlands School of Economics). He has written many articles and several books—most recently *Effective Organization Research for Development*, 1982.

Andreas W. Falkenberg is assistant Professor at the Graduate School of Business at Michigan State University, USA.

Krzyztof Obtój is presently associated with the University of Warsaw in Poland. He has also taught and researched in the USA.

Ian Nicholas is originally from Australia. Dr Nicholas was associated with Asbridge Management College in England and is presently a management consultant.

Robert Locke held the ESSO Management Chair at EIASM in Brussels until recently. He is presently Professor of European History at the University of Hawaii. His most recent book is *The End of the Practical Man*, 1984.

Malcolm Warner is Professor at Henley: The Management College and Brunel University. He collaborated with one of the largest comparative studies in Europe—IDE, and has published numerous books and articles on organizational behaviour and industrial relations.